The Internet For Windows® 98 For Dummies®

E-Mail Concisely

Microsoft's Outlook Express, Netscape's Messenger, and Qualcomm's Eudora are the three most widely used e-mail programs. Here's how to get basic e-mail tasks done in each program.

Outlook Express

To read your messages: Click the Inbox folder, just under Outlook Express in the left pane of the Outlook Express window. The top of the right pane becomes a list of messages. Click a message to read it.

To respond to a message: Click the Reply to Author button on the toolbar. Click the Send button on the toolbar when you're done. Don't forget to click the Send and Receive button to send your message out on the Internet.

To write a new message: Click the Compose Message button on the toolbar or choose the Compose⇨New Message command.

Netscape Messenger

To read your messages: Click the message in the upper pane of the Messenger window. The message appears in the lower pane. Messages with a little plus sign (+) beside them have follow-up messages. Click the plus sign.

To respond to a message: Click the Reply to Author button on the toolbar, [...] the message's [...] everyone who got a copy. Click the Send button when you're done. If you are online, your message is sent immediately. Otherwise, don't forget to choose the File⇨Go Online command to send your message out on the Internet.

To write a new message: Click the New Msg button on the toolbar.

Eudora

To read your messages: Eudora normally shows you your inbox; check the icons at the bottom of the Eudora screen. Click a message subject in the top pane of the inbox window and the message appears in the lower pane.

To respond to a message: Click the Reply button on the toolbar; it's the one with the single blue arrow pointing to the left. Or choose the Message⇨Reply command. To send your message, click the Send button at the top of the message. If you're online, your message is sent immediately. Otherwise, choose the File⇨Send queued messages command to send your mail out on the Internet.

To write a new message: Click the New Message button on the toolbar or choose the Message⇨New Message command.

Internet Settings in Windows 98

To look at your Windows 98 Dial-Up Networking connections: Choose the Start⇨Programs⇨Accessories⇨Communications⇨Dial-Up Networking command.

To check settings, such as the telephone number and the DNS numbers for a connection: *Right*-click the connection and choose the Properties command.

To test your modem: Choose Start⇨Settings⇨Control Panel to display the Control Panel, and then click Modems. Click the Diagnostics tab in the Modems Properties dialog box. Select a modem and click the More Information button.

To look at your Internet connection settings: Choose Start⇨Settings⇨Control Panel to display the Control Panel, and then click Internet. Click the Connections tab in the Internet Properties dialog box and click the Settings button. You can see your username (but not your password) in this dialog box, along with other settings that control when your computer will dial the Internet.

...For Dummies: #1 Computer Book Series for Beginners

The Internet For Windows® 98 For Dummies®

Cheat Sheet

Fill In Information about Your Internet Account

Your e-mail address: _____ @ _____

Your Internet provider's data phone number (the number your software dials):

_____

Your Internet provider's technical-support phone number (if you want to talk to a human being):

_____

Your Internet provider's technical-support department's e-mail address:

_____ @ _____

Your IP address (you may not have one assigned): _____

Your Internet provider's DNS (domain name server numbers, such as 204.127.160.1):

_____

Your Internet provider's SMTP mail gateway (for outgoing mail): _____

Your Internet provider's POP mail server (for incoming mail): _____

Your provider's news server (for Usenet newsgroups): _____

Useful Web Pages

http://www.yahoo.com	Yahoo! Web directory
http://altavista.digital.com	AltaVista Web search page
http://www.infoseek.com	Infoseek Web directory
http://www.tucows.com	The Ultimate Collection of Windows Software (also for Macs)
http:// cws.internet.com	Stroud's Consummate Winsock Applications
http://www.infobeat.com	Sign up to get news via e-mail
http://home.netscape.com	Netscape Communications home page
http://www.microsoft.com/ie	Microsoft Internet Explorer home page
http://www.liszt.com	Liszt Directory of E-Mail Mailing Lists
http://www.unitedmedia.com/comics/dilbert	Dilbert
http://att.net/dir800	AT&T 800-number directory
http://www.four11.com	Four11 phone and e-mail directory
http://maps.yahoo.com/yahoo	Maps of U.S. street addresses
http://weather.yahoo.com	World weather info
http://www.usps.gov	U.S. Postal Service zip codes and postage rates
http://mail.yahoo.com and http://www.hotmail.com	Free e-mail via the Web
http://wwwscout.cs.wisc.edu/scout	InterNIC Scout Report
http://www.us.imdb.com	Internet Movie Database
http://net.gurus.com	Updates to this book

...For Dummies: #1 Computer Book Series for Beginners

TM

References for the Rest of Us!®

BESTSELLING BOOK SERIES FROM IDG

Are you intimidated and confused by computers? Do you find that traditional manuals are overloaded with technical details you'll never use? Do your friends and family always call you to fix simple problems on their PCs? Then the *...For Dummies*® computer book series from IDG Books Worldwide is for you.

...For Dummies books are written for those frustrated computer users who know they aren't really dumb but find that PC hardware, software, and indeed the unique vocabulary of computing make them feel helpless. *...For Dummies* books use a lighthearted approach, a down-to-earth style, and even cartoons and humorous icons to diffuse computer novices' fears and build their confidence. Lighthearted but not lightweight, these books are a perfect survival guide for anyone forced to use a computer.

> *"I like my copy so much I told friends; now they bought copies."*
>
> — Irene C., Orwell, Ohio

> *"Quick, concise, nontechnical, and humorous."*
>
> — Jay A., Elburn, Illinois

> *"Thanks, I needed this book. Now I can sleep at night."*
>
> — Robin F., British Columbia, Canada

Already, millions of satisfied readers agree. They have made *...For Dummies* books the #1 introductory level computer book series and have written asking for more. So, if you're looking for the most fun and easy way to learn about computers, look to *...For Dummies* books to give you a helping hand.

TM

IDG BOOKS WORLDWIDE

4/98

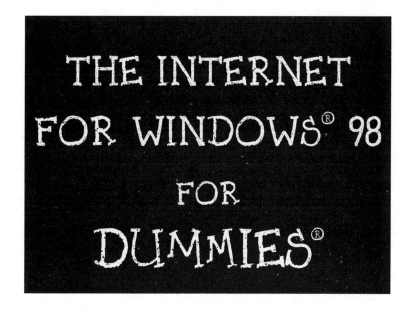

THE INTERNET FOR WINDOWS® 98 FOR DUMMIES®

by Margaret Levine Young, John Levine,
Jordan Young, Carol Baroudi

IDG Books Worldwide, Inc.
An International Data Group Company

Foster City, CA ♦ Chicago, IL ♦ Indianapolis, IN ♦ New York, NY

The Internet For Windows® 98 For Dummies®

Published by
IDG Books Worldwide, Inc.
An International Data Group Company
919 E. Hillsdale Blvd.
Suite 400
Foster City, CA 94404
www.idgbooks.com (IDG Books Worldwide Web site)
www.dummies.com (Dummies Press Web site)

Library of Congress Catalog Card No.: 98-85437

ISBN: 0-7645-0350-2

Printed in the United States of America

10 9 8 7 6 5 4 3 2 1

1B/SS/QV/ZY/IN

Distributed in the United States by IDG Books Worldwide, Inc.

Distributed by Macmillan Canada for Canada; by Transworld Publishers Limited in the United Kingdom; by IDG Norge Books for Norway; by IDG Sweden Books for Sweden; by Woodslane Pty. Ltd. for Australia; by Woodslane Enterprises Ltd. for New Zealand; by Longman Singapore Publishers Ltd. for Singapore, Malaysia, Thailand, and Indonesia; by Simron Pty. Ltd. for South Africa; by Toppan Company Ltd. for Japan; by Distribuidora Cuspide for Argentina; by Livraria Cultura for Brazil; by Ediciencia S.A. for Ecuador; by Addison-Wesley Publishing Company for Korea; by Ediciones ZETA S.C.R. Ltda. for Peru; by WS Computer Publishing Corporation, Inc., for the Philippines; by Unalis Corporation for Taiwan; by Contemporanea de Ediciones for Venezuela; by Computer Book & Magazine Store for Puerto Rico; by Express Computer Distributors for the Caribbean and West Indies. Authorized Sales Agent: Anthony Rudkin Associates for the Middle East and North Africa.

For general information on IDG Books Worldwide's books in the U.S., please call our Consumer Customer Service department at 800-762-2974. For reseller information, including discounts and premium sales, please call our Reseller Customer Service department at 800-434-3422.

For information on where to purchase IDG Books Worldwide's books outside the U.S., please contact our International Sales department at 650-655-3200 or fax 650-655-3295.

For information on foreign language translations, please contact our Foreign & Subsidiary Rights department at 650-655-3021 or fax 650-655-3281.

For sales inquiries and special prices for bulk quantities, please contact our Sales department at 650-655-3200 or write to the address above.

For information on using IDG Books Worldwide's books in the classroom or for ordering examination copies, please contact our Educational Sales department at 800-434-2086 or fax 817-251-8174.

For press review copies, author interviews, or other publicity information, please contact our Public Relations department at 650-655-3000 or fax 650-655-3299.

For authorization to photocopy items for corporate, personal, or educational use, please contact Copyright Clearance Center, 222 Rosewood Drive, Danvers, MA 01923, or fax 978-750-4470.

is a trademark under exclusive license to IDG Books Worldwide, Inc., from International Data Group, Inc.

About the Authors

Unlike her peers in that 40-something bracket, **Margaret Levine Young** was exposed to computers at an early age. In high school, she got into a computer club known as the R.E.S.I.S.T.O.R.S., a group of kids who spent Saturdays in a barn fooling around with three antiquated computers. She stayed in the field throughout college against her better judgment and despite her brother John's presence as a graduate student in the computer science department. Margy graduated from Yale and went on to become one of the first microcomputer managers in the early 1980s at Columbia Pictures, where she rode the elevator with big stars whose names she wouldn't dream of dropping here.

Since then, Margy has co-authored more than 16 computer books about the topics of the Internet, UNIX, WordPerfect, Microsoft Access, and (stab from the past) PC-File and Javelin, including *Dummies 101: The Internet For Windows 98, Dummies 101: Netscape Communicator, Internet FAQs: Answers to Frequently Asked Questions, UNIX For Dummies,* and *WordPerfect 8 For Windows 95 For Dummies* (all published by IDG Books Worldwide, Inc.). She met her future husband, Jordan, in the R.E.S.I.S.T.O.R.S., and her other passion is her children, Meg and Zac. She loves gardening, chickens, reading, and anything to do with eating and lives near Middlebury, Vermont (see `http://www.gurus.com/margy` for some scenery).

John R. Levine was a member of a computer club in high school — before high school students, or even high schools, had computers, where he met Theodor H. Nelson, the author of *Computer Lib/Dream Machines* and the inventor of hypertext, who reminded us that computers should not be taken seriously and that everyone can and should understand and use computers.

John wrote his first program in 1967 on an IBM 1130 (a computer roughly as powerful as your typical modern digital wristwatch, only more difficult to use). He became an official system administrator of a networked computer at Yale in 1975. He began working part-time, for a computer company, of course, in 1977 and has been in and out of the computer and network biz ever since. John got his company on Usenet (the Net's worldwide bulletin-board system) early enough that it appears in a 1982 *Byte* magazine article on a map of Usenet, which then was so small that the map fit on half a page.

Although John used to spend most of his time writing software, now he mostly writes books (including *UNIX For Dummies* and *Internet Secrets,* both published by IDG Books Worldwide, Inc.) because it's more fun and he can do so at home in the tiny village of Trumansburg, New York, where he is the sewer commissioner (Guided tours! Free samples!) and play with his baby daughter when he's supposed to be writing. John also does a fair amount of public speaking. (See his home page, at `http://iecc.com/johnl`, to see where he'll be.) He holds a B.A. and a Ph.D. in computer science from Yale University, but please don't hold that against him.

Jordan Young has been knocking around the computer industry for about 25 years. He learned to program by flipping the switches on the front panel of a PDP-8 one night, and since then it has been second nature. Early on, he realized that he enjoyed explaining computers more than using them and has been helping people use them effectively ever since, including a stint in what he fondly calls IBM's State Department and a few years in international marketing at Data General (which used to make minicomputers).

Over the years, he has done everything from software product development to press conferences announcing new computers to operating systems training courses in English and Spanish to lectures on OLAP software in Portuguese. Most enjoyable has been watching two children grow, a long trip down the Amazon River, a weekend spent on Easter Island, and camping in the Andes. Now he spends his time helping Margy with the occasional *...For Dummies* book, working on their Internet storefront at GreatTapes.com, and teaching computer classes. When he's not writing about or explaining computers to people, he likes to cook, tend to the chickens, and contemplate the nature of life, God, and the Universe.

Carol Baroudi first began playing with computers in 1971 at Colgate University, where two things were new: the PDP-10 and women. She was lucky to have unlimited access to the state-of-the-art PDP-10, on which she learned to program, operate the machine, and talk to Eliza. She taught Algol and helped to design the curricula for computer science and women's studies. She majored in Spanish and studied French, which, thanks to the Internet, she can now use every day.

In 1975, Carol took a job doing compiler support and development, a perfect use for her background in languages. For six years, she developed software and managed software development. For a while, she had a small business doing high-tech recruiting (she was a headhunter). Though she wrote her first software manuals in 1975, she has been writing for a living since 1984. Carol has described all kinds of software, from the memory-management system of the Wang VS operating system to e-mail products for the PC and Mac. For the past several years, she has been writing books, including *Internet Secrets and E-Mail For Dummies* (both published by IDG Books Worldwide, Inc.), for ordinary people who want to use computers. She enjoys speaking to academic, business, and general audiences about the impact of technology on society and other related topics. (Check out her home page, at `http://iecc.com/carol`, to see what she's up to.)

Carol believes that we are living in a very interesting time when technology is changing faster than people can imagine. She hopes that as we learn to use the new technologies, we don't lose sight of our humanity and feels that computers can be useful and fun but are no substitute for real life.

Dedication

John dedicates his part of the book (the pages with the particularly dumb jokes) to Sarah Willow, who still doesn't sleep, and to Tonia, who stays up with her, showing the dedication only a mother could have.

Carol dedicates her part of the book to Joshua, with all her love, and to her friends, who remind her that there's more to life than writing books.

Margy and Jordan dedicate their part of this book to Professor Jordan Young and Dionir Sousa Gomes Young.

ABOUT IDG BOOKS WORLDWIDE

Welcome to the world of IDG Books Worldwide.

IDG Books Worldwide, Inc., is a subsidiary of International Data Group, the world's largest publisher of computer-related information and the leading global provider of information services on information technology. IDG was founded more than 25 years ago and now employs more than 8,500 people worldwide. IDG publishes more than 275 computer publications in over 75 countries (see listing below). More than 60 million people read one or more IDG publications each month.

Launched in 1990, IDG Books Worldwide is today the #1 publisher of best-selling computer books in the United States. We are proud to have received eight awards from the Computer Press Association in recognition of editorial excellence and three from *Computer Currents'* First Annual Readers' Choice Awards. Our best-selling *...For Dummies®* series has more than 30 million copies in print with translations in 30 languages. IDG Books Worldwide, through a joint venture with IDG's Hi-Tech Beijing, became the first U.S. publisher to publish a computer book in the People's Republic of China. In record time, IDG Books Worldwide has become the first choice for millions of readers around the world who want to learn how to better manage their businesses.

Our mission is simple: Every one of our books is designed to bring extra value and skill-building instructions to the reader. Our books are written by experts who understand and care about our readers. The knowledge base of our editorial staff comes from years of experience in publishing, education, and journalism — experience we use to produce books for the '90s. In short, we care about books, so we attract the best people. We devote special attention to details such as audience, interior design, use of icons, and illustrations. And because we use an efficient process of authoring, editing, and desktop publishing our books electronically, we can spend more time ensuring superior content and spend less time on the technicalities of making books.

You can count on our commitment to deliver high-quality books at competitive prices on topics you want to read about. At IDG Books Worldwide, we continue in the IDG tradition of delivering quality for more than 25 years. You'll find no better book on a subject than one from IDG Books Worldwide.

John Kilcullen
CEO
IDG Books Worldwide, Inc.

Steven Berkowitz
President and Publisher
IDG Books Worldwide, Inc.

Eighth Annual Computer Press Awards ≥1992

Ninth Annual Computer Press Awards ≥1993

Tenth Annual Computer Press Awards ≥1994

Eleventh Annual Computer Press Awards ≥1995

IDG Books Worldwide, Inc., is a subsidiary of International Data Group, the world's largest publisher of computer-related information and the leading global provider of information services on information technology. International Data Group publishes over 275 computer publications in over 75 countries. Sixty million people read one or more International Data Group publications each month. International Data Group's publications include: **ARGENTINA:** Buyer's Guide, Computerworld Argentina, PC World Argentina; **AUSTRALIA:** Australian Macworld, Australian PC World, Australian Reseller News, Computerworld, IT Casebook, Network World, Publish, Webmaster; **AUSTRIA:** Computerwelt Osterreich, Networks Austria, PC Tip Austria; **BANGLADESH:** PC World Bangladesh; **BELARUS:** PC World Belarus; **BELGIUM:** Data News; **BRAZIL:** Annuário de Informática, Computerworld, Connections, Macworld, PC Player, PC World, Publish, Reseller News, Supergamepower; **BULGARIA:** Computerworld Bulgaria, Network World Bulgaria, PC & MacWorld Bulgaria; **CANADA:** CIO Canada, Client/Server World, ComputerWorld Canada, InfoWorld Canada, NetworkWorld Canada, WebWorld; **CHILE:** Computerworld Chile, PC World Chile; **COLOMBIA:** Computerworld Colombia, PC World Colombia; **COSTA RICA:** PC World Centro America; **THE CZECH AND SLOVAK REPUBLICS:** Computerworld Czechoslovakia, Macworld Czech Republic, PC World Czechoslovakia; **DENMARK:** Communications World Danmark, Computerworld Danmark, Macworld Danmark, PC World Danmark, Techworld Denmark; **DOMINICAN REPUBLIC:** PC World Republica Dominicana; **ECUADOR:** PC World Ecuador; **EGYPT:** Computerworld Middle East, PC World Middle East; **EL SALVADOR:** PC World Centro America; **FINLAND:** MikroPC, Tietoverkko, Tietoviikko; **FRANCE:** Distributique, Hebdo, Info PC, Le Monde Informatique, Macworld, Reseaux & Telecoms, WebMaster France; **GERMANY:** Computer Partner, Computerwoche, Computerwoche Extra, Computerwoche FOCUS, Global Online, Macwelt, PC Welt; **GREECE:** Amiga Computing, GamePro Greece, Multimedia World; **GUATEMALA:** PC World Centro America; **HONDURAS:** PC World Centro America; **HONG KONG:** Computerworld Hong Kong, PC World Hong Kong, Publish in Asia; **HUNGARY:** ABCD CD-ROM, Computerworld Szamitastechnika, Internetto online Magazine, PC World Hungary, PC-X Magazin Hungary; **ICELAND:** Tolvuheimur PC World Island; **INDIA:** Information Communications World, Information Systems Computerworld, PC World India, Publish in Asia; **INDONESIA:** InfoKomputer PC World, Komputek Computerworld, Publish in Asia; **IRELAND:** ComputerScope, PC Live!; **ISRAEL:** Macworld Israel, People & Computers/Computerworld; **ITALY:** Computerworld Italia, Macworld Italia, Networking Italia, PC World Italia; **JAPAN:** DTP World, Macworld Japan, Nikkei Personal Computing, OS/2 World Japan, SunWorld Japan, Windows NT World, Windows World Japan; **KENYA:** PC World East African; **KOREA:** Hi-Tech Information, Macworld Korea, PC World Korea; **MACEDONIA:** PC World Macedonia; **MALAYSIA:** Computerworld Malaysia, PC World Malaysia, Publish in Asia; **MALTA:** PC World Malta; **MEXICO:** Computerworld Mexico, PC World Mexico; **MYANMAR:** PC World Myanmar; **NETHERLANDS:** Computer! Totaal, LAN Internetworking Magazine, LAN World Buyers Guide, Macworld Netherlands, Net, WebWereld; **NEW ZEALAND:** Absolute Beginners Guide and Plain & Simple Series, Computer Buyer, Computer Industry Directory, Computerworld New Zealand, MTB, Network World, PC World New Zealand; **NICARAGUA:** PC World Centro America; **NORWAY:** Computerworld Norge, CW Rapport, Datamagasinet, Financial Rapport, Kursguide Norge, Macworld Norge, Multimediaworld Norge, PC World Ekspress Norge, PC World Nettverk, PC World Norge, PC World ProduktGuide Norge; **PAKISTAN:** Computerworld Pakistan; **PANAMA:** PC World Panama; **PEOPLE'S REPUBLIC OF CHINA:** China Computer Users, China Computerworld, China InfoWorld, China Telecom World Weekly, Computer & Communication, Electronic Design China, Electronics Today, Electronics Weekly, Game Software, PC World China, Popular Computer Week, Software Weekly, Software World, Telecom World; **PERU:** Computerworld Peru, PC World Profesional Peru, PC World SoHo Peru; **PHILIPPINES:** Click!, Computerworld Philippines, PC World Philippines, Publish in Asia; **POLAND:** Computerworld Poland, Computerworld Special Report Poland, Cyber, Macworld Poland, Networld Poland, PC World Komputer; **PORTUGAL:** Cerebro/PC World, Computerworld/Correio Informático, Dealer World Portugal, Mac*In/PC*In Portugal, Multimedia World; **PUERTO RICO:** PC World Puerto Rico; **ROMANIA:** Computerworld Romania, PC World Romania, Telecom Romania; **RUSSIA:** Computerworld Russia, Mir PK, Publish, Seti; **SINGAPORE:** Computerworld Singapore, PC World Singapore, Publish in Asia; **SLOVENIA:** Monitor; **SOUTH AFRICA:** Computing SA, Network World SA, Software World SA; **SPAIN:** Communicaciones World España, Computerworld España, Dealer World España, Macworld España, PC World España; **SRI LANKA:** Infolink PC World; **SWEDEN:** CAP&Design, Computer Sweden, Corporate Computing Sweden, Internetworld Sweden, it.branschen, Macworld Sweden, MaxiData Sweden, MikroDatorn, Natverk & Kommunikation, PC World Sweden, PCaktiv, Windows World Sweden; **SWITZERLAND:** Computerworld Schweiz, Macworld Schweiz, PCtip; **TAIWAN:** Computerworld Taiwan, Macworld Taiwan, NEW ViSiON/Publish, PC World Taiwan, Windows World Taiwan; **THAILAND:** Publish in Asia, Thai Computerworld; **TURKEY:** Computerworld Turkiye, Macworld Turkiye, Network World Turkiye, PC World Turkiye; **UKRAINE:** Computerworld Kiev, Multimedia World Ukraine, PC World Ukraine; **UNITED KINGDOM:** Acorn User UK, Amiga Action UK, Amiga Computing UK, Apple Talk UK, Computing, Macworld, Parents and Computers UK, PC Advisor, PC Home, PSX Pro, The WEB; **UNITED STATES:** Cable in the Classroom, CIO Magazine, Computerworld, DOS World, Federal Computer Week, GamePro Magazine, InfoWorld, I-Way, Macworld, Network World, PC Games, PC World, Publish, Video Event, THE WEB Magazine, and WebMaster; online webzines: JavaWorld, NetscapeWorld, and SunWorld Online; **URUGUAY:** InfoWorld Uruguay; **VENEZUELA:** Computerworld Venezuela, PC World Venezuela; and **VIETNAM:** PC World Vietnam.   3/24/97

Author's Acknowledgments

As you can tell from the cover, writing this book was a collaborative process. Arnold Reinhold's was the principal hand behind Chapters 13, 15, 16, 17, and 19, and he put Chapters 8 through 10 into their current form. Kathy Werfel originated Chapter 14. By the time a book is done, though, everybody's fingerprints are pretty much everywhere. Hy Bender was also involved in thinking about this book in its early stages.

All the authors particularly thank our editors at IDG Books Worldwide, Inc., especially Rebecca Whitney, Diane Steele, and Mary Bednarek. There's much lamenting nowadays over the lost art of editing, and we thank Rebecca for shoveling against the tide. You're about to read a much better book because of her efforts. It's a cliché to say that it takes a cast of thousands to make a big project like this one happen, but it's true. Although we've met only a few of the dedicated folks listed on the Publisher's Acknowledgments page, we're very thankful that they and their coworkers made this book happen.

The entire contents of this book were submitted by the authors to the publisher over the Internet. Edited chapters were returned for review in the same way. We thank the Finger Lakes Technology Group (Trumansburg, New York), MediaOne (Woburn, Massachusetts), LightLink (Ithaca, New York), STCO.NET (Shoreham, Vermont), and SoVerNet (Bellows Falls, Vermont), our Internet providers.

Many thanks to the Internet community for its support.

Publisher's Acknowledgments

We're proud of this book; please register your comments through our IDG Books Worldwide Online Registration Form located at http://my2cents.dummies.com.

Some of the people who helped bring this book to market include the following:

Acquisitions, Editorial, and Media Development

Project Editor: Rebecca Whitney

Acquisitions Editor: Michael Kelly

Technical Editor: Bill Karow

Editorial Manager: Mary C. Corder

Editorial Assistant: Paul E. Kuzmic

Special Help

Suzanne Thomas

Production

Associate Project Coordinator: Tom Missler

Layout and Graphics: Lou Boudreau, J. Tyler Connor, Angela F. Hunckler, Maridee V. Ennis, Jane E. Martin, Drew R. Moore, Brent Savage, Janet Seib

Proofreaders: Christine Berman, Kelli Botta, Michelle Croninger, Rachel Garvey, Nancy Price, Rebecca Senninger, Ethel M. Winslow, Janet M. Withers

Indexer: Richard T. Evans

General and Administrative

IDG Books Worldwide, Inc.: John Kilcullen, CEO; Steven Berkowitz, President and Publisher

IDG Books Technology Publishing: Brenda McLaughlin, Senior Vice President and Group Publisher

Dummies Technology Press and Dummies Editorial: Diane Graves Steele, Vice President and Associate Publisher; Mary Bednarek, Director of Acquisitions and Product Development; Kristin A. Cocks, Editorial Director

Dummies Trade Press: Kathleen A. Welton, Vice President and Publisher; Kevin Thornton, Acquisitions Manager

IDG Books Production for Dummies Press: Beth Jenkins Roberts, Production Director; Cindy L. Phipps, Manager of Project Coordination, Production Proofreading, and Indexing; Kathie S. Schutte, Supervisor of Page Layout; Shelley Lea, Supervisor of Graphics and Design; Debbie J. Gates, Production Systems Specialist; Robert Springer, Supervisor of Proofreading; Debbie Stailey, Special Projects Coordinator; Tony Augsburger, Supervisor of Reprints and Bluelines; Leslie Popplewell, Media Archive Coordinator

Dummies Packaging and Book Design: Robin Seaman, Creative Director; Jocelyn Kelaita, Product Packaging Coordinator; Kavish + Kavish, Cover Design

♦

The publisher would like to give special thanks to Patrick J. McGovern, without whom this book would not have been possible.

♦

Contents at a Glance

Cartoons at a Glance

By Rich Tennant

"Sales on the Web site are down. I figure the servers chi is blocked, so we're fudgin' around the feng shui in the computer room, and if that doesn't work, Ronnie's got a chant that should do it."

page 317

"I have to say I'm really impressed with the interactivity on this car wash Web site."

page 7

"Just how accurately should my Web site reflect my place of business?"

page 227

"You'd better come out here — I've got someone who wants to run a banner ad on our Web site."

page 105

"Face it Vinnie — you're gonna have a hard time getting people to subscribe online with a credit card to a newsletter called 'Felons Interactive!'"

page 155

Fax: 978-546-7747 • E-mail: the5wave@tiac.net

Table of Contents

Introduction

∙ ∙

*W*elcome to *The Internet For Windows 98 For Dummies*. Windows 98 marks a watershed of sorts for the Internet: For the first time, the most popular computer software comes with everything you need to connect to the Internet *and* cruise the World Wide Web. The arrival of Windows 98 marks a time when people begin to assume that a computer is not living up to its potential unless it's connected to the whole world of computers out there.

We think that it's vital for people to understand what the Internet is, especially if the Internet turns out to be as important as we think it is (and we have a great deal of company in thinking that it will stay important). The Internet is about more than just computers. Sure, it started as a way to connect some computers together, but what no one realized at the time is that when computers are hooked together, they provide people with a new way of communicating. That's why, sooner or later, almost every discussion about almost any subject seems to come around to the Internet and the World Wide Web: The Net and the Web are really about communication, and communication is relevant whenever two or more people try to do something, understand something, talk about something, buy or sell something, or do practically anything together.

Yes, this book is about the details of getting your computer hooked up to the Internet and learning how to surf the Web, but it's also about the ways that people communicate on the Internet and what kinds of information you can find out there.

About This Book

Microsoft would like to include with Windows 98 everything you need to use the Internet and the World Wide Web. As you may have heard, however, this development has created some controversy, everywhere from the U.S. Department of Justice to the Senate to the attorneys general of quite a few states. Whether it's good or bad for business to have all this software wrapped up in one package, though, it certainly is convenient for us computer users. We've been writing about the Internet for quite some time now, and for the first time we can give you step-by-step instructions for getting your computer hooked up to the Net and getting information from the Net because, for the first time, all the software you need is already on your computer.

We don't limit ourselves to Microsoft software, however. You may have some choices about what software to get when you buy a computer with Windows 98 in it. As we write this book, no one knows for sure what choices the Department of Justice will force Microsoft to make. Even if the Netscape Navigator program and Communicator suite of programs don't come as options on your new computer, though, they provide excellent alternatives for people looking to surf the Web. Also, Eudora (from Qualcomm) has set the standard for e-mail programs. We talk about all these software programs in this book.

Different people will want different things from this book, and you yourself will want different things from it at different times. Here's an overview of what you'll find:

- An explanation of what the Internet is
- Tips for figuring out which service to use to connect to the Internet
- Instructions for sending and receiving e-mail (electronic mail)
- The World Wide Web explained without (we hope) too much jargon
- Straight talk about channels, subscriptions, push technology, cookies, and other World Wide Web hype
- Enough information to put your very own home page on the World Wide Web
- The ins and outs of shopping on the Web

How to Use This Book

This book is designed so that you can read just the parts you're interested in. If you're just starting with Windows 98 and the Internet, however, you'll probably find that you want to read Part I first. (That's why we put it at the beginning.) It steps you through the process of selecting, signing up with, and setting up an Internet connection on your Windows 98 system. From there, you can hop around the book as you please. Sometimes a topic is too big to fit in one chapter and you find chapters with words like *More* or *Advanced* in their titles. You may want to read the chapter preceding these first, unless you already know what's going on.

Although we try hard not to introduce a technical term without defining it, sometimes we slip. Sometimes too, you may read a section out of order and find a term we defined a few chapters before that. To fill in the gaps, we include a glossary.

Because the Internet is ever-changing, we have expanded our book to include an online area to help keep it up-to-date. Whenever you see our special Whoosh icon, it means that we have more up-to-the-minute information available on our Web site, at

```
http://net.gurus.com
```

Whenever you have to type something, it appears in the book like this: **Hello, Internet!** Or else we put in on a line of its own, like this:

```
cryptic command to type
```

Type the command just as it appears. Use the same capitalization we do — some systems care deeply about CAPITAL and small letters. Then press the Enter or Return key. The book tells you what should happen when you give each command and what your options are.

If you have to follow a complicated procedure, we spell it out step by step wherever possible, with the stuff you have to do also highlighted in **boldface.** We then tell you what happens in response and what your options are.

When you have to choose commands from menus, we write File⇨Exit when we want you to choose the File command from the menu bar and then choose the Exit command from the menu that appears.

Who Are You?

In writing this book, we assumed that

- ✔ You have a computer running Windows 98.
- ✔ Your computer has a modem, and you've plugged your modem into the telephone line.
- ✔ You're pretty comfortable using Windows 98. You don't have to be a whiz at Windows; you just have to be able to get around.
- ✔ You have or would like to have access to the Internet.
- ✔ You want to get some work done with it. (We consider the term "work" to include the concept "play.")
- ✔ You are not interested in becoming the world's next great Internet expert, at least not this week.

How This Book Is Organized

This book has five parts. The parts stand on their own — although you can begin reading wherever you like, you should at least skim Part I first to get acquainted with some unavoidable Internet jargon and find out how to get your computer on the Net.

Here are the parts of the book and what they contain:

In Part I, "Getting on the Net with Windows 98," you find out what the Internet is and why it's interesting (at least why we think it's interesting). Also, this part has stuff about vital Internet terminology and concepts that help you as you read through the later parts of the book. Part I discusses how you get on the Internet, gives some thoughts about children's use of the Net, and tells you everything (we think) you need to know to sign up with an Internet service provider. For most users, by far the most difficult part of using the Net is getting to that first connection, with software loaded, configuration configured, and modem modeming. After that, it's (relatively) smooth sailing.

The rest of this book deals with what you can do on the Internet. Part II, "Mail and Gossip," jumps right to the heart of what the Internet is about: people talking to people. We get you set up with an e-mail account, teach you some e-mail tricks, and tell you how to fill up your e-mail box with messages from all sorts of mailing lists. If you prefer reading bulletin boards, we also tell you about Usenet Newsgroups, the bulletin-board system of the Internet.

Part III, "Windows 98 Web-Whacking," dives into the World Wide Web, the part of the Internet that has powered the Net's leap from obscurity to fame. We discuss how to get around on the Web, including how to look at all sorts of things people never expected you to want, like radio broadcasts and movies. We also talk about finding stuff (which is not as easy as it should be). Finally, we talk about channels, that feature of Windows 98 through which you can have Web pages magically appear on your computer at particular times.

Part IV, "Other Stuff You Can Do on the Internet," looks at the other important and useful Net services. Getting a file full of information from the Internet to your computer is something you have to (or want to) do at some point. Sitting down at the keyboard and typing messages while others do the same is a way many people have found to meet like-minded souls. From there, it's just a short hop to conducting a business meeting "live" on the Internet. And no one's public life is complete without a Web home page. Part IV tells you how to make your own.

A compendium of ready references and useful facts is in Part V, "The Part of Tens" (which, we suppose, suggests that the rest of the book is full of useless facts).

Icons Used in This Book

 Lets you know that some particularly nerdy, technoid information is coming up so that you can skip it if you want. (On the other hand, you may want to read it.)

 Indicates that a nifty little shortcut or time-saver is explained.

 Gaack! We found out about this information the hard way! Don't let it happen to you!

 Points out a resource on the World Wide Web that you can use with Netscape, Internet Explorer, or other Web software.

 Points you to more up-to-the-minute information on our very own Web site. Hey, this book is *alive*.

What Now?

That's all you need to know to get started. Whenever you hit a snag using the Internet, just look up the problem in the table of contents or index in this book. You'll either have the problem solved in a flash or know where you need to go to find some expert help.

Because the Internet has been evolving for almost 30 years, largely under the influence of some extremely nerdy people, it was not designed to be particularly easy for normal people to use. Don't feel bad if you have to look up a number of topics before you feel comfortable using the Internet.

Feedback, Please

We love to hear from our readers. If you want to contact us, please feel free to do so, in care of

> IDG Books Worldwide
> 7260 Shadeland Station, Suite 100
> Indianapolis, IN 46256

Better yet, send us Internet e-mail at `internet98@gurus.com` (our friendly robot answers immediately; the human authors read all the mail and answer as much as we can), or visit this book's Web home page, at `http://net.gurus.com`. These electronic addresses put you in contact only with the authors of this book; to contact the publisher or authors of other ...*For Dummies* books, visit the publisher's web site, at `http://www.dummies.com`, send e-mail to `info@idgbooks.com`, or send paper mail to the address just listed.

Part I
Getting on the Net with Windows 98

"I have to say I'm really impressed with the interactivity on this car wash Web site."

In this part . . .

Someday, you will get a computer, plug it in, and have access to the Internet. That day is not now. As a prelude to getting connected to the Net, we talk a little about what the Internet is, what you can do there, and how it got that way. Then we dive in to the nitty-gritty of getting your Windows 98 system connected to the Internet: the choices you have to make and the magic spells you have to cast. After you're on the Net, we give you some tips for how to keep the "Netty" bits of Windows 98 out of your hair.

Chapter 1

Welcome to the Net

- -

In This Chapter

▶ What is the Internet?

▶ What makes it different from any other network?

▶ Why is the Internet such a big deal?

▶ What does the Internet have to do with Windows 98, anyway?

▶ How safe is the Internet?

- -

*W*hat is the Internet? We skip the suspense and jump directly to the simplest answer: The *Internet* is a whole bunch of computers connected together, sharing information. That definition doesn't mean that every computer is part of the Internet or even that every computer that is connected to another computer is part of the Internet. In this chapter, we flesh out this answer and explain exactly what the Internet is (and isn't). You get our opinion about why the Internet has captured people's imaginations so quickly, and we talk about what people do with the Internet. We also talk about why the Net is different from other forms of communication. Because this is a book about Windows 98, we also introduce the Internet features of Windows 98 and explain why the Internet and Windows 98 are bound in a relationship that looks more like something from a daytime soap opera than from the world of business and technology. We end with a few tips to keep in mind to make your Internet experience a safe and happy one, along with a little history.

First, give yourself a break. The things we talk about in this book are, mostly, not complicated. When they are complicated, we explain them as simply as we can. Despite that, the whole subject of the Internet and Windows 98 can still be confusing. The reason is that many of the ideas here are completely new. Even if you're familiar with Windows 98, the Internet parts may be new to you, and we may take you to parts of Windows 98 you haven't looked at. If you're familiar with the Internet, it may not be obvious just how parts of the Internet appear in Windows 98. Many people find it helpful to read through the entire book quickly one time to get a broader perspective of what we're talking about. Others plow through a page at a time. Whatever your style, remember that it's new stuff — you're not supposed to understand it already. Even for many experienced Internet users, it's a new world.

One last point before we jump in: Even if you're an experienced computer user, you may find the Internet unlike anything you've ever tackled. The Internet is not a software package and doesn't easily lend itself to the kind of step-by-step instruction we can provide for a single, fixed program. When we talk about Windows 98, we can be very step-by-step. When it comes to the Internet, however, it's more like describing a living organism that's mutating at an astonishing rate. After you get set up and get a little practice, using the Internet seems like second nature; in the beginning, however, it can be daunting.

What Exactly Is the Internet?

Let's take a closer look at that quick answer to "What is the Internet?" We said that it's a whole bunch of computers connected together. Technically, when you connect two or more computers together, that's called a *network*. This type of network is similar to other networks you're probably familiar with. Radio and television networks connect stations all over the country so that they can all transmit Rush Limbaugh's program or *All Things Considered* or *The X-Files* at the same time. That's called a *broadcast network:* a single message (*The X-Files,* for example) is sent to all the points on the network at the same time.

The telephone network is even more similar to a computer network. All the telephones in the country are connected by wires, radio, or some other medium, just as many computers are connected. Any individual phone can tell the network that it wants to connect to any other individual phone; that's what you do when you dial a phone number. Similarly, any individual computer (connected to a network) can tell the network that it wants to connect to any other computer on the network. After the two computers are connected, they can have a conversation, just as two people would when they're connected by telephone.

Some computer networks consist of a central computer and a bunch of remote stations that report to it (a central airline-reservation computer, for example, with thousands of screens and keyboards in airports and travel agencies). Others, including the Internet, are more egalitarian and permit any computer on the network to communicate with any other. These kinds of networks have been around for 20 or 30 years or more (depending on who's counting and what they're counting).

So what makes the Internet different? For one thing, the Internet isn't really one network — it's a network of networks. "Great," you say, "and what exactly is that?" When you connect one computer to another computer, you get a computer network. When you connect computer networks together, you get networks of networks.

The Internet connects more than 100,000 networks all over the world, including university and college networks, big corporate networks, and lots of publicly accessible networks. It connects millions of computers from around the world — no one knows exactly how many.

Why Is Everybody Talking about the Net?

The Net is everywhere. It's a rare advertisement that doesn't include a line like `www.ourcompany.com`. Radio programs say "Write to us at our e-mail address: `ourshow@ourstation.org`." Almost everybody's business card has an e-mail address on it. All we're talking about here is a network of networks — it's not a miracle cure-all for the common cold. From the amount of press it's getting, however, and from the amount people are talking about it, it may as well be. Why?

Just about everyone, from pop psychologists to big-name economists, gives a different explanation. One of our favorites is the shift to the service economy. Many (some say most) jobs now deal with information, and the Internet has changed the way people can gather information more than anything since television, and some would say more than anything since the printing press. Others say that the Internet is a marketing executive's dream: just like television except that you show your advertisement only to exactly the people you think should see it. Still others say that the Internet is Big Brother come to life: "Someone" "out there" could conceivably keep track of all the information you look at. Others say that it's the beginning of the democratization of information: All the information that exists is equally available to anyone with a Net connection.

The Internet and the service economy

We're talking sociology and economics here. In the 1970s, the economy in the United States changed in a way that was not entirely foreseen: For the first time, more people made their living performing services for other people (everything from hair-cutting to lawyering) than made their living producing things. This shift parallels the shift at the end of the 1800s from farming to manufacturing. As the end of the 1800s and the beginning of the 1900s brought a shift from subsistence (grow it on the farm, eat it on the farm) to manufacturing commerce (work in the factory, eat food processed by Chicago meat processors), the 1980s and 1990s have brought a shift from manufacturing commerce to "knowledge commerce." Just as the late 1800s and early 1900s saw the creation of companies to deliver manufactured goods (supermarkets and five-and-dimes), the 1980s and 1990s have seen the creation of a new mechanism to deliver information: the Internet.

All these visions have some truth in them. Which is the most important depends mostly on who you are and what you do. All come from the same basic premise, however: The Internet is a *big* network, and with networks, size counts for a good deal.

What Do People Do with the Internet, Anyway?

Most people don't get all worked up over big economic changes or major new marketing opportunities. What makes people enthusiastic about the Internet is what they can do, what they have found, and whom they have met. The Internet's capabilities are so expansive that we don't have room to give a complete list in this chapter (indeed, it would fill several books larger than this one), although here's a quick summary:

- ✔ **The World Wide Web:** When people talk these days about surfing the Net, the Web is what they're talking about. What's the difference between the World Wide Web and the Internet? When we define the Internet earlier in this chapter, we never mention the World Wide Web. To latch on to a tired metaphor for the Internet, think of the Internet as the highway and the World Wide Web as just one of the kinds of services (or information) available on this highway. The Web, unlike earlier information services on the Internet, combines text, pictures, sound, and even animation. Its most important feature is that it lets you move from one *Web page* (or screenful of information) to another with a click of your computer mouse — the information you click to go to doesn't have to be on the same computer or even on the same continent as the information you're looking at. New *Web sites* (sets of Web pages) are growing faster than you can say "advertising budget," with new sites appearing every minute. In 1993, when we wrote our first Internet book, the Internet had 130 Web sites. Today, it has tens of millions, and, although all statistics about the Web are a little suspect, some data indicates that the number of Web sites is doubling every two months. To use the World Wide Web, you need a *browser* program, usually Netscape Navigator or Microsoft Internet Explorer. We introduce them in Chapters 8 and 9.

- ✔ **Electronic mail (e-mail):** E-mail is the workhorse of the Internet. Although all sorts of fancy new technologies (like the World Wide Web) have gotten people's attention, millions of people have been exchanging e-mail, some since before 1970. It's simple — all you need is your recipient's address. It's easy to create — you just type, like typing a memo. It works on almost every computer that's on the Net — no fancy pictures or sounds to worry about. (You can get fancy if you want, of course, although you don't have to.) E-mail is a whole new form of communicating: not quite as formal as a letter but often more convenient than a phone call. People use e-mail for anything for which they may use paper mail, faxes, special delivery of documents, or the telephone: gossip, recipes, rumors, love letters — you name it. (We hear that some people even use it for stuff related to work.) Electronic *mailing lists* enable you to join in group discussions with people who have similar interests and meet people over the Net. Chapters 5, 6, and 7 have all the details.

✔ **Chatting:** Remember the CB craze in the late 1970s? That's when many of the uses for the Internet were dreamed up. Someone realized that you could use a computer network like a CB channel, only with typing rather than talking. Things have gotten fancier, and now in addition to a zillion channels, it has private chat rooms for intimate groups, or meetings with that one special someone. Chat rooms are popular on services that predate the popularity of the Internet, like America Online and CompuServe. *Internet Relay Chat (IRC)* is a chat facility available to almost anyone on the Internet. We tell you how to use it in Chapter 13.

✔ **Information retrieval:** Remember that the Internet started as a tool for researchers at universities. And university-types *love* information. They collected documents and information and shared them on the Net. As a result, many computers have files of information that are free for the taking. The files range from U.S. Supreme Court decisions and library card catalogs to the text of old books, digitized pictures (most suitable for family audiences), and an enormous variety of software, from games to operating systems. So much free information is on the Net that people have created special tools known as *search engines, directories,* and *indices* to help you find stuff. Lots of people are trying to create the fastest, smartest search engine and the most complete Net index. We tell you about two of the most useful, AltaVista and Yahoo, so that you get the picture. As mentioned in the Introduction to this book, you see a Web icon here and there; it points to resources you can retrieve from the Net, usually as World Wide Web pages, as described in Chapter 12.

✔ **Electronic commerce:** You can buy stuff on the Internet. Heck, some of us even *sell* stuff on the Internet. Some people think that the Net will revolutionize commerce, just like supermarkets and no-haggle pricing did for groceries in the late 1800s. A dizzying array of stuff to buy is already out there, from books to videos to stock in microbreweries. You can already pay in lots of ways for what you buy, ranging from fancy "digital cash" to plain old credit cards. In fact, you can send your credit card number over the Internet in lots of ways, some about as safe as using your credit card over the telephone and others so safe that even the National Security Agency couldn't get its hands on it (at least that's the theory). We talk about the relevant issues later in this chapter and in Chapter 10.

✔ **Games:** A type of game that many people can play at the same time called a *MUD (Multi-User Dimension* or *Multi-User Dungeon)* can easily absorb all your waking hours and an alarming number of what otherwise would be your sleeping hours. In a MUD, you can challenge other players who can be anywhere in the world. Much less exotic but more relevant to many of us, you can also play traditional games like chess and backgammon on the Net.

✔ **Gossip:** No list of Internet uses would be complete without a mention of Usenet. Another one of those relics from the Internet's university days, *Usenet* refers to thousands of bulletin-board-like discussion groups available on the Internet: People post messages, and other people read them and respond, more or less politely, and with more or less useful information. Usenet discussions range from the sophomoric to the perverse to the technical to the arcane. Because almost anyone can set up a newsgroup, it's a good way for a company to promote discussions about its products or for people with offbeat interests to find one another. All the details are at our Web site, at

```
http://net.gurus.com
```

Is It Really Different, or Is It All Hype?

A great deal of hype *does* exist about how different the Internet is from previous forms of communication. But come on now, "the most important change in information since the printing press"? (We said that a couple of pages ago, in case you didn't notice.) This section tells you why we think so.

It's immediate

Although people say many things about lifestyles these days, one thing they all seem to agree on is that the pace of life in information-rich societies is faster than it has ever been. Put another way, like Alice in Wonderland, we're all running faster to stay in the same place. At the same time, information is becoming a more and more important part of our lives (there's the service economy, again). So the question becomes, "How do you want to get that information?"

Want some information from a manufacturer? You can call a company on the telephone, and if you want just a fact or two or a price, *if you can find the right person,* you get your information right away. Of course, the person taking your call may be busy, in which case you get his voice-mail and he gets back to you. If you want just a fact or two, however, you probably don't want to make it into a big project, but you have to. If you want a great deal of information, you won't get it in a telephone call. You want it in a form you can go back to and review, like a fax or a brochure, so you call the manufacturer and have someone send you a fax or some paper mail. When you get the info, you hope that you asked for the right thing and that it's still relevant to what you're doing.

Or you go to the World Wide Web and see the manufacturer's Web site. On a well-organized site, in just a few mouse clicks, you have your information. You still remember why you want it, and you can check right away to ensure that you've found the information you need.

It's democratic (with a small "d")

Anyone can put information out on the Internet, in a Usenet newsgroup, on a web page, in e-mail, in a chat room, or in any other forum that appears. And believe us, anyone already has. This situation is good and bad. It means that you, the reader, have to be responsible for evaluating what you read. It's probably fair to say that the monks copying manuscripts when Gutenberg came along felt the same way. Suddenly any fool with a printing press could print a book, many fools did, and it wasn't even authoritative.

The flip side of this issue, of course, was that anyone could read a book. Books no longer had to be protected as treasures because they no longer took years to produce. Historians have spent lives debating whether the wider dissemination of books, starting with the Bible, was responsible for everything from the Reformation to the French Revolution. The effect of information-for-everybody, however, was clearly dramatic.

A couple of things will probably result from the fact that everyone can publish and everyone can find the vast quantities of information on the Internet. First, people will get savvier about what they believe. When former Presidential press secretary Pierre Salinger waved around a printout from *the Internet* which "proved" that TWA flight 800 was shot down by a missile, the Net-savvy rolled their eyes while the rest of the world began to wonder, "Just what does it mean that information is on the Internet, anyway?" This incident was an important part of the learning process for all those people just becoming familiar with the Internet: Anyone can put information out there. Second, people will get savvier about how they present what they believe. The person who posts messages to a serious Usenet newsgroup in capital letters, insisting that there's a government conspiracy against him, gets as much credibility as the disheveled, unshaven guy standing on the soapbox on a city street. The person with the slick-looking Web site, with links to supporting materials and with lots of links from others to his site, suddenly looks much more credible.

It's as deep as you want it to be or as shallow as you want it to be

The idea of *hypertext* is about as old as the "modern" computer, although you may never have heard the term. Essentially, it's a way of connecting related pieces of information.

Back in the 1950s and 1960s, some pioneering thinkers suggested that soon too much information would be available, even for people interested in a particular subject — sort of like going to the encyclopedia to look for one fact and finding a ten-page article instead. You should, they said, be able to skim over the information and just zoom in on the exact facts you're looking for. The Internet, particularly the World Wide Web, begins to work that way. On a well-designed World Wide Web site, you should find one page giving you the big picture. You should then be able to dive in to exactly the subjects you're interested in. Not all Web sites work this way because organizing information this way takes much more work than writing traditional prose (we know; we do both).

Usenet newsgroups organize information by topic too, although with notable lapses. In Usenet discussions, people start a discussion with a topic. Suppose that one of us starts a discussion about lame chickens (you get interested in this kind of thing when you have pet chickens). People respond with their experiences or suggestions, and soon the Usenet discussion group has a *thread* (an ongoing discussion) or heading about lame chickens. People seeing the topic can decide whether they're interested in diving deeper into the subject.

It's chaotic

Chaos is good. Really. Chaos on the Internet means that things are never the same twice: The amount of time it takes to get information from here to there is different every time you send it; the collection of Web pages you may find on a particular subject may be different every time you look for the subject; the information on a particular computer may change from one visit to the next, and certainly the number of computers on the Net will be different. All this is good because it means that what's out on the Internet is the sum-total of the latest things people are thinking about.

It also means that the Internet is very different from a library. Most of us think of a library as a repository of information. We rest easy at night knowing that if we want to look at a 1948 copy of *The New York Times*, we can go to the library and see it on microfilm. The novel you took out of the library last year is usually still there next year if you want to reread it. The Internet is much more like a forest: Plants and animals (or information, in the case of the Net) come and go; you never know what you're going to see when you venture in, although the whole system is growing on its own.

The corollary to this concept, of course, is that if you find something you like, make a copy for yourself because you never know whether it will be there later. The most famous case is that of the Pentagon's files on Gulf War syndrome, which were posted on the Pentagon's Web site for about six months in 1995, before the Department of Defense decided, "Oops — those were classified" and removed them. By that time, of course, many people had copied them to their own Web sites, and the documents continued to be available.

Chaos has a less exotic side too, one that enables the Net to mirror real life. Two of us authors run a site that sells children's videotapes. If we get one copy of a tape (as we do sometimes, of used tapes that are out of print), we can advertise it on the Web site until someone buys it and then delete the ad. We could never do that if we had a printed catalog. By the same token, if you search for the tape *Babar the Elephant Comes to America* today, you may find it. Tomorrow, it may be gone.

It's ungovernable

The uncontrollable nature of the Internet is one of its most widely hyped aspects, and it's one area in which the hype matches reality. The Internet was designed to function even if one or more of the links that hold it together was broken. This design comes from its Cold War heritage, and we talk more about it at our Web site, at `http://net.gurus.com`. That design also means that it's very difficult to control where information goes on the Internet.

The current popular examples are Vietnam and China, both of whose governments are eager to join the modern information revolution but reluctant to allow people full access to all the information on the Net. Both have tried to set up "firewalls" so that they can monitor all the data that flows in and out of their countries. The betting in the Internet community is that they will fail. They can set up their own little Net "islands," with no access to or from the rest of the world, in which case they will find the Net less useful than the rest of the world does. Or they will find that information trickles in and out regardless of what they try. Like water, information on the Net flows through channels big and small; after a channel rejoins the main stream of information, though, you have no way of knowing how it got there: through the officially sanctioned channel or through someone's dial-up networking connection to a small Internet access point somewhere.

In the West, concerns over the *governability* of the Internet have focused more around the propriety of what people can access on the Net. If information is obscene or seditious or illegal here (wherever "here" is), governments have a reasonable chance of controlling that information on computers here: Computers can (and have been) seized and people thrown in jail for providing illegal information. What if the computer is overseas, though? How does a government know whether that information is coming into the country? By the time the information is chopped up and sent over the Internet, it's very hard, even for computers, to scan it for content.

Like it or not, after information is on the Internet, it goes anywhere people want it to go. And, unless the whole world is willing to live by the same set of laws regarding what's appropriate content, content that someone thinks is inappropriate will always be available on the Net.

It's rich in content but driven by the consumer

This point is obscure, although actually pretty important. *Rich in content* means that something communicates in many different ways. A page of typewritten text is not rich in content, though it may contain a great deal of information. The information is harder to absorb than, for example, a page of this book. Although a page in this book contains written information as well, we've *enriched* it by adding a table of contents, headings, icons in the margins, lists, and sidebars. All these elements help you find the information you want without having to read through 350 pages of gray text, although we hope, of course, that you read through the text anyway because we think that it's all interesting.

Traditionally, a magazine with pictures and different kinds of layouts is considered *richer* than a plain textbook, and TV is considered the richest medium of all, with sight, sound, and sometimes even text combining to communicate a message.

The "richer" the communications medium, the more costly it is to produce that medium. A minute of TV costs much more than a minute of radio, which costs more than a page of text. A minute of TV has to reach a much wider audience than a minute of radio, or than a page you type on your typewriter or word processor. Millions of people sit back on Thursday night and absorb one of a small number of TV shows, with broadcasters secure in the knowledge that those very expensive minutes of video are worth the expense.

The Net is different. As a medium, it has become richer and richer, starting with pages of text and text-only e-mail messages in the 1980s and now including pictures, sound, and moving pictures, just like television. Rather than have millions of people watch the same thing, however, people see what they want to see; people *go to* the programming they want to see rather than have that programming come to them at a time determined by someone else. *You the consumer* determine what you're going to see and when. If you don't like it, you don't have a choice of just the four or five other broadcast channels or 100 cable channels. Instead, you have the choice of millions of other web pages on the same or other subjects. This situation is new. Exactly what it will do to traditional media, no one knows. Although there are as many opinions as pundits, the only thing they all agree on is that it will make a big difference.

The Internet and Windows 98

At the time we write this chapter, Windows 98 isn't even an official product yet, and already it has a long and checkered history regarding the Internet. The reason is that much of Windows 98 crept out the door from Microsoft in the $2^1/_2$ years between the official release of Windows 95 and the official release of Windows 98. Some of what crept out the door had much to do with the Internet, and some people (including those at the Department of Justice) didn't like what they saw. Although it's hard to believe, when Windows 95 came out, the Internet was still a relatively small, relatively techie kind of thing. Although it was already useful, you really had to fiddle with the guts of your computer to get connected. Windows 95 made it easier to get connected, as did a host of software packages from other companies.

Adding the Internet to Windows

Along the way to Windows 98, Microsoft released Service Pack 1 for Windows 95, and later, OEM Service Release 2, known as OSR2. In December 1995, Bill Gates outlined a new Internet strategy for Microsoft that centered around the Internet, and over the succeeding months it became clear that Microsoft intended to integrate the web browser software into Windows itself.

No one knew quite what this intent meant until Windows 95 OSR2 was released in the fall of 1996. Now we've discovered that it means two or three very different things. To Microsoft, it means that the same program you use to look at information on the Internet should be used to look at information on your own computer — to make your computer easier to use and less confusing. To Netscape, the manufacturer of the competing web browser software, it looks like a ploy to require that everyone who buys Windows also have a copy of the Microsoft web browser — after you've done that, why buy another one from Netscape? The Justice Department seems to be seeing the question the Netscape way.

To users, combining Windows and Internet software looks confusing. Because people don't feel that the Net is an extension of their personal computer, the "integration" of the World Wide Web into the Windows 98 desktop doesn't feel seamless. Most people seem to want to "go to the Net" consciously rather than find that half the information they're looking at comes from the Web and half comes from their personal computer. We're not surprised, for several reasons.

First, information on the Net isn't organized in any particular way, and you have no control over what's where or how long it will be there. Information on your computer doesn't change unless you change it; information on your computer is organized the way you want it organized; and you get to filter and control what's on your computer.

Second, most of us don't have permanent connections to the Internet from our home computers. Although we talk more about this subject in Chapter 2, suffice it to say that, particularly if you only have one telephone line in your house, you don't want your computer dialing out to the Internet whenever *it* feels like it. You want to dial out to the Internet when *you* want to.

What Windows 98 comes with

All that having been said, what *does* Windows 98 give you relative to the Internet?

- ✔ An easy way to choose an Internet service, with the Internet Connection Wizard
- ✔ An easy way to connect to an Internet service you may already have, with the Internet Setup Wizard
- ✔ The Microsoft web browser, Internet Explorer (or, depending on what Microsoft and the Justice Department work out, you may have Netscape Navigator instead or also)
- ✔ The Microsoft e-mail program and Usenet newsreader, Outlook Express
- ✔ A couple of other Internet programs, including FrontPage Express (the Microsoft Web page editor), Microsoft Chat, and NetMeeting
- ✔ Access to broadcast-like features of the Internet, called *channels*
- ✔ Online updates if newer software for your computer is released

The nice thing about Windows 98 is that you get, for the first time, everything you need to connect to the Internet. Let's repeat that for emphasis: *If you have Windows 98, you already have everything you need to connect to the Internet.* Legalities and technicalities notwithstanding, that's a pretty nice situation. You don't have to run all over the computer store gathering hardware and software from different places just to get on the Internet.

What's the Department of Justice's beef with Microsoft, anyway?

Like most things legal, our story goes back a little in time. Back in 1990, first the Federal Trade Commission and later the Department of Justice began investigating Microsoft for possible antitrust actions. The investigation isn't too surprising: Any company as big as Microsoft, with as dominant a position as Microsoft has, is bound to be investigated sooner or later. What is telling is that, after all the dust settled, Microsoft was willing to sign an agreement with the U.S. government.

In this agreement, Microsoft agreed to a great deal of stuff. For Windows 98 and the Internet, the most important thing it agreed to was that it "shall not enter into any License Agreement in which the terms of that agreement are expressly or impliedly conditioned upon the licensing of any other Covered Product, Operating System Software product or other product (provided, however, that this provision in and of itself shall not be construed to prohibit Microsoft from developing integrated products)."

In English: Microsoft can't make you sell one of its products if what you really want to sell is another one of its products. It can develop "integrated" products, however. The thinking

at the Justice Department was that if Microsoft wanted to make serious inroads on a competitor, it might force anyone who wanted to sell Windows on its computer to also include the Microsoft answer to the competitor's product. For example, it would be illegal for Microsoft to insist that if you bought Windows, you had to buy Microsoft Word too. What it left open, of course, is "What is an integrated product?"

The Department of Justice claims that Microsoft was forcing PC manufacturers to include Internet Explorer on people's computers and prohibiting them from including other browsers, such as Netscape Navigator, if they wanted to sell Windows 95. Microsoft claims that Internet Explorer is an "integrated product" with Windows 95 OSR2. The early maneuvering in court seems to indicate that things are going the Department of Justice's way.

Fortunately, for you the user of the software, it doesn't matter much. As long as you have a web browser on your computer — Internet Explorer, Netscape Navigator, or another browser — they can all let you surf the Web. More importantly, after you have one, it's easy to get another — right off the Web!

The Windows 98 Active Desktop

The Active Desktop is supposed to be one of the keys to integrating Windows 98 and the World Wide Web. Here's what it boils down to in real life:

✔ **If you configure Windows 98 to use the "Web style" desktop, all the places you used to double-click in Windows 95 you now single-click in Windows 98.** Those of us who have tried to teach people when to double-click and when to single-click think that this feature is a *good thing* because the distinction in Windows 95 was so muddled that you couldn't get much beyond "try single-clicking, and if that doesn't work, try double-clicking."

✔ **You can use a Web page for wallpaper on your desktop.** By *Web page,* we mean stuff written and updated by someone "out there" on the World Wide Web. By *desktop,* we mean your computer screen when no programs are being displayed; your desktop usually has a bunch of icons on it (like My Computer and your favorite programs). *Wallpaper* is what Windows 98 shows when no programs are being displayed. The wallpaper appears behind whatever program icons are on your desktop; think of them as pictures hanging on (and therefore in front of) the wallpaper. Using a Web page as your wallpaper makes sense, however, only if you have a permanent connection to the Internet (through cable TV, a DSL telephone line, or a Local Area Network — we talk more about that subject in Chapter 2) or you're willing to have your computer be on the telephone frequently.

Is it worth it? In general, we think so. The single-clicking alone is worth the price of admission, and you can skip the other stuff if you want. Admittedly, now you have to learn when to *right*-click and when to *left*-click, but we think that you can handle that.

Windows 98 channels

You thought that channels were just on your TV? Think again. Remember awhile ago when we said that the Net has rich content but is driven by you, the consumer of that content? This situation does not sit well with the advertising and marketing types who became such an important part of the Net landscape in 1997.

The communications types who think about such things have described the Net as a *pull* medium. (They're the same people who describe the content as "rich.") What they mean by pull is that you go out and ask for the information; you *pull* it in to your computer. If you're interested in information about a new car or a book or some software, you go and look for it. Wouldn't it be neat, people thought, if you had another way to get information over the Net: What if it came to you?

This idea makes sense for some kinds of information, like stock market tickers and the weather. After the camel's nose is under the tent, however, all sorts of things can get *pushed* on to your computer screens. Advertisements immediately come to mind. Suddenly the World Wide Web looks a great deal like TV. And so, like TV, the content needs to be organized. That's where we got channels on the Windows 98 desktop.

Although channels and push were going to be the big thing in 1997, it hasn't quite worked out that way. Whether it's because people don't have the software for it or they don't have high-speed Internet connections in their homes or their bosses object to their watching the Discovery Channel (one of many out there) on their computer at work or they find push inherently obnoxious, push and channels have continued to wait for the next big thing. Still, they appear on your Windows 98 desktop unless you specifically ask them not to. Figure 1-1 shows what our desktop looks like with the channel bar on it.

Channel bar

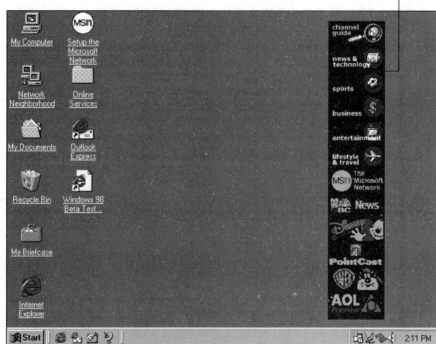

Figure 1-1:
Our
Windows 98
desktop
with the
channel
bar. Who's
buying?

It's a Jungle Out There
(Safety and Privacy on the Net)

Although this question may sound peculiar, the first thing to ask yourself about safety and privacy on the Net is "How much do you want?" At the extremes are two possibilities: Be completely private, an anonymous user traveling through the Internet like a knife through water, leaving not a trace. Or be a totally identifiable person, stamping "Kilroy was here" on every web site, discussion group, and Internet store you visit. The good news is that the Internet gives you the option of going either way. The bad news is that you have to think about it and decide where you want to be on the privacy scale.

Privacy and safety go, in some measure, hand in hand. If you're totally anonymous, you're likely to be pretty safe. After all, no one knows who you are, though you still have to watch out for some things, most of which are under the heading of "Safe computing," later in this chapter. On the other hand, if you're totally "out there," you may want to think about some things so that your online life and your physical life don't collide too violently.

How anonymous are you on the Net?

Let's start with some things people and Web sites *don't* know about you as you use the Internet. Unless you tell them, no one knows your name, your age, your sex, your physical stature, your handicaps, or your fabulous looks. You can project any image you want. On the other hand, all they know about you is what you say and how you act on the Net. Although your acne doesn't set you at a disadvantage, your dashing smile doesn't distract anyone from the bonehead remark you just made either.

All computers on the Internet have a number, sort of like a telephone number, called an *IP address*. It's the number that the Internet uses to make sure that the information you want gets to your computer. You may think that people could trace information back to you by tracing your IP number. Unlike your telephone number, however, your IP number changes every time you call in to the Internet. That's not true if your Internet connection is through a Local Area Network or other permanent connection, as it would most likely be if you're using the Net from your office. On the other hand, if you're using the Net from the office, you have lots of other things to worry about too, so keep reading.

Let's talk about what they *do* know about you — mainly, your e-mail address. Many Web pages ask you to register your e-mail address when you visit the page. This system is innocuous, unless the person who wrote the page decides to put you on an e-mail junk-mailing list. In that case, your e-mailbox fills up with about as much annoying junk as your paper-mailbox does during the Christmas catalog season.

People, inquisitive beasts that they are, may want to find out more about you. Sooner or later, you have a conversation with someone online — perhaps a technical-support person or a person at an online store or you wander into one of the many discussion groups or chat groups on the Net. If you're unlucky, you run into an unscrupulous person who wants to know more about you than he can find out from your computer. The most famous scam of this type is to pose as someone from "customer support" at some online service or e-mail service like AOL or Yahoo! (if you don't know what they are, don't fret; we get to them in the next chapter). Having established their "credentials," they ask you for your password or perhaps even a credit card number.

Never, ever, tell someone your password online. Ever. No one needs that information legitimately. People who claim otherwise are just admitting that they don't have the right to do whatever it is they want to do. Although most online services are good about reminding you not to give out your password, every year someone forgets, and then the Associated Press gets to write a story about how someone was presented with a $10,000 bill for online services stolen by a thief. Don't be that person.

Credit cards and the Internet

Credit cards are one of the hottest topics in the whole subject of buying and selling on the Internet. The discussion of credit cards and the Internet has four sides: merchants, fearmongers, hackers, and credit card companies. Merchants want you to use your credit card on the Internet. Face it: Credit cards are an easy way to pay for things, and the "transaction cost" (how much it really costs to "run" the charge) isn't that big. You can actually charge for things that cost $5, and everybody wins: You the customer get to make the purchase you want, and the merchant gets paid.

Why doesn't everybody use their credit card on the Net? Because of the fearmongers. The Internet is new technology. It's *sca-a-a-ry*. You type your information into that computer, and who knows where it may go or what may happen to it? People who are uneasy with the Internet seem to have focused much of their fear on what may happen to their credit card information between them and the merchant they're sending it to. They don't seem to worry about handing their actual physical cards with their handwritten signature to gas station attendants wearing distinctive outfits in bright colors not found in nature, to servers at restaurants, and to clerks at all sorts of stores. Do they know what those folks do with the card before they give it back to them? Do they worry about it? They certainly don't seem to spend much time warning you not to let your credit card out of your sight. Besides, there's a good living to be made as a fearmonger.

The malicious hackers play right into the hands of the fearmongers. Is it *possible* to snatch a credit card number from the Internet as it goes whizzing from place to place? Sure, it is. Lots of *crackers* (malicious hackers who like to break in to other people's computers) would like to tell you just how they would do it. Then lots of code nerds and virtuous hackers are dying to tell the crackers just how they would make that impossible. Then the malicious types find some other way they *may* be able to snatch a credit card number, and they go on and on. Although these guys are playing their games of one-upsmanship, the rest of us just want to order a book or CD or videotape on the Internet, and we do so with complete calm. Let's just point out that anyone with a radio scanner can pick up your credit card number if you're using a cordless or cell phone, as some politicians found out some time back. If you worry about ordering from a catalog while you're on a cordless phone, by all means worry about sending your credit card over the Internet. For the rest of us, the tiny risk is worth it.

Credit card companies have their own fish to fry. First of all, if someone ends up with your credit card, the companies are the ones responsible for the charges (sometimes after a $50 limit, which you pay). Second, they're not too comfortable with the Internet. The joke in the computer business says that as soon as banks get comfortable with double-entry bookkeeping (introduced in the 1400s), they'll get with this computer thing. On the other hand, the banks figure that there's money to be made on the Internet. So they (and, to be fair, many other folks) want to create some new payment system that they control. That way, they get their cut of every purchase.

We say, "The heck with them all." All of us have used our credit cards to buy things on the Internet, from $3 items to hundreds of dollars, and we've never had any problems. Furthermore, no documented cases have been recorded in which a credit card was used fraudulently as a result of an Internet transaction. It hasn't happened. Not once. Plain old scams? Sure: "Send us your credit card number, and we'll charge the shipping on the great prize you just won!" But you can do that on the telephone just as well.

Cookie crumbs

The crumbs of information web browsers can find out about you are not enough for the data-hungry sites of the Internet. Internet sites want to be capable of identifying you (uniquely) when you come to visit. Sometimes they even want to remember information about you, for a couple of good reasons. First, if you're using a service you pay for, they want to be able to identify the fact that you're you without having to ask every time you visit — no more of this "Enter your username and password" business. Second, if you've been shopping at a Web site and have items in your "shopping cart," the site wants to be able to remember from screen to screen who you are and what you're planning to buy. The same idea applies if you've been playing a game or chatting with people or making an airline reservation.

For some technical reasons, the only way an Internet site can do all that is to ask you who you are. Obviously, because asking you to enter your name over and over again would be annoying, the folks who make Internet browser software came up with another scheme: They leave some identifying information on your computer, and whenever they need to know who you are, they just ask your computer rather than ask you. They call those little bits of identifying information *cookies*.

Cookies can store all sorts of information about you, but only the information you give to the computer that's putting the cookie on your computer. Programs and Web sites are can read only cookies that they wrote. On the other hand, a cookie may contain *any* information you gave to the Web site that created the cookie as well as information the Web site provided. Most cookies contain incomprehensible strings of numbers, although some certainly could contain stuff that made sense if you looked at it.

People have very different feelings about cookies. Some of us don't care what any computer remembers about what we told it, so one of our computers is loaded with cookies — 67, to be exact. Another of us is conservative about cookies and routinely tells computers that they can't put cookies on his machine. (We talk about how to do that in Chapter 9, in the section about keeping cookie crumbs off your computer).

Safe computing

The greatest risk to safe computing from the Internet comes in the form of viruses — not the human little-strand-of-DNA kind, but rather the digital little-strand-of-computer-programming kind. Fortunately, if you stay in polite society, you aren't likely to come across much in the way of viruses. Even so, it's good to have a plan in mind for viruses. Most of this advice is actually prudent care-and-feeding of your computer advice, regardless of whether you use the Internet.

Make backups

Depending on what you do, making backups can be as simple as saving your documents to a floppy disk when you also save them on your hard disk or as fancy as copying your whole hard disk to tape every night. Obviously, to do a tape backup, you have to have a tape drive, and that costs money. Think for a moment, though, how much time you would waste when your computer's disk becomes unusable. Note that we say *when,* not *if.* At least once in the life of every computer user, whether because of lightning, a brownout, a Windows 98 configuration that suddenly refuses to work, a hard disk that suddenly makes a loud and fatal noise, or a virus, you find that you can't read from your hard disk.

If you have a tape backup, you just get the hardware to work, load enough software to "see" the tape drive, and reload that tape. With luck, you're done in an hour-and-a-half. If you don't have a tape, you run around and gather all the software you loaded on your computer, load it again, and find all the floppy disks on which you saved all your documents (except the one you really need, of course). Load all those disks, and you're off to the races. One day, no problem; $150 for a tape drive should be starting to look attractive. If you have more money to spend, you could consider an external hard drive (4MB for about $300) or a do-it-yourself CD recorder (starting at about $400 — but a great investment for the self-publishing musician.)

Use virus-protection software

Microsoft used to include virus-protection software with Windows, but, for reasons known only to itself, it doesn't anymore. (What? It *unbundled* something?) That's okay; plenty of better virus scanners are out there, some of them free and almost all of them costing less than $100. Most of them can automatically look at files you download from the Internet and check them for viruses before they can do any harm.

A virus does no harm to your computer until you either run the program that contains it or open the document that contains it. (Yes, some kinds of documents, notably Microsoft Word documents and Microsoft Excel spreadsheets, can contain viruses too.) If a virus scanner can look at the program (or document) containing the virus *before* you run the program or open the document, the scanner can alert you before any damage is done.

Virus checkers that work with your browser program automagically look at the files you download and warn you if you are downloading a file with a virus in it. Other offline virus scanners can be scheduled to run when your computer is idle or at a particular time during the day or night. How careful you choose to be about virus scanning depends on what you download and where you download them from. If you download only popular programs from well-established commercial sites, you can be somewhat relaxed about it — someone else generally finds the problems before you do, and they get fixed quickly.

If you are the adventurous sort and choose to troll the Internet's lesser-known sites for more obscure software, we recommend being careful.

Keeping your real life and your Internet life separate

For a number of good reasons, you may want to keep your real life and your Internet life separate. Usually, that's pretty easy to do. Because you can identify yourself by whatever name you want and because you are what you say on the Net, you're responsible for how much of your physical life leaks over into your Internet life. In fact, you probably do not want your physical life and your Internet life to be instantly identifiable with one another. The Internet is a whole new way of communicating, and people generally seem to want to create personalities just for the Internet. This concept isn't so strange when you think about it; it's kind of like what happened with the telephone. Now that we have the technology for picture telephones, no one seems to want them. Some of us *like* being able to sound businesslike and authoritative while in pajamas. Your telephone identity comes from your voice and your previous dealings with people.

That's why, when it comes time for you to decide what your username will be on the Internet, you may not want to choose something that identifies you too clearly: IthacaJoe gives people the idea rather than something more identifiable with you, like JoeSmithIthacaEnvironmentalLawyer — besides, that's a whole lot to type. For a couple of more substantive reasons, you may want to retain some online privacy:

✔ You're a professional — a physician, for example — and you want to participate in a mailing list or newsgroup without being asked for your professional opinion.

✔ You want help with an area of concern that you feel is private and would not want your problem known to people close to you who may find out if your name were associated with it.

✔ You do business on the Net, and you socialize on the Net. You may want to keep those activities separate.

Finally, here's a list, mainly of "don'ts" — things not to do when you're creating relationships online:

✔ Don't give anyone any password over the Internet. We said that already, although it bears repeating.

✔ Don't give out your address or telephone number unless you're willing for it to be totally public information. In all likelihood, your name, address, and telephone number are already publicly available on the Internet (we talk about that subject in Chapter 10). Except for people who know you, however, they're not associated with you the person or even you the personality on the Internet. If that guy who insulted you in the chat room last night has easy access to your phone number, your phone is likely to ring at 3 a.m. Or worse.

✔ Safeguard information about your kids. A chat room or a Web site can be run by anyone. If a reputable manufacturer of kids' games wants to know how old your kids are in order to send them demonstrations of age-appropriate software, that idea isn't such a bad one. People are so paranoid about information regarding kids, however, that no company would ask. On the other hand, anyone can set up a "kids' chat Web site" and ask for that same information in order to "register" for the site. Disclosing that much info about your kids in an unknown setting is not a good idea. The trick, of course, is getting your kids to be as prudent.

You've probably heard about some terrible thing that happened to someone who met somebody she had been corresponding with on the Internet. These things do happen, although they're very, very, very rare. Many more wonderful things have happened too — they just don't get so much press. We've met some of our best friends over the Net, and some people have met and gotten married — no kidding! We just want to encourage you to use common sense when you set up a meeting with a Net friend. Here are a few tips:

✔ Talk to the person on the phone before you agree to meet. If you don't like the sound of the person's voice or you feel nervous, don't do it.

✔ Depending on the context, try to check the person out a little. If you've met in a newsgroup or chat room, ask someone else you know whether they know this person. (Women, ask another woman before meeting a man.)

✔ Meet in a well-lit public place. Take a friend or two with you.

✔ If you're a kid, take a parent with you. Never, ever meet someone from the Net without your parents' explicit consent.

Surfing from the office

A couple of special concerns arise if you surf the Net from your office. The first, of course, is company policy. It may be against company policy for you to use the computer on your corporate desk to surf the Net for anything other than the most boring business purposes. Companies are more or less stringent about enforcing this kind of policy, depending on their corporate culture. If you're about to start surfing the Net from work and you don't know anyone else who is, you may want to ask around about the local policy.

Why would a company prohibit Net surfing implicitly or explicitly? Many good ideas and discussions are out there. Any company big enough to have a policy manual, however, may make it clear that viewing sexually explicit material on the office computer is a serious no-no. Even if the company doesn't care whether a coworker looks over your shoulder and sees offensive stuff, that may be enough to prove sexual harassment.

We have some friends who have done computer support at somewhat straight-laced major U.S. corporations, and they have been appalled at what they have found on people's hard disks. Do you want to be explaining what the picture-of-the-month is doing on your hard disk when you really want the support person to be helping you recover that big slide presentation for tomorrow's meeting? Let's get the details straight: If you're using the company's computer and Internet connection:

- ✔ Yes, they can read your e-mail.
- ✔ Yes, they can look all over your hard disk.
- ✔ Yes, they can keep track of what web sites you visited.
- ✔ Yes, in many cases they can listen to your telephone calls.

You work for the company, the computer belongs to the company, and you are using the computer on company time, so your privacy rights don't apply. We thought that we ought to warn you.

That's the last of the gloom and doom you hear from us regarding the Internet. We think that it's a cool place, and we spend a great deal of time there (our friends sometimes say too much time).

Where Did the Internet Come From?

If you want to know more abou the history of the Internet, zip over to our Web site, where we give you all the details:

    http://net.gurus.com

Chapter 2

How May I Connect to Thee? Let Me Count the Ways

- -

In This Chapter

▶ Ways to connect to the Internet from Windows 98

▶ What you need to connect to the Internet

▶ How to choose an ISP

▶ Programs that talk over the Net

- -

*W*ith all the hoopla around Windows 98 and its integration with the Internet, people often forget that after you get Windows 98 installed, *you* still have to connect it to the Internet. In a sense, it's a throwback to the days of yore, when computers arrived with no software installed and a big stack of boxes filled with software you had to load, configure, and make work all by yourself. Nowadays, Microsoft Office packages, rather than Corel or Lotus packages, come preloaded on the hard disk. (You may wonder why that is; some of us do. Perhaps the Department of Justice is wondering too.)

No Internet connection comes preloaded because you can connect your computer to the Internet in too many ways for one of them to be the "obvious" choice, even for Microsoft. The reason is partly that no single Internet provider is a local telephone call from everywhere in the United States and partly that an Internet connection is a service you pay for every month rather than software you buy once. The best deal for you depends on what you are going to do, how much support you want, where you live, and often what local or long-distance telephone plan you have.

In this chapter, we introduce you to the different ways you can connect to the Internet, and we tell you what tools normally found around the home you need in order to connect. *Hint:* An electric drill is *not* one of them — we're talking software tools here. In Chapter 3, we give you step-by-step instructions for getting connected to the type of account you choose.

If you already have an Internet account you're happy with and for which you don't pay huge long-distance bills, we give you permission to skip this entire chapter and go directly to Chapter 3. On the other hand, you may want to read this chapter anyway, to find out what your alternatives are.

Ways to Connect to the Internet from Windows 98

To connect your computer to the Internet, you have two major choices — or three, if you're lucky:

▶ **Choice 1: Sign up with an online service, such as America Online.** Online services tend to be easier to use, and they provide information in a more organized way. They usually don't give you the full range of Internet services, however. Unless services have a flat rate for unlimited use, they can be expensive if you use them for more than a few hours a month. Because demand is growing faster than some providers can support, access is sometimes slow.

▶ **Choice 2: Sign up with an Internet provider for an Internet account.** These folks are the main "on-ramp" to the Internet nowadays. They give you the basic account you need to put your computer on the Internet. If you decide that you want to deepen your Internet experience, most Internet providers allow you to put up a web page, though exactly how varies from provider to provider. What these folks give you is a PPP account (we promise to explain it in a few paragraphs), which is what you need to use a web browser (Internet Explorer or Netscape Navigator), an Internet mail program (Outlook Express, Eudora or Netscape Communicator), and all the other new things cropping up on the Internet, from telephones to whiteboards.

▶ **Choice 3 (if you're lucky): Sign up for cable TV access.** We say "if you're lucky" because cable access is not widely available yet. If it's available in your area, however, all you have to do is call your cable company and arrange for someone to come and install a network card in your computer and some cable in your home (if you don't already have cable TV). If you choose this option, you can skip the rest of this chapter and just gloat. You don't need a phone, you don't need a modem, and you don't need a TV.

This section takes them one at a time.

Are you already on the Internet?

If you have access to a computer running Windows 98, it may already be on the Internet. If you're just upgrading to Windows 98 from Windows 3.1 or Windows 95, you may also already be on the Internet. Here are some ways to check:

✔ If you have an account on an online service, such as CompuServe, America Online (AOL), Prodigy, Microsoft Network (MSN), or MCI Mail, you already have a connection to the Internet. At the least, you can send mail, and some online services provide relatively complete Internet connections.

✔ If you use a computer at your company or school, it may well have an internal e-mail system. If it does, it can probably send mail to and from the Internet. Ask a local mail expert.

✔ If your company or school has a local computer network, it may be connected directly or indirectly to the Internet, for either just mail or a wider variety of services. Because networks of PCs (even Windows 3.1, Windows 95, and Macs) usually use the same type of networking the Internet does, connection is technically easy. Some networks of PCs or Macs use different types of network setups (most commonly Novell Netware or AppleTalk). For them, it's more difficult, but still possible, for the people who run the network to hook it to the Internet.

Prodigiously computing and serving America online

Back in the old days (and it's amazing how recent those old days were), the Internet was only for serious computer geeks. Everyone else who wanted to be online used (we show our age here) The Source or, later, CompuServe or, even later, America Online and Prodigy. Those online services did a few important things to earn the two or three (or, early on, even ten) dollars an hour they charged their customers.

First, they provided local telephone numbers in most of the major regions where people live. That capability was often important. Even if your company or university had a computer you could dial in to from home, if you lived any distance away, the long-distance telephone charges could mount up fast. (For more information about long-distance charges, see the sidebar "How important is my ISP's telephone number, really?" later in this chapter.) Even if you were adventurous and signed up with a bulletin-board system, after you traveled away from home, it was long-distance time again.

Second, the online services provided easy-to-use software for electronic mail. For a long time, you could only trade mail with people on the same online service as you, although that capability could still be useful. Third, they provided "chat" facilities — the same online kind of CB-type chats we talk about in Chapter 1. Fourth, they created communities of people with similar interests, ranging from the technical to the social. Online services were a decent deal: many of the most popular Internet services with much less hassle.

With the growth in popularity of the Internet and new packages that make it easy to sign on, CompuServe, AOL, and Prodigy decided to make themselves "gateways" to the Internet, providing all the services they had traditionally provided and adding Internet access. Because they implemented this decision in fits and starts, you may have heard of lots of things you can't do if you use one of these three services as an Internet gateway; by the time you read this chapter, however, they all will offer nearly all the services that most direct Internet connections do — in addition to all the services you can get only from them.

The pros and cons of AOL and CompuServe as Internet providers

Here are some reasons you may want to use AOL or CompuServe to access the Internet:

  ✔ **You already have an AOL or CompuServe account.** It's the best reason we can think of. If you've been using these services, you already have an e-mail address that people may know, and you probably have found stuff on these services you like (such as chat rooms or investment advice or movie reviews). Why bother learning that all over again? Continue to use what you know *and* use new things on the Internet: It's the best of both worlds.

  ✔ **AOL or CompuServe have local-access telephone numbers in your area, and no one else does.** This situation is very unlikely.

  ✔ **You travel frequently, particularly overseas.** CompuServe in particular has an excellent network of service points all over the world. Both AOL and CompuServe provide good national coverage in the United States. Using AOL or CompuServe enables you to get on the Net without having to rip out your Windows 98 Internet setup every time you visit a new location. (On the other hand, if you travel frequently, IBM's Internet service has even more international service points than CompuServe does.)

  ✔ **You want to post your own Web page without becoming an Internet whiz.** Although we take you through as much of the posting-your-own-web-page procedure as we can, every Internet provider is a little different. AOL makes it pretty easy.

Here are some reasons you may *not* want to use AOL or CompuServe to access the Internet:

- ✔ Some of the Internet services they provide are new to them, and our experience is that their technical support sometimes isn't up on the latest details.

- ✔ Access to Internet features, from searching the World Wide Web to downloading files, can be slower because everything you're doing has to go from the computer you're looking at to their computer to your computer.

- ✔ Your computer has an extra layer of software — although it's not *supposed* to get in the way, sometimes it does.

- ✔ Internet access isn't their main business, so if that's what you want to concentrate on, you may not have their full attention.

As you can probably tell from this list, we think that using CompuServe or AOL as your Internet provider works, although we're not enthusiastic about it. Although we have accounts on both online services, we mainly use a *real* Internet provider (read on).

What are AOL, CompuServe, and Prodigy doing on my Windows 98 Start menu?

For that matter, what are AOL Preview and Microsoft Network doing on the channel bar on your desktop? And hey, what *is* the channel bar? One thing at a time.

In Chapter 1, we talk about channels — the Microsoft way of organizing information it's going to "push" onto your computer. The channel bar is the Microsoft suggestion for what channels you may be interested in. You're not really "subscribed" to any of these channels, which we talk all about in Chapter 11.

The AOL Preview and MSN (Microsoft Network) channels are both "teasers" that try to convince you to buy the full service. The AOL Preview even has a button to sign up for the service. You also find AOL and MSN on the Windows

Start menu (by choosing Programs⇨Online Services), along with AT&T WorldNet, CompuServe, and Prodigy Internet. Each of these commands starts you down the road to signing up for a particular online service. We talk all about how to do *that* in Chapter 3.

For the record, AOL and CompuServe are online services that also function as Internet service providers if you really want them to. MSN and Prodigy Internet are both online services that changed themselves into Internet service providers; MSN still has a great deal of content you can get to only if you're a member using its own software. Of the services on the Programs⇨Online Services menu, only AT&T WorldNet is a basic Internet service provider.

Serving up the Internet

Companies that sell Internet accounts — accounts that connect your computer to the Internet — are called *Internet service providers* in geekspeak and are even more often abbreviated *ISP.* (We computer types just love TLAs — three-letter acronyms.) An ISP is similar to an online service, but with the important difference that its primary business is hooking people to the Internet. Because almost all ISPs buy their equipment and software from a handful of manufacturers, the features and services one ISP offers are much like those of another, with such important differences as price, service, and reliability. Think of it as the difference between a Ford and a Buick, with the differences between your local dealers being at least as important in the purchase decision as the differences between the cars.

What an ISP sells you is known as a *PPP account.* For all you TLA fans, PPP stands for Point-to-Point Protocol, if you must know. (An earlier scheme called SLIP worked the same way as PPP, although PPP is now universally offered and is more reliable.) When you connect to your provider with PPP, your computer becomes part of the Internet. You type stuff directly to programs running on your computer, and those programs communicate over the Net to do whatever it is they do for you.

The big advantage of PPP access is that you're not limited to running programs your Internet provider gives you. You can download a new Internet application from the Net and begin using it immediately — your provider acts only as a data conduit between your computer and the rest of the Net.

The disadvantage of PPP accounts used to be that they were difficult to set up. You had to know many arcane numbers and fiddle around in the guts of your computer's operating system. Windows 98 makes this process much easier with its Wizards, and we lead you through the process in Chapter 3.

If you're the type of person who likes to live on the edge, technologically speaking, you probably want the fastest Internet connection available so that you can play with all the fancy graphics and download sound and video. Graphics, video, and sound are all bits of information — lots and lots of bits of information — too many for most dial-up connections to handle. High-speed connections can provide greater *bandwidth,* the amount of data transferred in a specific amount of time. The good news is that high-speed connections are becoming available and affordable by mere mortals. And they are available from ISPs, not from online services.

And then there's the cable guy

Cable television companies have been working to provide Internet access and in some areas are successfully providing service. If cable Internet access is available in your community, it's worth checking out.

Here's how it works in the Boston area. You call the cable company. The technician comes and installs a network connection doozus (technical term) where your cable comes into your house, installs a standard network card in your computer if it doesn't already have one, brings a cable modem (Carol's looks like a laptop computer with a spike hairdo), and hooks them together. Magic.

If you have cable television, the cable is split, and one segment goes to your computer. If you don't have cable television, the cable company may have to install the actual cable too. When the technician goes away, however, you have a permanent, high-speed connection to the Internet (as long as you pay your bill, about $50 a month). In addition to the speed and constant access at a fixed price, you aren't tying up a phone line.

Essentially, the cable TV company serves as your Internet service provider. This setup is nice because it gets one company out of your Internet equation. With a PPP account from an ISP (that's what we describe in the preceding section), you use the phone company to get in touch with the Internet. With a cable modem, your computer talks directly to the cable company's box. Because they're the folks supplying the Internet data to you, one less company is involved (the telephone company gets left out of the play).

Firewalls: Computing inside a box

Lots of PCs in big companies are loaded up with Internet software and have network connections with a hookup to the Internet, so if you're so blessed, you can run programs on your computer and hook right up to the Net. Right? Not quite.

If you're in a large organization that has (not altogether unreasonable) concerns about confidential company secrets leaking out by way of the Internet, a *firewall* system placed between the company network and the outside world may limit outside access to the internal network.

Because the firewall is connected to both the internal network and the Internet, any traffic between the two must go through the firewall. Special programming on the firewall limits which type of connections can be made between the inside and outside and who can make them.

In practice, you can use any Internet service that is available within the company; for outside services, however, you're limited by what can pass through the firewall system. Most standard outside services — such as looking at Web pages, copying files from one computer to another, and sending and receiving electronic mail — should be available, although the procedures, involving something called a *proxy server,* may be somewhat more complicated than what's described in this book.

Often, you have to log in to the firewall system first and from there get to the outside. It's usually impossible for anyone outside the company to get access to systems or services on the inside network (that's what the firewall is for). Except for the most paranoid of organizations, electronic mail flows unimpeded in both directions.

Keep in mind that you probably have to get authorization to use the firewall system before you can use *any* outside service other than mail.

What You Need to Connect Windows 98 to the Internet

Just about any computer that can run Windows 98 can connect to the Internet. In addition to your Windows 98 machine, however, you need three items to make this Internet trick work:

- ✔ A modem to hook your computer to the phone line
- ✔ An account with an online service or Internet provider, to give your modem somewhere to call
- ✔ Software to run on your computer

We look at each of these items in turn.

Choosing a Modem

If you went the cable TV route we just talked about in this chapter, you don't need a modem, so skip this section.

No matter whether you sign up with AOL, CompuServe, or an Internet service provider (ISP, remember?), your computer calls their computer over the telephone. How fast information comes and goes to and from the Internet is determined by three things: how fast your computer can squirt the information into the telephone, how fast the telephone company can carry that information to the provider you signed up with, and how fast it can suck that information from the phone. The "thing" that connects your computer to the telephone (and, on the other end, the telephone to the service's computer) is called a *modem*.

Shapes, sizes, and speeds

Modems come in all sorts of shapes and sizes. Some are separate boxes, known as *external* modems, with cables that plug in to the computer and the phone line with power cords. Other, *internal* modems are inside the computer, with just a cable for the phone, and some of the newest ones (*PC Card* modems) are tiny credit-card-card-size things you stuff into the side of your computer. (They still have a cable for the phone — some things never change.)

Matching the variety of physical sizes is an equal variety of internal features. The speed at which a modem operates (or the rate at which it can stuff computer data into a phone line) ranges from a low of 2400 bits per second (bps, commonly but erroneously called baud) to 33,000 and even 56,000 bps. (These big numbers are usually abbreviated as 33K and 56K, and the bps part is dropped.) Notice that in all these cases, we're talking *bits* per second here; divide by eight to get bytes (or characters) per second. So your 56K modem transfers a maximum of 7,000 characters per second to and from the Internet (and that's if you're *very* lucky). Some modems can act as fax machines, and some can't. Some have even more exotic features, such as built-in voice jail, er, mail.

Nearly any modem made in the past ten years is adequate for an initial foray on the Net, and most computers sold in the past couple of years come with built-in modems. If you already have a modem, use it. If you have to buy a modem, get the fastest thing you can afford — 14,400 bps (the slowest you can buy nowadays) is just barely adequate. While you're shopping, be sure to get a cable to connect the modem to your computer, and be sure that it has connectors which match the connectors on computer — three different kinds are used.

Note to laptop computer owners: If your computer has credit-card-size PC Card slots but no built-in modem, get a PC Card modem that fits in a slot so that you don't have to carry around a separate modem when you take your computer on the road. Although it costs more, it's worth it.

When is a modem not a modem?

You may have heard that you can connect your computer to the Internet in faster ways than using a modem. In theory, that's true, although reality is usually another story. Here's the scoop: The pair of phone wires that runs between your house and the phone company has remained unchanged in design since about 1900. They work just fine for voice applications, such as ordering pizza, but leave something to be desired for transmitting Internet data. In the early 1980s, AT&T developed what was supposed to be the next generation of telephones, called *ISDN,* alleged to be short for Improvements Subscribers Don't Need. ISDN uses the same phone wires (which is important because phone companies have about 100 million of them installed) and puts boxes at each end that transmit *digital* data rather than the older *analog* data. In this arrangement, an ISDN line can transmit 128K bits per second, a considerable improvement over the 33K or 56K that a regular line permits.

Does your computer need its own telephone line?

No. If you're planning on doing serious surfing, however, you may want to get it one. You don't *have* to, but let's clear up some common misconceptions. Then, you can decide whether you *want* to.

When your computer is connected to the Internet, it is talking on the telephone. Even though nobody in the house has a handset glued to an ear, your telephone is in use. People calling you get a busy signal, just as though the cat had knocked the receiver off the cradle. If you pick up the telephone, you hear a great deal of static, which is what information actually sounds like as it streams down the telephone line. The computers (yours and the one you called) usually resent the intrusion and hang up on each other. If you've been getting a large program from the Internet for later use on your computer ("downloading," as explained in Chapter 12) and you're 45 minutes into a 50-minute download, you won't be very happy about the hang-up.

Think about the following when you're deciding whether to get a second telephone line: If you live with other people, is it okay with them for the telephone to be tied up for hours at a time? Even if you live alone, is it okay with you not to be able to receive telephone calls for hours at a time? Finally, if you're new to computers and need some technical support about an Internet program, it can be convenient to talk to technical-support people *while* you're on the Internet and using their program. You can only do that if you have two telephone lines.

If you can afford it and if you think that you'll be online for any length of time, we strongly recommend a second telephone line. If you decide not to get one, however, you may want to get voice-mail service from the telephone company if it's available in your area. Although we normally like our trusty answering machine, if you're on the Internet, people calling you get a busy signal and the answering machine never gets the call. With voice mail, the telephone company takes the message while you or your computer are on the phone, without the caller ever getting a busy signal. Then, when you're done surfing the Net, you can deal with the dozens of irate friends wondering who the heck you were talking to on the telephone for all those hours.

Although the idea was good, phone companies, unfortunately, utterly botched the way they made ISDN available. For one thing, ISDN installation is fantastically complicated; we know full-time managers who have been unable to find anyone at their local phone company who knows how to install it. For another, ISDN is overpriced in most places: in New York, for example, an ISDN line costs about twice as much as a regular line, and every call you make, even a local call, costs extra. For this reason, unless you have a local Internet provider that arranges the details of an ISDN connection for you and knows the incantations to mutter at the phone company to make the per-call charges go away (phrases such as "multilocation Centrex"), we don't think that ISDN is worth the bother.

Wait! ISDN uses 1970s computer technology, and these are the 1990s! In the meantime, the communications wizards have invented ADSL, SDSL, and HDSL — the DSL stands for Digital Subscriber Loop, and the first letter is a minor variation on the theme. *xDSL*, as it has come to be called, can take the same pair of phone wires and run not at a piddling 128,000 bits per second but at two, three, and even five *million* bits per second using 1990s technology. ADSL was originally intended to provide "video on demand"; telephone companies soon discovered, however, that when people demand video, they satisfy their own desire not with ADSL from the telephone company, but by turning on cable TV or running down to the store to rent a movie. ADSL has now been reborn as yet another high-speed Internet gateway.

Phone companies are still in the early stages of advanced planning for their ADSL roll-out strategies. (Or, in English, they don't yet have a clue about how or when to offer ADSL, so they're doing experiments.) They do know that they have to do something soon or else the cable-TV crowd will steal all their Internet customers.

So the answer to when a modem isn't a modem is, "When it connects to an ISDN line — then it's a *terminal adapter*." People got over this silliness when it came to xDSL, so the box you use with an xDSL line is still called a modem.

Marrying an Internet Service Provider

Okay, you've decided not to go the cable-modem route, and you've decided not to go the AOL or CompuServe route. Your decision means that you have to pick an Internet service provider. This selection may seem as mystifying to you as picking a dentist from the telephone book seems to some of us. We can shed some light on the problem, however. This section tells you what to think about and look for.

First, it would be nice to get your selection right the first time. Because your ISP's name is part of your e-mail address, you don't want to change too often, or else your friends will get tired of trying to follow you around. Still, if you find that you have to move, it's not too big of a problem if you do so before 600 people have your e-mail address in their address books.

Second, it's almost impossible to actually, substantively compare ISPs. Although a little mini-industry out there of programs and services claims to measure ISP performance, they really rate only the national or large regional ISPs, and the performance they measure may or may not have anything to do with the performance you experience.

Third, the most important thing about an ISP is its telephone number. If an ISP isn't a local telephone call for you, don't consider it. In most places, that cuts the list to a handful of potential ISPs.

How important is my ISP's telephone number, really?

If you're not careful, you can end up paying more for the phone call than you do for your Internet service. One of the things you do when you sign up for an online service is to determine the phone number to call. *If at all possible, use a provider whose number is a free or untimed local call.* If you use a local or regional Internet service provider, that provider has a short list of phone numbers you can use. Of the national providers, IBM, AT&T, and CompuServe have their own national networks of dial-in numbers; the rest piggyback on other networks, such as Sprintnet, from Sprint; Tymnet, from MCI; and Alternet, from WorldCom. If one national provider has a local number, therefore, they probably all do because it's a Sprintnet, Tymnet, Alternet, or CompuServe number that works for any of them.

If you cannot find a provider that's a local call for you, your options are limited. If you have a long-distance plan, such as Sprint Sense (Sprint) or Friends and Family (MCI), you can put your provider's phone number on your list of frequently called numbers and get a low rate that should be less than ten cents per minute for nights and weekends. (That's still more than $5 per hour.) Be sure to compare rates for in-state and out-of-state calls because an out-of-state call is cheaper in many cases even though it's farther away.

Here's a real-life story that happened to one of our readers, who wrote to ask us to warn other people. She bought a new computer with Internet software already installed. When she started up the software, it said that it would find a local-access number for her. She entered her area code and the first three digits of her phone number to aid the search. The software found a number and configured her program to dial it automatically. She believed it, not unreasonably, when it said that it had found a local-access number. She found out differently, however, when her $500 phone bill arrived. To be sure that this situation doesn't happen to you, if you let your Internet provider's software find a local-access number for you, check that number before you let your computer dial it. Check for the availability of a truly local provider, as explained in the following section, "Who's eligible to be your ISP?" Call your long-distance carrier and find out, at minimum, your charge per minute.

Who's eligible to be your ISP?

A bunch of national ISPs exist — companies that have set out to provide Internet access over most (if not all) of the country. Their thinking is that, just as you want to use a long-distance calling card anywhere in the country, you will want to use your Internet account anywhere in the country. They also figure that if they own their own network, they can provide better-quality service than smaller companies. Not surprisingly, many of these national companies are in the communications business. Some of the more well-known are AT&T WorldNet, Concentric, IBM Internet Connection, MindSpring, and Sprint Internet Passport.

Finding a local Internet service provider is much like finding any other small- or medium-size business serving your community. Try the following:

- ✔ Check the business pages of your local newspaper for advertisements from local-access providers.

- ✔ Ask your public library's research librarian or online services staff.

- ✔ Look in your local yellow pages under Internet Services.

- ✔ Use a friend's Internet account, an Internet computer at the local library, or a trial account from a commercial provider to access the World Wide Web. Search for "Internet service providers." You can find numerous lists of them that you can then search for something close to home. We've compiled our own list of lists for you. Check our Web page about ISPs (at `http://net.gurus.com/isp`) for Web sites that list ISPs by state, area code, or country.

- ✔ Ask anyone you know in your area who already has access what she's using and whether she likes it.

Many cities also have *freenets,* a type of local community computer system that usually has a link to the Internet. Except in Los Angeles, freenets are indeed free (although they don't turn down contributions if you want to support them.) If you know anyone who already has access to the Web, maybe you can coax that person into checking out the following location, which provides a current list of freenets around the world:

`http://www.genealogy.org/NGS/netguide/freenets.html`

Choosing from among the eligible

After you've determined which companies are in your handful of ISPs, here are some things to think about as you try to select from among them. As usual, no hard-and-fast rule applies for choosing between a national ISP and a local one. National ISPs are convenient because they have lots of dial-in numbers across the country; this option can be handy if you travel much. AT&T, for one, has a handy toll-free number you can call that automagically tells you what telephone number to dial for Internet access, and it even makes a stab at telling you whether it's a local call. National ISPs also usually (but, sadly, not always) have an extensive support staff to help you. On the other hand, because local ISPs tend to compete in pricing more than the national ones do, you may get a better deal. And, because they stick to one geographic area, many offer community-oriented online materials.

When you're doing your comparison shopping, consider the factors discussed in the following sections.

Price

Pricing schemes have become more standard over the past couple of years, although what you're offered may still vary greatly. Some providers charge you by the hour, and others have a flat rate per month. Many have "blended" schemes: For a monthly charge, you get a set number of hours, and you pay by the hour if you use more than that. Most providers have a flat rate of $20 per month or less, which we recommend even if they also have a lower blended rate. If you do pick one with limited free hours, studies have shown that the average Internet use is about 18 hours per month. A few providers charge more for daytime use than for nights and weekends, although that's much less common than it used to be.

If you or your kids become regular online users, you will find that time stands still while you're online and that you use much more online time than you think you do. Even if you think that you will be online for only a few minutes a day, if you don't have a flat-rate plan, you may be surprised when your bill arrives at the end of the month.

Support

Call and talk to members of the support staff before you sign up. Good support means support 24 hours a day. That's a level of support you probably won't get from a local ISP, so you have to decide whether that single factor is enough to make you go with a national provider. Even if you do decide that it is, make sure that your national provider doesn't put you on hold for a long time. Perhaps even more important than the number of hours of support available is the *kind* of support you get. Your ISP should provide support people who don't think that your questions are stupid and can actually answer them. You would be surprised at how often they don't. We don't say this to knock support people; it's a hard job, and the people who do it are usually at the bottom of the pecking order. (We know; we've done it.)

Load

Two things concern you here: Do you get busy signals when you call, and does the information you're receiving from the Internet get stuck behind other people's information somewhere inside your ISP's facilities? Busy signals, you can test yourself. Even before you have Windows 98 all set up to call the Internet, you can call the ISP's access number (that's the number your computer calls) and see whether you get a busy signal. You shouldn't, even between 7 p.m. and 10 p.m., which is probably the Internet's busiest time. How fast information makes it through your ISP facility is hard to test, so this factor is just one to be aware of. If you're talking to someone who uses an ISP you're considering and they say that things seem slow for them, this could be the problem.

Modem speed

Modem speeds have been increasing dramatically, with new modem standards coming out about every year. Some providers haven't upgraded their equipment in a long time. It does you no good to have a fast modem if your provider's modem speed can't match it. Ask how fast the modem is at the local number you call to connect.

800 numbers

A few providers have toll-free numbers for use when you're on the road. Their hourly rates have to be high enough to cover the cost of the toll-free call, however, so it's almost always cheaper to dial direct back to your usual "local" number and pay for the call yourself. After all, someone has to pay for the toll-free call, and that someone is you. Access to a toll-free number can be attractive to people who travel frequently but sign on to the Internet only occasionally while they're on the road.

In the final analysis, whom you choose as an Internet service provider probably isn't that important. Within broad limits, they all work, though some more quickly than others. Just make sure that you have a pricing plan you can live with and that the Internet is just a local call away.

Payment plans

All ISPs (that we have ever heard of) take credit cards. For them, and for most customers, it's the easiest way to pay. If you're on a fixed-rate plan, they just charge your card once a month. Some smaller ISPs even wait and charge you for the *previous* three months, so you can get ahead a little. Other, larger ISPs have quarterly or yearly plans where they give you a little price break for paying in *advance*.

For some people, however, credit cards are not a good option. Some ISPs, usually smaller local ones, can arrange for you to pay ahead with a check. It's not a particularly common arrangement (computer types hate dealing with pieces of paper), although if you call around, you can probably find an ISP who's willing to do it.

Don't let the Windows 98 Internet Connection Wizard push you around

Windows 98 comes with a nifty Wizard that helps you get on the Internet. A *Wizard* is the mechanism by which Windows 98 asks you a bunch of questions and then sets up something based on your answers. Most hardware installation (and some software installation) in Windows 98 is done through Wizards. The process of getting connected to the Internet can have so many steps that the Internet Connection Wizard may call on the services of several other Wizards along the way. It's all confusing, although if you just keep answering questions, you end up on the Internet.

We go through all the steps in the Internet Connection Wizard in Chapter 3, although you should know about one important aspect of the Wizard. It's a nice feature: The Internet Connection Wizard asks you for your area code and the first three digits of your telephone number and then tries to find a local ISP for you. It may or may not succeed; if it can't find a local ISP, it finds the closest one it can, which can result in hefty long-distance charges if you surf the Internet much.

More important, the list from which the Wizard selects an ISP is far from complete. It includes many national ISPs and some regional ones, although none of our favorite local ISPs appears. If you select an ISP for yourself, you can still use the Internet Connection Wizard and its friends to set up Windows 98 to connect to your account.

Signing up for your Internet account

If you have decided to use AOL, AT&T WorldNet, CompuServe, the Microsoft Network, or Prodigy Internet, wait: We take you through their automated sign-up procedures in painful (just kidding) detail in Chapter 3. If you decide to use a local Internet service provider, you have to call and talk to someone there; ISPs usually sign up people over the telephone or sometimes by mail using actual pieces of paper. They take a credit card number (or check) and all the contact information they need for you and mail you a packet. The packet usually contains at least four things:

- ✔ The technical information you need in order to tell Windows 98 how you're planning to connect to the Internet.
- ✔ A list of telephone numbers your computer can call to connect to the ISP.
- ✔ Some cryptic instructions for how to get all this stuff set up. (In fairness, some of the instructions are getting better.)
- ✔ A great deal of software, including a web browser.

ISPs may also send you a ton of promotional material, special offers for other services, and the other typical stuff people try to get into your hands after they think that there's some chance you'll read it. This advice is important: *Unless the instructions they send you specifically discuss Windows 98 and are crystal-clear to you, ignore the software and their installation instructions!* The software is usually old, and you probably have better software on your Windows 98 system. The instructions range from the absurdly complicated to the pretty good. Even when they're good, however, they have to cover Windows 3.1, Windows 95, Windows 98 (if you're lucky), and the Macintosh. Chapter 3 covers only Windows 98 and does so in great detail. We think that you'll find it easier to follow.

You need much of the technical information the providers send you; a check-list at the beginning of Chapter 3 helps you figure out just what you need.

Winsock? Like at an airport?

No, Winsock is short for *Win*dows *sock*ets. It's like this: Back in the dark ages of PC networking, about 1990, several different software vendors wrote PC Internet packages. Each package provided functions so that other people could write Internet applications of their own that worked with the vendor's package.

Because each vendor's functions were, unfortunately, slightly different in the details, even though functionally they all did the same things, applications that worked with one didn't work with another. In 1991, a bunch of network vendors got together at a trade show and thrashed out a common, standard set of functions for Windows Internet applications. Every Internet software vendor, even Microsoft, quickly agreed to support this Windows sockets standard, or Winsock. (It's called *sockets* because its design is based on a well-established UNIX package by that name.)

In practice, any Windows Internet application you find that is *Winsock-compatible* (whether it's commercial, shareware, or free) should work with Dial-Up Networking, the Winsock-compatible Internet connection program that comes with Windows 98. If you have a PPP or cable Internet account, you can use any of a huge variety of Winsock-compatible programs. Most of the famous programs you've heard of — like Netscape Navigator and Internet Explorer — are Winsock-compatible, as are the Internet programs that come with Windows 98. America Online and CompuServe work with Winsock-compatible programs too.

In the annals of software development, this degree of compatibility is virtually unprecedented, so let's hope that it's a harbinger of things to come.

All Dressed Up and No Place to Go — What Programs Talk Over The Internet?

You have an account with an online service or an Internet service provider. You have a modem. You have a phone line. You're ready to roll. Wait — what about the software?

In Chapter 1, we talk about the programs that come with Windows 98. They let you do most of the important things that people like to do with the Internet — no fools, those folks at Microsoft! They've worked hard to make sure that you have almost every category of Internet software to avoid the horrifying (to them) possibility that you may use or, even worse, buy software from someone else. Still, they represent only one entrant in each of those categories. Let's review those categories with some looks at the other entrants:

- ✓ **Connection software:** Dial-Up Networking, the Windows 98 Internet connection program, works great. You have no reason we can think of to use any other connection program. We tell you how to set it up in Chapter 3.

- ✓ **Web browsers:** Netscape Navigator is still the world's most popular web browser, although Microsoft is pushing Internet Explorer hard. To the casual user (or even the not-so-casual user), they are equivalent. One or the other or perhaps even both almost certainly came with your Windows 98 system. We talk all about them in Chapters 8 and 9.

- ✓ **Web browser plug-ins:** Programs such as RealAudio, Shockwave, VXtreme, and their friends are "helper" programs for your web browser. You have to be running Netscape Navigator or Internet Explorer to use these and lots of other cool plug-in programs. The makers of many of these programs seem to be under some delusion that we actually care about them on their own. They're wrong. Don't misunderstand us: They're fine pieces of software, although they just work to extend what you can see on a web page to include sound and moving pictures. Unless you care about the innards of the technology, you can just think of them as part of the World Wide Web. Still, because they require some care and feeding, we talk about them in Chapter 9.

- ✓ **E-mail:** Outlook Express is the latest of several attempts Microsoft has made at the e-mail market, and it's homing in on it. Eudora is still queen of the hill, in our eyes, however. Netscape Messenger (part of Netscape Communicator) also holds its own in this category. Read more about them in Chapters 5 and 6.

- ✓ **Usenet, the Internet's bulletin board:** Outlook Express does double duty for Microsoft, covering this category as well as e-mail. The other program to look at here is Free Agent. Both these programs are great for reading Usenet newsgroups. You can also read your newsgroups over the World Wide Web at DejaNews.com. Netscape Collabra weighs in here too. We talk all about Usenet at our Web site at `http://net. gurus.com`.

- ✓ **Chatting on the Net:** We talk about the CB-radio-like features of the Net in Chapter 1. The Internet calls these online, real-time, flying-purple-conversations with lots of people at the same time conversations *IRC,* or *Internet Relay Chat.* mIRC is the most widely used Windows program that lets you do it. Windows 98 comes with Microsoft Chat, which lets you participate in IRC conversations *and* pretend that you're in a surreal comic strip at the same time (we're not making this up!). If this is your thing, look at Chapter 13.

- ✓ **Collaborative Working on the Net:** This category is one of the more interesting Internet applications to come along recently. Windows 98 comes with the Microsoft NetMeeting program, which rolls several

Internet communications functions into one package: Internet phone, videoconferencing, IRC, whiteboarding, and application sharing (where one person in a meeting controls an application that appears on the screens of all the participants in the meeting). This package is surprisingly cool, and we talk about it in Chapter 14.

Wrapping It Up: What You Need and What to Do with It

If you've been following along with us here, you should have at hand everything you need to connect your Windows 98 system to the Internet. Here's a quick review of what that stuff is that you need in order to do it. At the beginning of Chapter 3, you can fill out the checklist of information you can refer to as you set things up. Chapter 3 also has detailed instructions on how to do what you need to do.

You should have

✔ A computer running Windows 98. (Hey, we could assume that you know about this one, but you can't be too careful!)

✔ A modem to connect that computer to a telephone line.

✔ A telephone line to connect the modem to.

✔ An Internet service provider or online service you've decided to use.

✔ A web browser, which usually comes with Windows 98. All the rest of the software we talked about in the preceding section is available on the Internet if for some reason it didn't come with your computer.

After you've assembled these tools, commonly found around the home, you're ready to get connected. (See, just like we said at the beginning of the chapter: No electric drill required!) Here's the general overview of what's left to do:

✔ Make sure that Windows 98 knows about your modem.

✔ Make sure that the parts of Windows 98 which connect to the Internet were installed on your computer.

✔ Sign up for an account with a national ISP or an online service. If you've already signed up, don't worry. We show you how to tell Windows 98 all about your account.

✔ Finally, tidy up so that getting your PC on and off the Internet is as easy as possible.

Chapter 3

Setting Up Your Internet Account

• •

In This Chapter

▶ Simpler connections: The Internet Connection Wizard

▶ Stepping through the Internet Connection Wizard

▶ Signing up with a national Internet service provider (ISP)

▶ Telling Windows 98 about your modem

▶ Become your own wizard: Casting your own Internet connection spells

▶ Signing up with an online service

▶ Telling Windows 98 about an account you already have

▶ Determining when you don't need the Connection Wizard

• •

*F*or most people, the most difficult part of using the Internet is getting their Internet account set up. For approximately 10 percent of the U.S. population, a painfree alternative exists. If you're curious about whether you may be part of that lucky 10 percent, jump to the end of this chapter and read the section "Avoiding the Connection Wizard Altogether." If you know that you're part of the 90 percent who doesn't have the option of cable access or you naturally prefer doing things yourself, read on.

Introducing the Connection Wizard

To make the process of connecting to the Internet simpler, Microsoft created the Internet Connection Wizard. The Wizard's job is take you through all the steps in this chapter, from making sure that your modem is installed to signing you up on the Internet to getting you connected. Unfortunately, like all wizards, it's a little short on the explaining part of things — it just does them. Also, you can cast many of the same spells the Wizard uses, which can be handy when the wizardry flies by faster than you want.

In this chapter, you use the Internet Connection Wizard, which offers to take you down one of three separate paths: one to sign you up for a new account with an Internet service provider (ISP), one to use an existing account with an ISP, and one to use an Internet connection you may already have. We describe all three paths. We also show you how to cast all the same spells without using the Internet Connection Wizard.

The Wizard does not think highly of online services such as CompuServe or AOL, although your choice of providers is your own. Later in this chapter, we guide you through the process of signing up for one of those services and preparing to use one as your Internet connection.

You probably don't have to read this entire chapter. If you're lucky, Windows 98 correctly identifies your modem and loads its Internet dialing software so that you speed right through and quickly and easily sign up for an Internet account. In that case, you read about one-third of what's in this chapter. On the other hand, if things don't go so well, you may read the entire chapter, perhaps several times. When you think that you're done, however, you're done.

Care and Feeding of the Internet Connection Wizard

Running the Internet Connection Wizard is usually the easiest way to set up your Internet connection. As with all wizards, your first problem is to find it. If you're lucky, it's right on your Start menu, and you choose the command Start⇨Programs⇨Internet Explorer⇨Connection Wizard. If the command isn't there, try wandering around your menus to see whether you find something that says Connection Wizard. You know that you've found the Internet Connection Wizard when you see a screen that looks like the one shown in Figure 3-1.

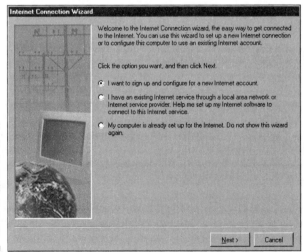

Figure 3-1:
How do you
want the
Internet
Connection
Wizard to
serve you?

The Wizard wants to recommend an Internet service provider

As you can tell from Figure 3-1, the Internet Connection Wizard does one of three things for you: It can set up an account for you with an ISP, set up a connection to an account you already have, or leave your accounts well enough alone. Click the appropriate option to indicate what you want the Wizard to do for you:

- ✔ If you already have an account with an ISP and you (or someone else) have set up that account on your computer, choose the last option, I Already Have an Internet Connection Set Up on This Computer and click the Next button. In this case, the Wizard disappears and you can skip to the beginning of Chapter 4.

- ✔ If you already have an account with an ISP but it's not set up on this computer, choose the second option, I Want to Set Up a New Connection to My Existing Internet Account, and join us again later in this chapter, in the section "Telling the Wizard that you're already signed up."

- ✔ If you need to choose an ISP, choose the first option, I Want to Choose an Internet Service Provider, and click Next to go comparison shopping, by letting the Wizard gather the information for you.

You have *plenty* of time to have second, third, and fourth thoughts before you spend any money. Windows 98 may have to reassure itself that it has all its marbles. If so, you see a screen telling you that the Wizard is beginning its automatic setup. Windows 98 may tell you that it needs to install some additional components so that it can get the information it needs to set up your Internet connection. On the other hand, it may not. It all depends on what got installed when Windows 98 was first put on your computer. If it has to install some additional components, it may also restart your computer, so make sure to close all the other programs you may have been using.

You may, in fact, see various screens (or the same screen several times) if Windows has to make many behind-the-scenes changes. Windows may want to know, among other things, which modem it should use to connect to the referral service. Make sure that the modem it selects is the one you want to use to dial the Internet, and then click OK. Windows may also want to confirm your area code so that it can look for local Internet service providers. If you see other messages, just keep pressing the Next button. Sooner or later, the text in the gray part of the dialog box changes to say "The Internet Connection Wizard will now connect to the Microsoft Referral Service." Toward the bottom of the dialog box, you see the telephone number the Wizard is trying to dial and a one-line message indicating what it's doing, such as "dialing" or "connecting to service."

When the Wizard is all done, the dialog box is replaced by a box similar to the one shown in Figure 3-2. On the left side of the window is a list of providers the Wizard thinks that you may be interested in; it may show you enough that you have to scroll up and down the list to see them all. The right pane shows you information about each Internet service provider. Click the ISP's name on the left to see information about it. You may have to scroll up and down to see all the information about a provider. Be prepared to spend some time with this list if you really want to comparison-shop; a great deal of information is there.

Figure 3-2:
The Internet
Connection
Wizard's list
of Internet
service
providers
for your
con-
sideration.

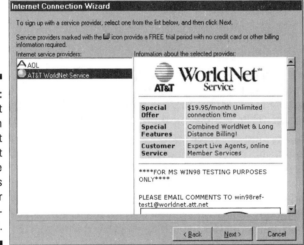

 Rather than see a list of recommended ISPs, you may see one of two other screens. If you see a dialog box that looks like Figure 3-3 and says "Could not connect," check out the advice in the section "How the Wizard Can Get Lost and Other Exciting Adventures," later in this chapter. If you see a dialog box that says "Install new modem," skip to the section "Making Sure That Windows 98 Sees Your Modem," a couple of sections ahead.

Signing up with an ISP by using the Wizard

When it comes to which ISP to sign up with, the choice is always personal. We've heard of most of the companies that appear on the lists for our area codes, and all the ones we saw there were perfectly reputable. If you have friends who are already connected in your area, ask them what provider they use and whether they're happy with the service. Another thing you can

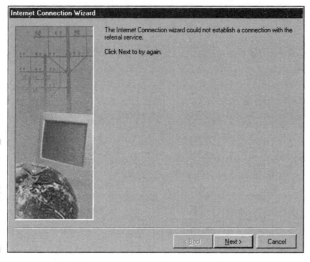

Figure 3-3:
The Wizard couldn't get through on the telephone.

do to boost your confidence is call and talk to several providers on the phone and ask about the services they provide. If they're courteous and helpful before you buy, that's a good place to start. If they're not, forget about them and find somebody who is.

After you've chosen a service, highlight its name in the left pane of the Internet Connection Wizard's window and click the Next button. Because the sign-up procedure is a little different for each provider, we can't give you step-by-step instructions after that. You generally have to fill in some forms containing the information the ISP needs to set up your account, including a credit card number. If you have read Chapter 1, you know how we feel about entering credit card numbers over the Internet: *It's plenty safe.* If you're still not comfortable with it, some of the sign-up pages may have a telephone number you can call to talk to a live human being.

Before you decide to go forward, we remind you one last time that the telephone number the ISP picks for you may not necessarily be a local telephone call. This situation should be clear if the Wizard lets you pick a telephone number from a list — you can check before you confirm that you want to use that telephone number. If the Wizard just picks a telephone number for you, however, be sure to check that the connection phone number is a local call — look on the confirmation screen before your card gets charged). If the ISP doesn't tell you the telephone number it's going to dial, you just have to trust it. After your account is set up, you can check the number and cancel if you need to. We show you how to cancel accounts at the end of Chapter 4, in the section about making Dial-Up Networking a little more convenient.

The information you need for each ISP is slightly different, although not particularly exotic. Here's what we provided to the ones we tested:

- ✔ Name.
- ✔ Address.
- ✔ Telephone number.
- ✔ The telephone number the computer is connected to. This number helps the ISP figure out what number your computer should dial. Some ISPs let you pick from a list of numbers in your area.
- ✔ A credit card number with expiration date.
- ✔ Some ISPs let you pick your own username and password, and others assign a username and password to you (we give you more info about this subject in a minute).
- ✔ An e-mail mailbox name. Although you can read more about this subject in the e-mail chapters, briefly, your e-mail address is whatever you pick, with your provider's name at the end. For example, our e-mail address here for *The Internet For Windows 98 For Dummies* is internet98@gurus.com; the "company" is gurus.com, and the e-mail mailbox name is internet98.

Somewhere in the sign-up process (usually at the end), you see a "summary" screen with your login name, password, e-mail mailbox name, and perhaps some technical information. *It is very important that you keep all this information!* Unfortunately, Microsoft makes it difficult to print this information. If you're feeling adventurous, you can press the Print Screen key on your keyboard to capture the information on your screen. Then choose Start➪Programs➪Accessories➪Paint to use the paint program that comes with Windows 98. Finally, use Paint's Edit➪Paste command to create a new Paint picture with your Internet account information. Finally, choose Paint's File➪Print command to print the information on your printer. On the other hand, if you're not feeling adventurous, you can just copy this stuff down with pencil and paper.

This screen of information is the only place where this information appears. If you need to call your ISP, you need this information. If you need to change any of the information in your Internet setup, you need this information. Please don't lose it.

At the end of the sign-up process, your Internet service provider may offer to set up an Internet connection for you by using your new account. By all means, allow it to. You should be all set to start sending and receiving e-mail (see Chapter 5) or surfing the World Wide Web (see Chapter 8), although you may want to take a look at Chapter 4 just to get the big picture of when your computer connects to the Internet and what you see when it does.

Things do not always go smoothly when you're sending information over the Internet, and you may as well learn that now as later. It's possible to get all the way through the sign-up process and, just before you think that you're done, have the whole process come to a grinding halt. (It has happened to us.) Make a note of the telephone number to call for customer assistance; it's on one of the sign-up screens.

Telling the Wizard that you're already signed up

Whether you got help from the Wizard in choosing an ISP or told it to skip that part, you should now see an Internet Connection Wizard dialog box labeled Set Up Your Internet Connection. If you don't, take a quick look at the beginning of the section "Care and Feeding of the Internet Connection Wizard," earlier in this chapter. Choose one of three options depending on whether you're shopping for an account, have an account you need to set up, or already have your account set up. If you're shopping, go to the section "The Wizard wants to recommend an Internet service provider," earlier in this chapter. If you already have an account with an Internet service provider *and* you (or someone else) have set up that account on your computer, skip to Chapter 4.

You may already have an account with an ISP, although it's not set up on this computer. The reason may be that you just signed up and have a welcome package from the ISP on your desk or that you were using the Internet from another computer and you're moving to a new computer. Or you may have an account set up on this computer but want to change some of the settings for it. In any case, you're in the right place. Follow along to see what the Wizard does next:

1. **In the Internet Connection Wizard's Welcome dialog box, choose the second option, I Want to Set Up a New Connection — to My Existing Internet Account and click the Next button.**

   The Wizard asks whether you're using just any old Internet connection or an Internet connection such as Microsoft Network or America Online. Microsoft Network and AOL have their own configuration programs that have nothing to do with the Wizard. To avoid confusion, the Wizard gets out of your way right now if you're using those services. If you're using one of these services to get to the Internet, click the second option, then the Next button, and then the Finish button to make the Wizard disappear. For more information about these services, see the section "Getting to the Internet from an Online Service Like AOL or CompuServe," near the end of this chapter.

2. **Select the first option in this dialog box — the one labeled Select This Option If You Are Accessing the Internet Using an Internet Service Provider or a Local-Area Network (LAN).**

That's assuming that you're using a *real* Internet service provider and not the Microsoft Network or AOL. Then click the Next button.

You see the Set Up Your Internet Connection dialog box, in which you can tell the Wizard whether you have a LAN connection or a telephone connection. You have a LAN connection if you're at the office (or school or the like) and your computer is connected via a high-speed network connection to other computers in the building, one of which is connected to the Internet. (We mention this subject briefly in Chapter 2 and in this chapter, in the section "Network spell 2: Setting up TCP/IP.") We assume that you will connect over the telephone.

3. **Make sure that the Connect Using My Phone Line option is selected and click the Next button.**

The Internet Connection Wizard asks you to choose a modem. In most cases, you have only one modem connected to your computer, and Windows 98 shows you the correct modem. If Windows 98 did not detect a modem attached to your computer, you take a detour to the Install New Modem Wizard; accordingly, you should take a detour to the section "Making Sure That Windows 98 Sees Your Modem," just ahead.

4. **Verify that Windows 98 is showing you the correct modem, and press the Next button.**

If you already have a Dial-Up Networking connection set up on this computer, the Wizard displays a dialog box in which you can choose to create a new Dial-Up Networking connection or select one of your existing ones. If you don't have a Dial-Up Networking connection on this machine, the Wizard skips directly to the Phone Number screen, where you tell it what number to dial; skip Step 6.

5. **If the Wizard asks you what to do about an existing connection, decide whether you want to create a new one or modify the existing one. Select the appropriate option, and click Next.**

If you select an existing connection, the Wizard asks whether you want to change the setting for it. This question strikes us as kind of silly because you wouldn't have selected this connection unless you wanted to change it, but hey, perhaps things in Redmond, Washington, are different from the way they are other places. If you decide that the answer is No, make sure that that option is selected and click Next. Skip ahead to Step 13, where we tell you why you should ignore mail for now. If you decide that you do want to change the existing connection, select the Yes option and click Next.

The Wizard may have to pause here to mess with the guts of your Windows 98 system. If it does, you see a message along the lines of "Installing files."

6. **Make sure that you have your Windows 98 CD handy, and let the Wizard do its thing.**

   When it's all done, you're looking at the Phone Number dialog box of the Internet Connection Wizard.

   The entries here are fairly straightforward, with the exception of the check box labeled Dial Using Area Code and Country Code. This entry is the telephone number that you want to make sure is a local call from where you are. If you never move your computer, it doesn't matter whether you check the Dial Using Area Code check box. Most people leave it checked, and that's fine. (This check box tells Windows 98 whether to use the dialing rules, which we talk about a little in the Chapter 4, in the section "Location, Location, Location.") Click the Next button when you've filled out everything; then you see the User Name and Password dialog box.

7. **Fill in the username you got from your ISP, along with the password it gave you, and click Next.**

   ISPs usually let you select your own username (except that you can't have one that's already in use), and often let you select your own password. Click Next when you've filled in the information; then you see the Advanced Settings dialog box.

8. **How brave are you? With most modern ISPs, you don't have to mess with this advanced stuff, so you should probably click No and then Next and move on to Step 13.**

   If your connection doesn't work, you can always get back here by starting the Wizard again and telling it that you want to change the settings for your Internet account.

   If you're still here, you're either curious or your setup didn't work on the first try. Click Yes in the Advanced Settings dialog box, and then click Next.

   The following four screens require information from your ISP, so if you don't have that stuff, you're out of luck. First, Windows 98 asks whether you have a SLIP or PPP account. As far as we can tell, no one should be using a SLIP account anymore; if you have one, your ISP can usually change it to a PPP account in one brief telephone call.

9. **Click the PPP option and click Next.**

   You also have to know how to log on. Some providers require you to run a little program known as a script. If your provider requires it, you have to get it from the provider. Generally, you can type by hand what you need. Most services don't require anything.

10. **Select the appropriate script option (if you're lucky, it's I Don't Need to Type Anything When Logging On), and then click Next.**

    You have to know whether you have a permanent IP address. Most people *don't* have one, and that's okay.

11. **If you do have a permanent IP address, type it here. Otherwise, leave selected the option labeled My Internet Service Provider Automatically Assigns Me One. In either case, click Next.**

    The same rules apply for the DNS Server Address. We give you more details about these four options in the section "Deep spells within TCP/IP, or reading the entrails," later in this chapter, where we cast our own spells.

12. **Click the Always Use the Following option and enter the DNS addresses you got from your ISP. Alternatively, leave the My Internet Provider Automatically Sets This option set. In either case, click Next.**

13. **If you're creating a new Internet connection, you have to give it a name. Click Next when you've chosen something. You don't have to name anything if you're modifying an existing account.**

    We usually use the name of the ISP just so that we don't forget what's what, although you can get as cute as you want.

14. **Now come three questions, to which you should answer No: No, you don't want to set up your Internet mail account; No, you don't want to set your Internet news account; and No, you don't want to set up your Internet Directory service.**

    We talk about mail in Chapter 5 and finding people in Chapter 10. We talk about news stuff at our Web site, at `http://net.gurus.com`. Meanwhile, hold your breath.

Congratulations! Your Dial-Up Networking connection is all set to call your ISP. In Chapter 4, we tell you how to make the connection, and we throw in a few tips to help you get connected more easily. The rest of this chapter gives you the ins and outs of the Wizard, along with details to help you out if problems crop up with your Internet connection.

How the Wizard Can Get Lost and Other Exciting Adventures

The Internet Connection Wizard must be able to dial the telephone if it's going to connect to anything. Figure 3-3 showed the dialog box you see if the Wizard can't get through on the telephone. If you don't see a dialog box that looks like that one, check to see whether Figure 3-4 looks more like it. If so, skip ahead to the next section; that's where we talk about setting up your modem in Windows 98.

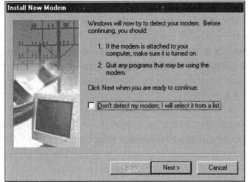

Figure 3-4:
The Modem
Connection
Wizard
magically
appears.

The Wizard may not be able to get through to its list of ISPs, for any number of reasons. Here are the most common:

✔ The modem is turned off. Most external modems have an On–Off switch somewhere on them. Some of the most popular have a little rocker switch right on top that's easy to push from On to Off. Check to see whether the modem has lights and, if it does, whether any of them are on. Also check the power cable to the modem and the power brick at the outlet.

✔ The cable from the computer to the modem is another place to check. Usually, it has little screw knobs that no one screws in to the back of the computer or the back of the modem. Make sure that the screw knobs are tight.

✔ The preceding are two of the reasons that internal modems are becoming more popular. It's still a good idea, however, to check both the connection from the telephone line to the modem and the telephone line at the wall jack.

✔ Does the telephone line have a dial tone? Plug in a telephone rather than the modem, just to check.

✔ Are you calling from inside an office? Do you have to dial 9 or something similar to get an outside line? You could press the Dialing Properties button in the Dial-Up Networking's Connect dialog box and become an expert. If your computer is a laptop that travels from place to place, that's just what you may have to do. We help you at the end of Chapter 4, in the section about making Dial-Up Networking a little more convenient. To sign up for an Internet account, you have to get this stuff right just one time. Click in the Number to Be Dialed portion of the Could Not Connect dialog box (the one that was shown in Figure 3-3), and type the digits you have to dial to get through to the Wizard's phone number.

> ✔ Do you have call-waiting? Did someone try to call while the Wizard was on the telephone? The Wizard doesn't take kindly to being interrupted. In the same Number to Be Dialed portion of the dialog box, enter the magic code you need to turn off call-waiting, usually *70. If you have to wait for a second or two afterward, follow the *70 with two commas — ***70,,** — each comma pauses the process for a couple of seconds. Sometimes 1170 works too.

None of those things helps? Then you need your neighborhood telephone guru. After you can get through to the phone number the Wizard is trying to call on a regular telephone and hear the whistle and hiss of the modem on the other end, go back and try the Wizard again.

Making Sure That Windows 98 Sees Your Modem

Unbeknownst to you, Windows 98 has not just one Wizard inside it, but a whole coven of them. The Install Modem dialog box, as shown in Figure 3-4, is the face of yet another one of those Wizards. If you reached this dialog box from the Internet Connection Wizard, then for some reason your modem wasn't installed in the Windows 98 software. No problem: The Modem Wizard is here to help. You can invoke it in a couple of other ways; we talk about them in the section "Casting Internet Connection Spells Yourself," a little later in this chapter.

Letting the Modem Wizard do the work

In most cases, the Wizard can get your modem installed for you. If it can't, you can wade in to the details and do it yourself. Before you click Next and let the Wizard look for your modem, follow its advice and make sure that it's turned on and plugged in, and in general look at the list of things that can go wrong, as described in the preceding section, "How the Wizard Can Get Lost and Other Exciting Adventures." If you prefer to wade in directly without even giving the Wizard a chance, look at the following section, "I'll do it my way."

Letting the Wizard search for a modem is the best thing to do, for several reasons. First, sometimes the Wizard can identify your modem more specifically than you can. Are you *sure* that you know the difference between a Courier 14,400 Dual Standard, Dual Standard PC, HST, HST PC, V32bis Fax, V32bis Fax PC, and V32bis-V42bis PC modem? And which exact one do you have? The Wizard can figure these things out. Second, the Wizard somehow occasionally identifies and installs a modem that doesn't appear on that list. Third, by letting Windows find the modem, you know that Windows can communicate with it, and that's a good thing.

Not much is involved in letting the Wizard find the modem. It may ask you for a hint about whether it's looking for a PC Card modem (also known as a PCMCIA modem card), although that's about it. PC Card modems are popular on laptop computers, so if you have a desktop computer, the answer is probably no. (See Chapter 2 for the lowdown on modems.) Windows 98 knows a great deal about PC Card devices, so as soon as you insert a PC Card modem, Windows 98 tries to install the relevant software for you. That's all the Wizard does for PC Card modems: tells you to stick them in and then waits for Windows 98 to do all the work.

If you're not installing a PC Card modem, the Wizard pokes around in all your hardware and eventually lets you know what it finds. If you agree with its choice, click Next to see a final dialog box which tells you that you're all done. If you don't agree with its choice, you can click the Change button and follow along in the following section, "I'll do it my way."

After you click the Finish button in the last Modem Wizard dialog box, you go back to where you came from — either the Internet Connection Wizard or the Modems Properties dialog box from the Control Panel (if you're casting your own spells).

I'll do it my way

You're doing it your way — telling Windows 98 exactly which modem you have — if the Wizard couldn't find your modem or if it chose the wrong modem or if Windows 98 doesn't come with software to support your modem. No matter how you get here, you see a dialog box like the one shown in Figure 3-5.

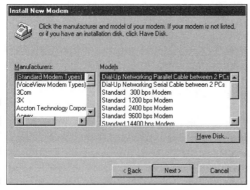

Figure 3-5:
Picking your modem yourself.

This dialog box has two columns. On the left, scroll down until you see the manufacturer of your modem. When you do, click the name. As soon as you click, you see a list of the modems it makes (at least the ones that Windows knows about) in the list on the right. Scroll through that list until you see your modem and click it. If you see too many modems with similar names, you may have to guess. It generally shouldn't make much difference if the modems are similar. If you're not sure, pick the one that sounds the simplest — it's the one most likely to work.

Your modem may not appear on the list. In fact, no modem remotely like your modem may appear on the list. For that matter, its manufacturer may not even appear on the list. If that happens, don't despair. *If* your modem came with a floppy disk or CD-ROM containing the *driver files* (little chunks of computer program) that Windows 98 needs to handle your modem, you're in luck. That's what the Have Disk button is for.

The Have Disk button tells Windows to look wherever you tell it for drivers for your modem. Usually, you tell it to look on a floppy disk (in drive A) or on a CD-ROM (usually in drive D). If the people who created the disk or CD have been cooperating, you can just type **A:** or **D:** in the box labeled copy Manufacturer's Files From. If they've squirreled away the drivers somewhere on the disk or CD, you have to fill in that box *and* press the Browse button. You have to click different folders until you get to one which has files that end in .INF. Windows doesn't let you click OK until you find one. After you do find a folder with .INF files in it and you click OK, the manufacturer's list and the modem list are replaced with just the items that are on your floppy disk or CD-ROM.

Whether you're selecting from the list that Windows 98 came up with or from the list for items on your floppy disk or CD-ROM, you are asked how this modem is connected to your PC. The Wizard didn't have to ask because it found the modem and knows where it found it. Your choices are usually COM1, COM2, or LPT1, and the answer is almost always COM1 or COM2. How can you tell which? There's no good way. You can hope that the plugs on the back of your computer are labeled, although they usually aren't. We suggest trial and error: Try COM1, and, if that doesn't work (we tell you how to test it in a minute), try COM2. (You have to look at the Modems Properties dialog box from the Control Panel to do it.)

After you click Next in this dialog box, your modem is installed, though you have to click the Finish button in the next box to get the Modem Wizard to go away. Just like when you let the Wizard do all the work, you whisk back to wherever it was you called the Wizard from.

With a double-click here and a single-click there

With the Internet taking more and more of people's attention, Microsoft wanted to make the Windows 98 desktop look as much like a part of the Internet as it could. One of the aspects of the Internet it adopted was *single-click actions*. Although in earlier versions of Windows, a single-click *selected* something and a double-click *activated* it, most of us found that distinction impossible to remember. Web pages on the Internet do away with that foolishness and just use single-clicks for everything: You point to something, you click it, it does its thing.

People who have used computers for a while and who are familiar with double-clicking hate the change. People who are just learning about computers love being able to click just once. Not wanting to offend anyone, Microsoft lets you have it both ways, which means that your computer may be set up differently from your neighbor's. In this book, we use single-clicks because we assume that most of you are just learning.

Here's how to make sure that your Windows 98 expects single-clicks:

1. *Right*-click your Windows 98 desktop.

   That is, click with the right mouse button a portion of your screen that is showing your desktop background color or wallpaper. (Do not click an icon or some text, or else Windows 98 thinks that you want to do something with that element.) A pop-up menu appears out of thin air from the desktop where you *right*-clicked.

2. Choose Properties from the pop-up menu, the last item on the menu. The Display Properties dialog box appears.

3. Click the Web tab, where you can tell Windows 98 how much you want your desktop to look like a Web page.

4. If the View My Active Desktop As a Web Page check box is *not* checked, click it to put a check mark in it.

   Checking this box tells Windows 98 to display Web pages (or portions of Web pages) on your desktop, behind your icons. Because this feature is the best way to get a sense for how Windows 98 and the Internet can work together, put a check mark in it.

5. Click the Folder Options button near the bottom of this dialog box.

   Windows 98 insists on asking whether you're all through with the Display Properties and are ready to move on to the Folder Options.

6. Click Yes.

   The Folder Options dialog box appears. The settings in this box determine how folders appear in many places in Windows, primarily in Windows Explorer but also on your desktop (which is a Windows Explorer window in disguise).

7. Make sure that the circle beside Web Style is filled in; if it's not, click it.

   You can always go back and change this setting later, if you prefer.

8. Click OK to accept this change.

   You're all set to single-click your way through Windows 98. If you haven't ever changed these settings, Windows 98 may ask whether you really want to.

9. If Windows asks you to confirm, click Yes and then OK.

Now you're really ready to single-click.

Casting Internet Connection Spells Yourself

Wizards are wonderful things when they work. Unfortunately, much like wizards in the real world, the Windows 98 Wizards can be a little temperamental. In this section, we lay out all the separate spells you have to cast to get your Windows 98 PC on the Internet. Here are the things that must be installed and configured in Windows 98 in order for you to get on the Internet:

✔ A modem

✔ The networking pieces of Windows 98

✔ TCP/IP, the "language" computers speak to one another over the Internet

✔ Information about your Internet service provider (ISP)

For each of these elements, you may also have to know how to find out whether it has been set up properly in Windows 98 and, if not, how to fix it. At the end of this section, we tell you how to dial out to your ISP. The starting place for the first three items is the Windows 98 Control Panel; information about your Internet service provider has its home in a thing called Dial-Up Networking. The Windows 98 Control Panel is so important that it has its own place right on the Windows 98 Start menu: You choose Start➪Settings➪Control Panel. Figure 3-6 shows the Control Panel.

Figure 3-6:
The
Windows 98
Control
Panel.

Controlling modems from the Control Panel

The Control Panel contains modem central for your Windows 98 system. Clicking the Modems icon shows you everything Windows 98 knows about modems on your computer. (This is the first time we've done any clicking where the new Windows 98 *Web style* makes a difference. If you click Modems and nothing happens, look at the sidebar titled "With a double-click here and a single-click there," earlier in this chapter.) After you click Modems, if Windows 98 doesn't know about *any* modems on your computer, it launches — as a bonus — the Modem Wizard we describe in the section "Making Sure That Windows 98 Sees Your Modem," earlier in this chapter.

If Windows 98 knows that you have a modem, you see the Modems Properties dialog box, from which you can add new modems, remove old ones, and find out about the ones you already have. Figure 3-7 shows both tabs in the Modems Properties dialog box.

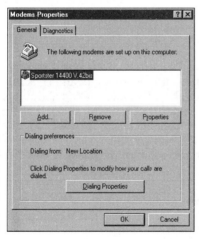
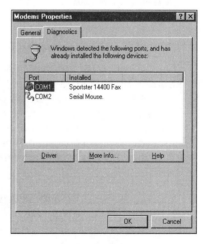

Figure 3-7: Both tabs in the Modems Properties dialog box.

This dialog box lists each modem installed on your system. If a modem is plugged in to your computer and it's not listed here, Windows 98 doesn't know about it. Fortunately, that situation is easy to fix. Just click the Add button, and the handy Modem Wizard appears. The section "Making Sure That Windows 98 Sees the Modem" talks about that process.

Testing your modems

In the section "Making Sure That Windows 98 Sees Your Modem," earlier in this chapter, we tell you that the only good way to tell whether your modem is connected to COM1 or COM2 is by trial and error. The Diagnostics tab in the Modems Properties dialog box is the place to do it. There, Windows 98 lists all the ways that it thinks a modem can be connected to your computer — it calls those ways "ports" for getting data into and out of your computer. It also lists what it thinks is connected to each port.

Click the port you want to test and click the More Info button. If you see a dialog box full of information, your modem is working. (The exact information you get is arcane and not all that interesting to most of us.) Alternatively, you may see a message saying that your modem is not responding. Windows 98 gives you two suggestions, one for internal modems and one for external modems. For internal modems, it recommends that you check for interrupt conflicts. Fixing interrupts gets you deep into the guts of Windows 98 — we suggest calling whoever installed your internal modem in your computer, your local computer whiz, the people who made your modem, or the people who made your computer.

For external modems, checking that the modem is turned on is a good suggestion, although we figure that you already tried that. Our bet is that you've told Windows 98 that your modem is connected to the wrong place. Check out the modem's properties to fix that.

The properties of a modem

On the General tab in the Modems Properties dialog box is a Properties button. Highlight the modem you want to learn about and click this button. You see a dialog box with several tabs full of information about this modem in particular. Figure 3-8 shows the properties for a typical external modem. The dialog box you see may have more tabs because the properties depend on the modem and the software driver that was written for it. The General tab contains the only stuff you're interested in for purposes of this discussion.

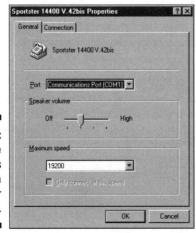

Figure 3-8:
The
properties
for a
particular
modem.

For an internal modem (including PC Card modems), all you can usually do is turn the speaker on and off. For an external modem, however, you can click the Port setting and choose among the ports where Windows 98 thinks that your modem can be (usually COM1 and COM2). If you get no response from the port you have picked, try picking another one. Then click OK to close the properties for this modem, and try the diagnostics again. (For the dangerously curious, we talk about dialing properties in Chapter 4, in the section about making Dial-Up Networking a little more convenient.)

Network spell 1: The networking pieces of Windows 98

As you know, Windows 98 comes with everything you need to get con- nected to the Internet. Unfortunately, some of that stuff may still be on your Windows 98 CD. You can find out by looking for Dial-Up Networking on your Window 98 Start menu. Usually, you can find it by choosing Start➪ Programs➪Accessories➪Communications➪Dial-Up Networking. If you don't find it there, look around on your Start➪Programs menu; it may be somewhere else. If you do find it, you're in luck: You can skip this whole spell and move on to the next, checking whether TCP/IP has been set up on your computer.

If you're still here, you have to see whether Windows 98 Dial-Up Networking was installed when Windows 98 was installed on your computer. Just as for modems, the Control Panel is the place to check:

1. **If your Control Panel isn't already running, use the Start➪Settings➪ Control Panel command to get it.**

2. **Click the Add/Remove Programs icon.**

   You see the Add/Remove Programs Properties dialog box with three tabs; on the middle tab, labeled Windows Setup, you can investigate which parts of Windows 98 got installed on your computer.

3. **Click the Windows Setup tab, and be prepared to wait a little while Windows wanders around your computer looking for parts of itself.**

   When Windows 98 is done, you see a list like the one shown in Figure 3-9. Each of the major topics with a check box beside it represents a part of Windows 98. Most of these parts are made up of subparts. A white, blank check box means that the entire part of Windows 98 was *not* installed; a white checked check box means that the entire part of Windows 98 *was* installed. A gray check box (with a check mark) means that some of the subparts for that part of Windows 98 were installed.

Figure 3-9:
The
Windows
Setup tab of
the Add/
Remove
Programs
Properties
dialog box.

4. **Look for the Communications part of Windows 98; in most cases, its check box is gray with a check mark in it. Click the Communications.**

    Do *not* click the check box; that action removes from your computer all the parts of Windows 98 that have to do with communications. If you do clear the check box by mistake, click Cancel immediately, and then click the Add/Remove Programs icon again.

5. **After you click the Communications line, click the Details button.**

    You see a list of subparts of Windows 98 having to do with communications. One of the first of these parts is Dial-Up Networking.

6. **Make sure that this box has a check mark in it, and click OK. You return to the main Windows Setup screen, where you can click OK again.**

    If Dial-Up Networking was not installed on your computer, it is now. You may have to find your Windows 98 CD, and Windows may decide to restart your computer.

Now you're ready to tell Windows 98 how to talk over the telephone. You may be able to do it by using the Internet Connection Wizard. Try going to the section "Care and Feeding of the Internet Connection Wizard," earlier in this chapter, and telling the Wizard that you already have an Internet account you want to set up. The Wizard may do the plumbing and deep spells for you.

Network spell 2: Setting up TCP/IP

This procedure is, without a doubt, the most complicated piece of setting up an Internet connection, and one of the major benefits of using the Internet Connection Wizard is that it saves you the trouble of doing this part of the job. If you're having to read this section, either the Internet Connection Wizard didn't do its job for you or for some reason your Internet connection doesn't work or you're just curious. No matter; we go through the procedure one step at a time, and you will, in all likelihood, get online eventually. Setting up TCP/IP has two parts. One is just getting TCP/IP on your computer and hooked up right. The other is making sure that Windows 98 is, deep in its guts, looking in the right place for the right Internet stuff. We discuss each aspect in turn.

Getting TCP/IP hooked up to the plumbing

As with most of the other spells we cast here, the Windows 98 Control Panel is the place to begin. (If your Control Panel isn't already running, choose the Start⇨Settings⇨Control Panel command to see it.) Here are the tasks before you:

- ✔ Make sure that the Dial-Up Networking adapter is installed; if it isn't, install it.
- ✔ Make sure that TCP/IP is configured to talk to another computer using the dial-up adapter.

Here's how you do it:

1. **Click the Network icon in the Control Panel.**

   You see the Network dialog box, as shown in Figure 3-10. What you're looking at is a list of the ways Windows 98 is prepared to talk to other computers. The list in this illustration is fairly extensive; your list may be much shorter or even blank. No matter: What you're looking for is an entry that says Dial-Up Adapter and another entry that says TCPIP -> Dial-Up Adapter.

   Notice that the list in Figure 3-10 does contain a dial-up adapter and a TCP/IP entry, although both are for use with the Microsoft Virtual Private Network (which is far out of ...*For Dummies* territory). If you don't see a line that says simply Dial-Up Adapter and another that says simply TCP/IP -> Dial-Up Adapter, you have to install them. On the other hand, if you *do* see Dial-Up Adapter and TCP/IP -> Dial-Up Adapter, you're all set. Proceed to the section "Information about your ISP," later in this chapter.

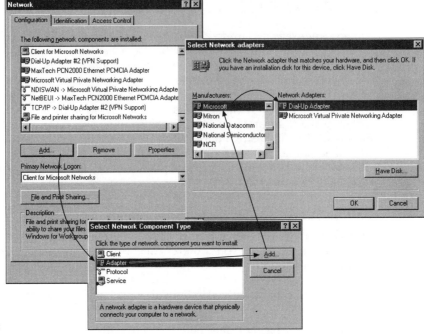

2. **If you don't have a dial-up adapter, click the Add button.**

   You see the Select Network Component Type dialog box.

3. **Select Adapter and click the Add button.**

   You see the Select Network adapters dialog box.

4. **Scroll down the list of manufacturers until you see Microsoft and click it. In the box on the right, click Dial-Up Adapter.**

   (We know — Microsoft didn't make your modem, although it did write the software you're about to install.) Figure 3-10 illustrates this series of steps.

5. **Click OK to finish.**

6. **If you don't have a TCP/IP -> Dial-Up Adapter, click the Add button.**

   You see the Select Network Components dialog box.

7. **Select Protocol and click the Add button.**

   You see the Select Network Protocol dialog box.

8. **Click Microsoft in the list of manufacturers. In the box on the right, scroll down to Dial-Up Adapter and click it.**

9. **Click OK to finish.**

10. **Click OK to close the Network Properties dialog box.**

    Windows 98 may ask you to restart your computer, or it may ask for the Windows 98 CD-ROM; when it's done whirring and clicking, you're almost ready to talk on the Internet.

This is also the last you see of the Control Panel (at least for setting up your Internet connection). Choose the File⇨Close command (or the Close button, the X, in the upper-right corner) to close the Control Panel.

Deep spells: The guts of TCP/IP, which you should ignore if at all possible

When your computer calls your Internet service provider, your computer connects to the Internet. Several million computers worldwide may have to be capable of finding your computer and talking to it more or less instantaneously. To enable the rest of the computers on the Internet to find your computer, you have to enter some additional information if it hasn't been set up automatically. You may have received one or more of the following pieces of information from your Internet service provider:

- ✔ **A permanent IP address:** Your computer's address on the Internet — in the form 123.45.67.89 (computers love to think in numbers). If you didn't get one, every time your computer calls, your Internet service provider assigns it a temporary IP address.

- ✔ **One or more Domain Name Server (DNS) addresses:** The address (or addresses) of computers your computer can use to ask for the IP addresses of other computers — kinda like Internet directory assistance.

- ✔ **A domain name:** The name of the family of computers your computer is a member of. It's usually a name related to your Internet service provider (ISP). Because one of our ISPs is TIAC, for example, one of our domain names is tiac.net.

- ✔ **A hostname:** The name by which your computer is known on the Net. You don't use the hostname unless you do some really geeky stuff.

All your Dial-Up Networking connections live together in your computer. You can peek at them by choosing the Start⇨Programs⇨Accessories⇨Dial-Up Networking command. You see the Dial-Up Networking window, as shown in Figure 3-11. You can tell Windows 98 about this technical stuff from the Dial-Up Networking windows.

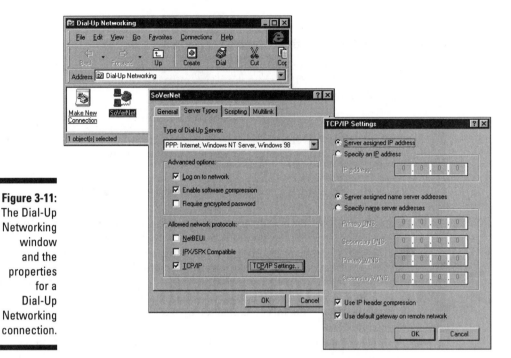

Figure 3-11:
The Dial-Up
Networking
window
and the
properties
for a
Dial-Up
Networking
connection.

1. **From the Dial-Up Networking window (refer to Figure 3-11),** *right-* **click your connection name.**

   You see a pop-up menu that includes Properties.

2. **Choose Properties.**

   You see general information about this connection.

3. **Click the Server Types Tab.**

4. **Click the TCP/IP Settings button.**

   This dialog box is the place to type your permanent IP address and your Domain Name Server IP addresses, if you know them. In many cases, neither Windows 98 nor your Internet service provider cares if you don't bother.

5. **If your Internet service provider gave you this information, type it in the box. If your ISP didn't tell you a permanent address, click Server Assigned IP Address.**

6. **Click OK until you're back at the Dial-Up Networking window.**

When you're looking at the properties for a connection, you can click the Server Type button. Notice that the Server Types dialog box, shown earlier, in Figure 3-11, has check boxes for NetBEUI and IPX/SPX Compatible. You can clear these check boxes and speed up your network communications a little.

Making a LAN connection to the Internet

Although this entire subject can be mind-numbingly complicated, all the pieces you need to connect a PC that's already on a LAN to the Internet are part of Windows 98, so you can probably get things working with the help of your local network manager.

Here's a one-sentence summary: You set it up the same way as Dial-Up Networking, except that rather than use a dial-up adapter, your network connection uses whatever networking card is installed in your computer. Connecting via a LAN is a little simpler than dial-up because you don't need phone numbers, logins, or passwords. Whoops — that was more than one sentence; it really is kind of complicated.

Information about your ISP

You may have wondered just what it was that the Internet Connection Wizard was offering to do for you at the end of the sign-up process, when it asked whether it should set up an Internet connection for you. You're about to find out. It's not all that grisly, and it's a good thing to know about so that your Internet connection isn't entirely magic.

Windows 98 collects all the information it needs to dial an Internet service provider into a thing it calls a *Dial-Up Networking connection*. You're about to create one. To do it, you must be signed up with an ISP and know the telephone number to dial to connect to that ISP:

1. **Choose Start⇨Programs⇨Accessories⇨Communications⇨Dial-Up Networking from the taskbar.**

   If this is the first time you've run Dial-Up Networking, yet another Wizard immediately appears to guide you through the process of creating a connection.

2. **If a Wizard doesn't appear, invoke it by clicking the Make New Connection icon in the Dial-Up Networking window.**

   The Dial-Up Networking window and the first words of the Wizard are shown in Figure 3-12. The Wizard wants to know only three things about your Internet connection.

3. **Give your connection a name. Don't just say it out loud — type it in the box.**

   What's it called? Because our Internet service provider is named the Sovereign Vermont Network, we call ours *SoVerNet*— creative, huh?

   You see the description of your modem in a list box. If you have only one modem, skip the next step.

Figure 3-12:
The Dial-Up
Networking
window,
with the
Wizard
active.

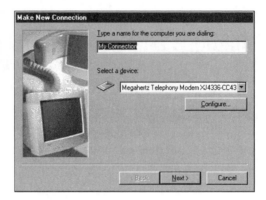

4. **Choose the modem you want this connection to use.**

   Click the modem name to see a list of modems installed on your computer. Click the correct one.

5. **Click Next to proceed to the next step in the Wizard.**

6. **Type the telephone number your computer dials to connect to your ISP. Make sure that the Country code is right.**

   Notice the boxes for your area code and country. Windows 95 wants to know where your ISP is so that it can figure out whether to dial the area code and things like that. That's all in Chapter 4, in the section about making Dial-Up Networking a little more convenient.

7. **Click Next to proceed to the next step in the Wizard.**

8. **Click Finish.**

   The Wizard adds your connection to the list of available connections, and you're done.

That was painless, right? We talk about *using* that Internet connection in Chapter 4.

Getting to the Internet from an Online Service Like AOL or CompuServe

In Chapter 2, we go over a couple of reasons you may want to get your Internet access from an online service like AOL, CompuServe, Microsoft Network (MSN), or Prodigy. Briefly, although they are just becoming *full* Internet service providers, if you plan to spend most of your time using their special services (like the AOL chat rooms) and want the flexibility to occasionally use any Internet programs you want, using your online service as an ISP may be a good solution for you. Online services have spent more time and effort on becoming easy to use and easy to sign up for than most Internet providers, so we don't go step-by-step through each sign-up procedure. This section gives you the overview of what you have to do, along with some pitfalls.

You can choose Start➪Programs➪Online Services to find all the online services that come with Windows 98. If you live outside the United States, you may see a different list from the ones we describe here.

America — and the rest of the Internet — Online

The AOL sign-up process is easy to use and thorough; by the end, you're signed on to America Online and, through that service, can access the Internet. (Chapter 4 has instructions for starting an Internet connection by using AOL.) For ease of use, AOL is hard to beat. We still get more busy signals there than with most ISPs, though. Also, because the AOL connection is not really an Internet connection, some software may not work seamlessly with it — we occasionally have to tell programs that we really are connected to the Internet. We also find that it's slow. A major disadvantage at the time we write this book is that you're stuck with the AOL mail program; although you can use other programs to read Usenet newsgroups (described at our Web site, at `http://net.gurus.com`) and you can use a standard Web browser, AOL does not support standard mail.

AT&T WorldNet

Unlike America Online and CompuServe, AT&T WorldNet is a real, honest-to-goodness Internet service provider. We include it in this part of the chapter because it has a good sign-up package you can reach by choosing Start➪Programs➪Online Services from the menu. Just like the Internet Connection Wizard, it creates a Dial-Up Networking connection for you. It also creates its own Dial-Up Networking connection if you choose Start➪Programs➪AT&T WorldNet Software➪Connect to AT&T WorldNet Service. Although some of its dialing screens therefore look a little different, deep down, they're doing the same thing as Dial-Up Networking.

CompuServe

CompuServe has taken a middle route between AOL and AT&T: With CompuServe, you get the value-added content from an online service along with a true Internet connection. The software sign-up procedure isn't as slick as with AOL, and changing telephone numbers is a little more complicated. The connection is reasonably fast, though, and all the standard Internet programs – including e-mail programs — are perfectly happy to work with CompuServe. (At least, CompuServe was testing its mail connection, called a POP server, at the time this book was written.) Because AOL recently bought CompuServe, you can expect CompuServe to eventually become more AOL-ish.

Prodigy Internet

Prodigy started as an online service, and its online service, now called Prodigy Classic, still exists. Its ISP service is called Prodigy Internet, which is the sign-up that comes with Windows 98. It's hard to distinguish between Prodigy Internet and other ISPs because it *is* an ISP. Like MSN and AT&T WorldNet, it's an Internet-based service, and like MSN and AT&T WorldNet, it creates a true Dial-Up Networking connection for you so that other Internet programs work well. The sign-up process is not flashy, although it works well.

The Microsoft Network (MSN)

The Microsoft service began as an online service competitor to AOL and CompuServe but quickly became Internet-based. As with AT&T, you can sign up either from the Internet Connection Wizard or by choosing Start⇨Programs⇨Online Services from the taskbar. As with CompuServe, you end up with a real Internet connection, so other programs work well. MSN is so Internet-oriented, in fact, that you use it through the Microsoft Explorer Web browser (described in Chapters 8 and 9). Using a browser is nice because it means that you don't have to learn how to use another program in order to use MSN. (Because both AOL and CompuServe came out before Web browsers even *existed,* the program you use to communicate with them is their own — one more thing to learn.) MSN Internet mail is the most standard of the three online services, although not as standard as a regular ISP's.

Moving on

By hook or by crook, you have a connection to the Internet now. You're either going through an online service, in which case things were probably simple to set up, or you chose one of the Microsoft-recommended ISPs or you're using an ISP you chose yourself. In any case, you have a Dial-Up Networking connection. In Chapter 4, you get online and learn some tips about making dial-up connections more convenient under Windows 98.

Avoiding the Connection Wizard Altogether

For some small but ever-growing percentage of the population, high-speed access to the Internet is available using cable modems. In many areas of the United States, cable-television companies are providing cable access to the Internet. Here's what's so cool about that:

- ✔ Cable modems are significantly faster than dial-up modems.
- ✔ The cable company comes and installs your cable modem and sets up your Internet connection. You could skip this whole chapter as well as the next.

The cost and availability of cable access varies all over the country. For some, it costs as little as $40 a month; for others, it's close to $70. But before you plug your ears and run away, listen to why it may be worth it to you.

Cable access does not use a telephone line. It means that you can use your computer and talk on the phone at the same time. (Or someone else could use the phone, or someone could call you.) People who use the Internet frequently often install a second phone line. Cable access may be cheaper than a second phone line. (To get an accurate comparison, add the monthly cost of the second phone line to the monthly cost of your Internet service provider.)

Cable access is always there — you're always connected. You don't have to have your computer dial in every time you want to check your e-mail or look at a Web site. You click — it's there.

Unfortunately, we can't tell you whether cable is available in your area. You have to call your cable television company and ask. We do know that it's available in the greater Boston area and parts of upstate New York, and we like it a lot.

One bit of warning, however, if you do go the cable route. Cable technology puts you on a Local-Area Network connecting all the cable modem customers in your neighborhood. Make sure that your computer doesn't have file-sharing or print-sharing enabled, unless you really want all your neighbors to look at your disk or print on your printer.

Chapter 4

Dialing In and Out

*G*etting ready to dial out to the Internet can be quite an adventure. You may have created a Dial-Up Networking connection, successfully confronted the Internet Connection Wizard, cast some Internet connection spells, and who-all knows what else. Now you're ready to see whether the whole thing works. In this chapter, we go through the basics of how to use your Dial-Up Networking connection. We also give you some tips on what can go wrong when you try to get connected. After you're connected, hanging up isn't hard to do, although you have to know where to click. We also talk about programs that are smart enough to hang up for you and ones you have to tell that you're through. Also, if you ask nicely, Windows 98 can tell you how things are going with your Internet connection, and we tell you how to ask.

You can make Dial-Up Networking more convenient in a number of ways, including making your connections easier to find and making Windows 98 dial automatically without bothering you. We tell you how to do these things, and we talk more about local telephone numbers and dialing locations. In case you haven't noticed, new area codes are springing up like mushrooms after a spring rain and now you may have to dial an area code just to make a local call about as often as you're not *allowed* to dial an area code to make a local call. The Windows 98 dialing locations deal with all this stuff, although to do so they have to be kind of complicated. Still, they're probably worth reading about, just so that you know what they're about when you need them.

Starting Up Your Dial-Up Networking Connection

Until you spruce up your desktop and menus (described later in this chapter, in the section "Making Dial-Up Networking a Little More Convenient"), the Windows 98 Dial-Up Networking window is your key to getting on the Internet. Here's how to use it to get online:

1. **If the Dial-Up Networking window isn't open, open it by choosing Start➪Programs➪Accessories➪Comunications➪Dial-Up Networking from the taskbar.**

   Figure 4-1 shows our Dial-Up Networking window after we've created Dial-Up Networking connections for all the online services that came with our copy of Windows 98, plus our local ISP. Your Dial-Up Networking window probably has only two icons in it: Make a New Connection and the connection for the ISP or online service you signed up for. Note that we have no AOL icon even though we signed up for it. The reason is that, as we say in Chapter 3, AOL doesn't give you a true Internet connection.

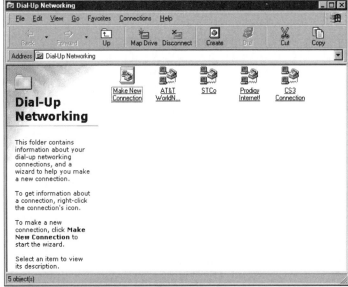

Figure 4-1: The Dial-Up Networking window with a number of Dial-Up Networking connections.

2. **Click the connection name.**

   Back when you created the connection, Windows 98 suggested My Connection for the name, although we hope you were more creative.

You see a Connect To dialog box, as shown in Figure 4-2. Windows 98 may or may not suggest a username, depending on whether you have other (non-dial-up) networking connections set up on your computer.

3. Make sure that the right username is in the box, and remember that cApiTaliZaTioN matters!

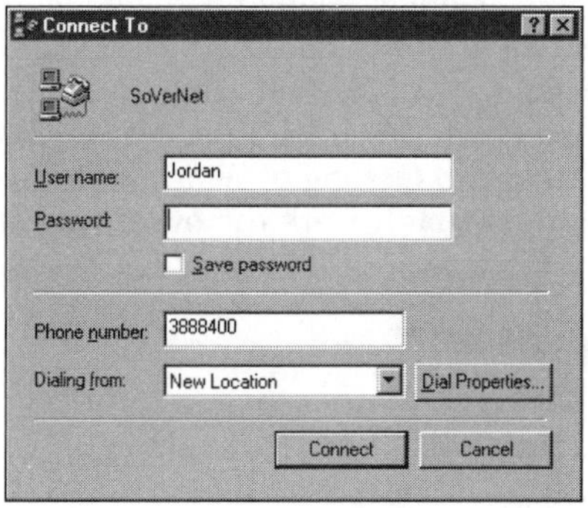

Figure 4-2:
The
Windows 98
Connect To
dialog box
dials the
phone and
makes the
connection.

Figure 4-2: The Windows 98 Connect To dialog box dials the phone and makes the connection.

4. Enter your password in the Password box.

For security reasons (who's that looking over your shoulder?), the password appears as asterisks, one per character you type.

5. Decide whether to check the Save Password check box so that you don't have to enter your password again.

Advantage: You don't have to type your password every time you want to call the Internet. *Disadvantage:* Anyone can walk up to your PC and sign on to the Internet as you. The Save Password check box may be gray and may not allow you to check it. If that's the case, read the section "Why doesn't Windows 98 save my Dial-Up Networking password?" near the end of this chapter.

6. Change the Phone Number and Dialing From boxes, if you need to.

The phone number should be familiar from the Make New Connection Wizard. You can type a new telephone number here, although you probably don't want to — you're better off modifying the telephone number permanently (see the section "Making Dial-Up Networking a Little More Convenient," near the end of this chapter) or creating a new connection.

The Dialing From box contains the name of the location where Windows 98 thinks that you are right now. It's usually New Location, unless you have a portable computer and have already set up different dialing locations for it (see the section referred to in the preceding paragraph).

7. **Click the Connect button.**

You see a series of messages beginning with `Initializing` and ending with `Connected`. Finally, you see the Connection Established dialog box, as shown in Figure 4-3.

It's a perfectly nice dialog box, although it's just a reminder about what we're about to tell you in the following section: how to disconnect from the Internet. If you don't mind seeing it, skip Step 8, which makes this dialog box go away forever. We prefer to click as few dialog boxes as possible when we want to get on the Internet. (Our thoughts turn to reading our e-mail or looking at whatever Web page it was that brought us to the Internet, not the care and feeding of Windows 98, although Microsoft, of course, may prefer that it were the other way around.)

Figure 4-3:
At last!
Connected
to the
Internet.

8. **Click the Do Not Show This Dialog Box check box, if you want not to see this particular dialog box every time you connect.**

9. **Click the Close button to make this dialog box go away.**

10. **Celebrate — you're finally connected to the Internet!**

What Microsoft is trying to tell you with the Connection Established dialog box, with its little icon of two computers, is that a new little icon appears on the system tray part of your Windows 98 taskbar (way over to the right, next to the clock). We call it the *dial-up icon,* and whenever Dial-Up Networking is connected to the Internet, that icon appears on the taskbar.

Hanging Up Your Dial-Up Networking Connection

It doesn't take much to hang up your Dial-Up Networking connection, though it can be kind of hard to figure out unless you know where to look: *Right*-click the dial-up icon (the little picture of the two computers on your taskbar, as shown later in this chapter, in Figure 4-5) in the system tray part of the taskbar (way over to the right). You see a menu with two items on it: Status, which shows you the connection statistics we just talked about, and Disconnect. Clicking the word *Disconnect* does just that. The astute reader (that's you, right?) also notices the Disconnect button on the Connection Statistics dialog box. Clicking it does the same thing.

Telling Windows 98 to Connect to the Internet Whenever It Wants

When you connect to the Internet, you want *Internet* things, such as e-mail or the Web, not Windows 98 dialog boxes. You can tell Windows 98 to connect automagically to the Internet whenever you ask for Internet-based information. Windows 98 remembers how you want to be connected to the Internet, and *most* (but not all) programs that access the Internet can induce Windows 98 to get connected all by itself. When you set up a dial-up Internet connection, the Dial-Up Networking Wizard automatically assumes that you want to use this connection for automatically dialing the Internet — or *autodialing*.

Are we done yet?

Some programs (most notably, Internet Explorer) offer to disconnect you from the Internet when you're done using them. A program generally makes this offer only if it was the one that initiated the connection to the Internet in the first place. In general, we find it to be a nice feature.

This feature can be a little confusing, however. For example, what happens if you start using Internet Explorer to browse the World Wide Web and then get involved in reading your e-mail? As soon as you decide to leave Internet Explorer, it offers to shut down your Web connection. If you're in the middle of downloading some mail, you probably don't want to disconnect just yet.

You don't have to *do* much about this; it just happens. What you do have to remember (if you told Internet Explorer *not* to disconnect from the Internet) is to disconnect yourself when you're done reading your mail (or whatever else it was that you were doing). Take a look at the section "Telling Windows How Long to Stay Connected," just ahead, to learn how to have Windows 98 disconnect from the Internet after you've walked away from your computer for a while.

Even though we jump ahead a little here, you can start yourself down the autodialing path by asking Internet Explorer to show you a Web page. We talk all about Internet Explorer in gruesome detail in Part III of this book, but just getting it started can't hurt, right? Here's what to do:

1. **Make sure that you are not connected to the Internet (disconnect if you need to).**

2. **Click the Internet Explorer icon, which is usually on your desktop or right beside the Start button on the taskbar, or you can choose Start⇨Programs⇨Internet Explorer⇨Internet Explorer from the taskbar.**

   The first time Windows 98 decides that it has to dial out to the Internet, you probably see the Internet Autodial dialog box, as shown in Figure 4-4. If you see this dialog box, you see it only once. After you tell Windows 98 that you want it to dial the Internet automatically, it is content to do so until you tell it to stop. (That's what the following sidebar, "Get your hands off my telephone — turning off Internet Autodial," is all about.) This is your chance to tell Windows 98 if you *don't* want it to dial out by itself.

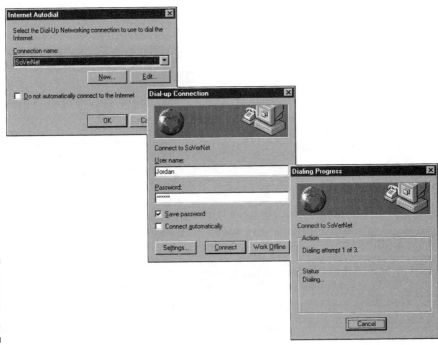

Figure 4-4:
Three steps
to autodial
the Internet.

Get your hands off my telephone — turning off Internet Autodial

You can turn off Internet Autodial in a slightly roundabout way. The key is in the Windows 98 Control Panel (choose Start⇨Settings⇨ Control Panel from the taskbar to open it). Click the Internet icon in the Control Panel to see the Windows 98 Internet Properties dialog box, and then click the Connection tabs in the dialog box. If you told Windows 98 to autodial the Internet, the button beside the Connect to the Internet Using a Modem option contains a check mark. You can disable autodialing by clicking the button beside the Connect to the Internet Using a Local Area Network option, *even if you don't have a local-area network!*

(Local-area networks, unlike telephones, don't have dials.) Click OK to close the Internet Properties dialog box, and close the Control Panel, by either choosing the File⇨Close command or clicking the Close button (the X) in the upper-right corner of the Control Panel.

Programs that need to access the Internet behave in one of two ways: They either tell you that they can't get to the Internet (like Internet Explorer) or go ahead and dial whatever Dial-Up Networking connection they think they need (like Outlook Express). You always have the option of connecting manually, which is, after all, what you said you wanted to do.

3. **If you *don't* want Windows 98 to connect to the Internet when it thinks that you may want to, click the Do Not Automatically Connect to the Internet check box. If you *want* Autodial to work, leave this check box blank.**

   Our opinion is that you *shouldn't* click this check box. It's kind of nice to have Windows start up your connection when you ask to check your e-mail or see a Web page. When Windows 98 wants to dial out, you have another chance to figure out whether your teenager is on the telephone.

   When Windows 98 tries to dial out to the Internet, you see the Dial-Up Connection dialog box, the middle dialog box shown in Figure 4-4. The username is the name you used to sign on to Windows 98.

4. **If the name you use with your Internet service provider doesn't appear in the User Name box, type the username it gave you.**

   The first time you see this dialog box, the Password box is blank because you have never told Windows 98 what your password is for this account.

5. **Type your password in the Password box (asterisks appear as you type).**

   After you enter a password, the Save Password check box is available, so you have to decide whether to trust that password to Windows 98. The first time you see this dialog box, the Save Password check box is *not* checked.

6. Decide whether to click the Save Password check box.

Convenience definitely dictates that you should click it. Your comfort level with the people who pass by your computer when you're not around determines whether you do.

If you let Windows 98 save your password, anyone who walks up to your computer can sign on to this ISP or online service as you. You get hassle-free connection to the Internet, however. Windows stores your password on your hard disk in an encrypted form, which means that casual passers-by can't read it, although it won't slow down the National Security Agency for long. Your computer is still protected by your Windows 98 password, which you type when you turn the computer on. We always let Windows store our password because we like uninterrupted access to the Net. We figure that the Windows password is good enough and that the number of malicious strangers who wander into our home office is usually low.

Finally, you have to decide whether you want Windows 98 to connect to the Internet totally automatically.

7. Decide whether to click the Connect Automatically check box.

Pluses and minuses abound. On the plus side is uninterrupted access to the Net. On the minus side is the fact that your computer may pick up the telephone at odd times, without knowing whether anyone else in the house is using it. If your computer is on its own telephone line, we definitely recommend automatic connection. If your computer shares a telephone line with human beings (you, for example), it depends on how upset people will get if the computer occasionally picks up the phone while they're talking. Although it doesn't do any harm, it can be annoying.

If you decide on automatic connection, you see the Dialing Progress screen (from the right side of Figure 4-4) every time Windows 98 decides to dial out to the Internet. If you change your mind and decide that you don't want to connect automatically at that time, you can click the Cancel button. Rather than go away entirely, the program's Dial-up Connection dialog box appears (the one in the middle of Figure 4-4). From there, you can uncheck the Connect Automatically check box.

8. After you've entered your identifying information and decided what Windows 98 should do with your password and connection, you're ready to click the Connect button.

You see the Dialing Progress dialog box, as shown on the right side of Figure 4-4. After you're connected to the Internet, the dialog boxes go away, and you're all set. Only the dial-up icon in the system tray part of the taskbar indicates that you're connected.

Telling Windows How Long to Stay Connected

One way to disconnect from the Internet is not to send or receive any information for a while. How long "a while" is depends. The sidebar "Get your hands off my telephone — turning off Internet Autodial," earlier in this chapter, contains the key: On the Connection tab of the Internet Properties dialog box in the Control Panel, click the Settings button. You see the Dial-Up Settings dialog box, where you can specify the name of the connection you want Windows 98 to use when it connects automatically, a check box to enable automatic disconnection, and a number box that says how many minutes to wait to disconnect. Before you are disconnected, however, you always have a chance to say something about it. After the required period of Internet inactivity, Windows 98 displays a dialog box telling you that it will disconnect in 30 seconds. You can either watch the time count down if you enjoy the suspense, disconnect immediately, or cancel the disconnect. If you cancel the disconnect, you remain online.

Monitoring Your Dial-Up Networking Connection

If the Internet were less congested and if modems were faster, you probably wouldn't care what goes on with your Dial-Up Networking connection. Instead, you would ask for information and it would appear instantly, and then you would send information out to the Internet and it would transmit in a flash.

Alas, most of us don't live in that world; we live in a world in which access to Web pages has been called "the World Wide Wait." You click a Web page or request some information from the Internet or check your mail, and your Internet connection seems to stop. Although the rest of your computer seems to be humming along fine, who knows what's happening between you and the Internet?

If your modem has lights, you can look and see whether any information is coming or going; external modems usually have SD (send data) and RD (receive data) lights that blink as data goes by. Most modems nowadays are internal, though, which means that they have no lights. (Who could find them in the dark inside a computer?) You may need some important information that you can't find out just from lights, anyway. Luckily, Dial-Up Networking can give you a little information about what's going on with your connection.

Remember the dial-up icon that appears near the right end of the taskbar when you are connected? The icon represents your computer and the computer you're dialed in to; when their screens flash, information is coming or going. (Are these guys cute or what?)

You can get some more specific information about your connection, too. If you pass your mouse pointer over the dial-up icon and pause for a second, a little message pops up telling you how many bytes your computer has sent and received. The message also tells you the speed at which your modem is communicating over the telephone, although we find the speeds it reports to be wildly optimistic. Figure 4-5 shows the taskbar with a dial-up icon on it, with the cursor on the icon and the pop-up information displayed.

Figure 4-5:
Connection
statistics
from the
Dial-up icon
and the
Connected
To dialog
box.

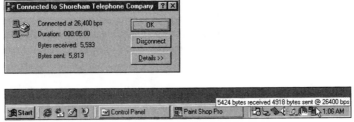

If you double-click the dial-up icon, you see the dialog box shown in Figure 4-5. Unlike the pop-up information, the information in the dialog box is "live." As information flows to and from your computer, the counts of bytes received and bytes sent are updated. You can click the Disconnect button to hang up or the OK button to make the dialog box go away. If you *really* want to know more, click the Details button.

Making Dial-Up Networking a Little More Convenient

Face it — choosing Start➪Programs➪Accessories➪Comunications➪Dial-Up Networking and the connection name every time you want to connect to the Internet is not convenient. Life is way too short to issue that command more than once! You can make your dial-up networking connection much easier to find by putting a shortcut to it on your Windows 98 desktop and on your Start menu.

You may not find this technique as useful as we do. Web browsers, such as Internet Explorer and Netscape Navigator, and mail programs, such as Outlook Express and Eudora, know how to tell Windows 98 to dial up the Internet. There's still a small advantage, however, to dialing before you start the program: If you're truly impatient, you can start dialing the Internet connection and *then* start the program. That way, the program starts *while* the Internet connection is dialing: Your computer does two things at one time, and you wait only half as long.

Some programs also hang up the telephone right after they're done doing whatever it was they did. For example, if you check your mail and then send some mail and then surf the Web, the automatic dialing procedure makes probably three telephone calls, wasting between 30 seconds and a minute of your time each time. If some of the e-mail you're reading contains Web addresses and you decide to look at those Web pages, you could be bouncing on and off the Internet any number of times. You may find it faster to dial up the Internet before you start, stay connected the whole time you're working, and then disconnect when you're all done.

Putting your connection on your desktop

Here's how to create shortcuts to your Dial-Up Networking connection. If you find that you don't use them, you can always delete the shortcuts later, with no effect on the Dial-Up Networking connection itself.

1. **Choose the Start⇨Programs⇨Accessories⇨Communications⇨Dial-Up Networking command to open the Dial-Up Networking window.**

   You see the window that was shown in Figure 4-1.

2. **Drag your favorite Dial-Up Networking connection to the Windows 98 desktop.**

   That's all there is to it! Windows 98 leaves your connection where it is and makes a shortcut on the desktop that runs the connection; now you have two icons for the same connection — one in the out-of-the-way Dial-Up Networking window and one right on your desktop.

3. **Leave your Dial-Up Networking window open if you want to put your Dial-Up Networking connection on your Start menu too. Otherwise, close it.**

If you're used to Windows 95, you notice that this process is quite a bit simpler in Windows 98. Remember that because what's on your desktop is a *shortcut* to the actual dial-up networking connection, you can delete it if you want.

Putting your connection on your Start menu

You may want to put your Dial-Up Networking connection on your Start menu too. This ability is less important than it used to be because you can return to your desktop at any time in Windows 98 by clicking the little picture of a desk blotter on the taskbar (on ours, it's just to the right of the Internet Explorer and Outlook Explorer icons — take a look at Figure 4-5). Still, we like to have our Dial-Up Networking connection on our Start menu so that we can get to it without messing up the desktop. Here's how:

1. **If your Dial-Up Networking window isn't still open, open it by choosing the Start⇨Programs⇨Accessories⇨Communications⇨Dial-Up Networking command.**

   As always, a button for the window appears on the taskbar too.

2. **Open your Start menu by choosing the Start⇨Settings⇨Taskbar & Start Menu command.**

   The Taskbar Properties dialog box appears; it has a tab labeled Start Menu Programs.

3. **Click the Start Menu Programs tab.**

   From this tab, you can control what's on your Start menu, by adding and removing things as you like. We can't go into all the details of the Start menu here.

4. **Take a deep breath and click the A̲dvanced button.**

   Don't panic. The Advanced button just opens a Windows Explorer window to part of your hard disk. If you've used Windows Explorer, this window should look familiar; if not, take heart: We don't get really fancy here. What you're looking at is the top pick on the Start menu (Programs), and, if anything appears above Programs on your Start menu, you see those items too. Figure 4-6 shows our Start menu and how it looks in Windows Explorer. In this figure, we clicked the little plus (+) sign beside the Programs folder to show you what's in the Programs folder.

   You have to decide where you want your Dial-Up Networking connection shortcut to go: right on the Start menu, on the Start⇨P̲rograms menu, or on a submenu.

5. **If you want it to go just above Programs on the Start menu, you're all set. If you want it to go under Programs, click the Programs folder; if you want it to go inside a folder in Programs, click that folder.**

   Click the Back button if you feel that you've gone too far into folders.

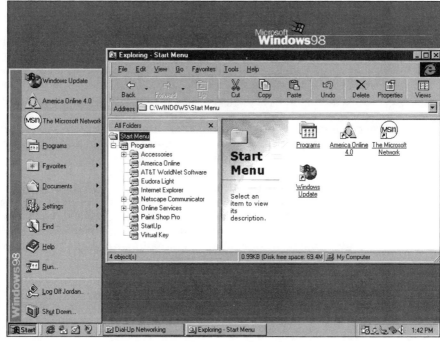

Figure 4-6:
The Start
menu, and
the same
Start menu
in Windows
Explorer.

6. **When you're looking at the folder in which you want to put the Dial-Up Networking connection, click the Dial-Up Networking button on the taskbar.**

   The Dial-Up Networking window appears on top of your Exploring — Start Menu window.

7. **Drag your Dial-Up Networking connection into the Exploring — Start Menu window.**

   That's all there is to it; you've created your shortcut. If you want to get rid of it sometime, just open the Exploring — Start Menu window the same way you did in Steps 2 through 5, *right*-click the shortcut, and choose Delete from the pop-up menu.

8. **Close the Exploring - Start Menu window by choosing the File⇨Close command or by clicking the Close (X) button in the upper-right corner of the window.**

9. **Close the Dial-Up Networking window the same way.**

10. **Close the Taskbar Properties window by clicking the Close button (the X) in the upper-right corner of the window.**

Now you can start your Internet connection by just cruising the Start menu. Very convenient.

Canceling your Internet account

Canceling an account with an Internet service provider is one of the few things you usually *can't* do over the Internet. When you sign up for an account with an Internet service provider, you usually get a package full of stuff, including software (which we ask you to ignore), instructions (which we recommend that you ignore), and some billing information (which you probably threw away). Somewhere in there was a telephone number for account inquiries or billing questions or administrative support or something like it. That's the telephone number you want to call to cancel your account with the Internet service provider.

If you signed up by using the Internet Connection Wizard, you probably had to click OK on a confirmation screen before your credit card number went whizzing over the Internet. You may also have seen a screen full of information after your account was successfully created. We recommend that you print those screens or copy the information from it on paper for moments just like this one.

One of the conveniences of paying with a credit card is that your credit card company helps you with any billing problems with the Internet service provider. The credit card company usually counts on you to have a telephone number or contact information for the Internet service provider, although it can, in a pinch, sometimes give you a contact phone number.

After you get in touch with the Internet service provider, a short conversation is all it usually takes to get your account turned off. It wants to be able to identify you, usually by your telephone number, credit card number, and perhaps other information you gave during the sign-up process. After it does, that's usually all there is to canceling your Internet account.

Fine-Tuning Your Connection

You can find out exactly what telephone number Windows 98 will dial to connect to the Internet. That way, you can check yourself to see that it is local. Although you may already know this number, if you signed up with a service that created your connection automagically, you may not.

Also, Windows 98 may save your Dial-Up Networking password so that you don't have to remember it. Sometimes it gets very stubborn and doesn't. We can tell you when (we think) it does and doesn't.

Making sure that the telephone number is local

If you typed the telephone number for Dial-Up Networking to use to connect to the Internet, you had a chance to look in your telephone book and see whether it's a local call for you. If you're not sure, call the telephone company. If you used an automatic sign-up wizard for an ISP, however, you may not have seen the telephone number. If that's the case, you can't be too careful: It's worth checking to make sure that your ISP is a local call before spending hours browsing the Web. We know true stories of people who signed up with what they thought was a local number until their first $500 phone bill arrived.

Here are the steps:

1. **Open up the Dial-Up Networking window to look at your connection (choose the Start⊏>Programs⊏>Accessories⊏>Communications⊏>Dial-Up Networking command) and click your connection.**

   You see the Connect To dialog box that was shown in Figure 4-2. If the telephone number in the Phone Number box looks like it has been modified by Windows 98, check out the section "Location, Location, Location," later in this chapter. In any case, this is the telephone number Windows 98 will dial.

2. **Check your local telephone directory or call your telephone company's business office to make sure that you won't be paying for the Internet by the minute.**

   If the number *is* long-distance and your ISP suggests a better number to use, type the number in the Phone Number box.

3. **To save any changes, you have to go ahead and connect to your Internet account by clicking Connect.**

   If you make changes and then click Cancel, Windows 98 throws your changes away.

"Why doesn't Windows 98 save my Dial-Up Networking password?"

Suppose that you want Windows 98 to save your Dial-Up Networking password. After all, it's convenient, even if it means that anyone who comes up to your computer can get on the Internet as you. (If you don't want Windows 98 to save your password, you can skip this section of the book.) Every once in awhile, Windows 98 does not save your password; it has been one of the most vexing questions for users of previous versions of Windows.

Several possible reasons exist for why the password isn't saved, only a few of which we can help you out with. The rest get you deep into the guts of Windows 98, a place where even experienced folks have been bitten by poisonous snakes occasionally and have the scars to prove it. The symptom you're most likely to see is a Connect To dialog box (like the one shown in Figure 4-2), where the Save Password check box is grayed out and you therefore cannot check it.

The most common reason for this situation is that you didn't log on to Windows 98 in the first place, so it has no idea who you are. When you started up your computer, Windows 98 most likely showed you a dialog box that said Welcome to Windows or Enter Network Password or something similar. In either case, you had the option of clicking the Cancel button. If you canceled this dialog box, Windows 98 still starts and you can still use it. You are not *logged in,* however. If you don't log in, Windows doesn't save passwords for you.

Luckily, you can talk Windows into saving your passwords, including your Internet password. Your best bet is to choose Start⇨Log Off from the Start menu. Windows 98 asks you to sign on again. When you enter your password this time, Windows 98 should save your Dial-Up Networking password the next time you connect.

If you've forgotten your password, you can sign on with a different name, in which case Windows 98 asks you for a new password. Any passwords Windows 98 had saved for you are no longer available, although as you work, Windows 98 asks you for the passwords it needs. If you remember all of them, before long, Windows 98 knows all the ones you need. We know of no way to get Windows 98 to tell you a forgotten password.

What if Windows never asked you to sign on in the first place? When you started Windows 98 for the first time, you may have pressed the Cancel button when you were asked to sign on for the first time. Windows 98 figured that you didn't care about saving passwords and resolved never to bother you again. All's well and good until now, when you want it to remember a password. No problem. Choose Start⇨Log Off, and then you see the Welcome to Windows sign-in dialog box. Enter a new username, and click OK *without* typing a password. Windows 98 asks you to confirm that you don't want a password (actually, it asks you to retype your "null" password), so just click OK. Now, whenever you start Windows, it's not supposed to ask you to sign on. If it does, you can just click OK. But now Windows saves your Dial-Up Networking passwords for you.

Windows 98 may ask for your password when you start up your computer and *still* not allow you to check the Save Password check box in the Connect To dialog box. If so, your password file may have gotten messed up (that's a technical term). It's time to call tech support, from either your computer manufacturer or Microsoft.

Location, Location, Location

If your computer moves around (as laptops typically do), you may find yourself calling the same Internet access number from places with different area codes. Dialing telephone numbers used to be so easy: If you were making a call inside your area code, you dialed seven digits, and if you were making a call outside your area code, you dialed 1, the three-digit area code, and the seven-digit telephone number.

Now, you make calls within your area code, and even some local calls require that you dial 1 plus an area code. In some places, you dial the 1 only sometimes — you have to know when. If you have a desktop computer, this situation isn't so bad: After *you* figure out what to dial to get to the Internet, you can just tell Windows 98 and be done with it. Because laptop computers move from place to place, however, the right way to dial a particular telephone number changes depending on where the computer is.

For laptop computer users (or anyone who moves her computer around frequently), Windows 98 has a baroque scheme for what it calls *dialing locations* that covers most, but not all, of the area code possibilities. This section first solves the most common desktop computer dialing problems and then looks at solutions for laptop computers. In either case, you have to look at your Dial-Up Networking connections again. If you've closed the Dial-Up Networking window, choose the Start⇨Programs⇨Accessories⇨ Communications⇨Dial-Up Networking command from the taskbar to get it back.

Dialing from your desktop computer

If your computer never moves, you only have to make sure that your Dial-Up Networking connection dials the right number when you set it up. To check which digits Windows 98 dials to connect to your ISP, click the Dial-Up Networking connection you want to check out. You see the Connect To dialog box that was shown in Figure 4-2.

The digits Windows 98 will dial are in the Phone Number box. Windows 98 may have added (or removed) the area code from the telephone number you gave it, and it may have added a prefix (like 9,) to get an outside line and a prefix (like *70) to turn off call-waiting. If Windows 98 modified the telephone number you gave it, someone (you, perhaps?) told it something about its Dialing location which made it think that it was the right thing to do.

The Dialing From box tells you where Windows 98 thinks that it's dialing from. For desktop computer users, this entry almost always says "New location." Windows creates this location for all computer users, and, if your computer never moves, it should be good enough. If you want to find out more about what's in this dialog box, look in the section "Dialing from your laptop computer," just ahead.

If the telephone number Windows 98 will dial is correct, you can click Cancel and skip the rest of this location business. If Windows 98 has gotten smart with you and done things to your telephone number that you don't like, you can tell it to keep its hands off. After you do, it's your job to tell Windows 98 about these tasks:

✔ Dialing 9 or something else to get an outside line

✔ Turning off call-waiting (call interrupt)

✔ Dialing an area code

✔ Dialing 1 before an area code

Follow these steps to tell Windows 98 exactly how you want your telephone number dialed:

1. **If you're still looking at the Connect To dialog box, click Cancel to forget about dialing out right now.**

2. **In the Dial-Up Networking window, right-click the Dial-Up Networking connection you're interested in.**

   After you perform Steps 3 through 6 in this list, Windows 98 forgets the username and password associated with this Dial-Up Networking connection. Before you proceed, therefore, make sure that you have them written down somewhere. Windows 98 tells you the username for this Dial-Up Networking connection (in the Connect To dialog box — that's the dialog box you just closed in Step 1 if it was still open). It does not tell you the password, however; it just indicates that it remembers the password by putting a few asterisks in the Password entry in the dialog box.

3. **Choose Properties from the pop-up menu.**

   You see a dialog box with a bunch of tabs describing the properties of your Dial-Up Networking connection. On the General tab, in the Phone Number section, you see the area code and telephone number you (or some fancy Internet setup Wizard) told Windows 98 to dial.

4. **Uncheck the Use Area Code and Dialing Properties check box.**

   By unchecking this box, you tell Windows 98 that you will give it exactly the right telephone number to dial and to keep its hands off your telephone number. As a result, the area code and country code entries become unavailable: They no longer affect the number your computer dials. Also, when you see the Connect To dialog box, the Dialing From entry is not available. The reason is that Windows 98 uses the location settings in the Dialing from box to decide how to mess up your telephone number; unchecking the check box labeled Use Area Code and Dialing Properties tells Windows 98 to keep its hands off your telephone number.

5. **In the Telephone Number box, enter the telephone number** *exactly* **as Windows 98 should dial it.**

   Include **9,** (a 9 with a comma) if you need to dial 9 for an outside line. Often, when you have to dial 9 to get an outside line, you have to wait until you actually get the line before you dial again. If you have to wait, you have to tell your computer to wait. Put the comma in to tell Windows 98 to pause. If you have trouble connecting, try putting in a second comma to extend the pause. Include ***70,,** (that's star 70 with two commas) if that's what you press to disable call-waiting. (Again, the commas tell Windows 98 to wait for the command to disable call-waiting to clear before it begins dialing the number.) Include the 1 and the area code if you need them.

6. **Click OK to keep your changes.**

   Presto! You're all set to dial out.

If you set up an additional Dial-Up Networking connection later, remember to uncheck the Use Area Code and Dialing Properties check box for that new connection, and fill in exactly what Windows 98 needs to dial up the Internet.

Dialing from your laptop computer

If your computer moves around frequently, changing the area code and other dialing instructions for each Dial-Up Networking connection every time you move your computer can become tedious. Windows 98 can figure out this stuff for you by defining a *dialing location,* which is basically a name and an area code. If you get fancy, a location can include things like dialing 9 to get an outside line and dialing *70 to turn off call-waiting. The simplest way to check out your locations is from the Connect To dialog box when you're about to dial.

 You can get to the Dialing Properties dialog box in several different ways. Windows 98 is sensitive about the order in which things happen. Make sure that you get to the Dialing Properties dialog box from the Dial-Up Networking dialog box; otherwise, some of the settings do not appear.

1. **In the Dial-Up Networking window, click the connection you want to check.**

   You see the Connect To dialog box, as shown in Figure 4-2.

2. Click the Dial Properties button.

You see the Dialing Properties dialog box, as shown in Figure 4-7.

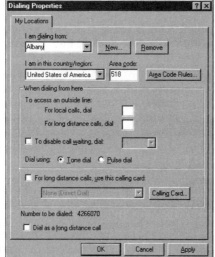

Figure 4-7:
Is this the
location
from which
I am
dialing?

The following sections describe common dialing problems and ways to solve them from the Dialing Properties dialog box.

Your computer may be in one of several different places when you want it to call the Internet

Click the New button in the Dialing Properties dialog box. Windows 98 creates a new dialing location with the same characteristics as the dialing location you were just looking at. Windows 98 gives the new location a creative name, like New Location (2). (Click OK to acknowledge the new location.) Type a more appropriate name, like **Office** or **Home**. Review the following dialing problems to see whether you need to change any of the settings for this new location.

You always have to dial 1 and the area code to reach this number, even though it's within your area code

If the area code you are dialing from (in the Area code box in the Dialing Properties dialog box) is the same as the area code of the number you are calling (that's the number you entered when you created the Dial-Up Networking connection you're working on), Windows 98 assumes that you don't have to dial 1 and the area code. You can tell Windows 98 to always dial this number as a long-distance call by checking the check box labeled Dial As a Long Distance Call. In the Dialing Properties dialog box is a field labeled For

Long Distance Calls, Dial. Windows adds the contents of that field as well as 1 and the area code to whatever telephone number you entered. Unlike the other settings in this dialog box, this check box applies to only the Dial-Up Networking connection you were looking at when you clicked Dial Properties in the Connect To dialog box.

You want to turn off call-waiting

Windows 98 is all set for this trick: In the Dialing Properties dialog box is a check box labeled To Disable Call Waiting, Dial. Make sure that this box has a check mark in it, and pick one of the call-waiting codes from the nearby list. If you dial a more creative code to disable call-waiting, type what you dial.

You want to dial the area code but not a 1 in front of it

You can't — at least not by using the dialing properties and locations in Windows 98. If you need to dial the area code without the 1, you probably live in Texas or dangerously close to Washington, D.C., and the most sensible thing to do is to move. If you can't, however, look at the section "Dialing from your desktop computer," earlier in this chapter, and tell Windows 98 *exactly* how you want your number dialed. You may have to define two Dial-Up Networking connections for the same telephone number if you sometimes dial it as area-code-plus-number (no 1 appears before the area code) and sometimes dial it as 1-plus-area-code-plus-number. For the no-1-before-the-area-code connection, follow the procedure in the section "Dialing from your desktop computer," a little earlier in this chapter. For the 1-plus-area-code-plus-number connection, use locations as we've described them in this section.

You want to use a telephone credit card

We prefer to create a new dialing location for each type of credit card call we make. That way, we can select the credit card as a dialing location directly from the Connect To dialog box (refer to Figure 4-2). If you like this plan, follow the instructions in the section "Your computer may be in one of several different places," earlier in this chapter, to create the location. Then click the For Long-Distance Calls, Use This Calling Card check box. Click the Calling Card button to select a calling card, and enter your calling card PIN. If your calling card is not listed, you can create a new one; examine the existing ones carefully, however, so that you can figure out what your calling card should do. If you need to create a new type of card, you just wandered out of the territory covered by this book — sorry!

You're happy with your location as it now appears

Click OK to accept the dialing location you've created or modified, and get rid of the Dialing Properties dialog box. The location you've been working on now appears as the Dialing From location in the Connect To dialog box, and it's available from any other Dial-Up Networking connections you've created.

Whom to Call (And Whom Not to Call) for Support

If you're having trouble getting Dial-Up Networking to work, we can't very well tell you to go look on the World Wide Web for support, can we? This situation is a shame because organizing and delivering this kind of information is just what the World Wide Web was designed for, and it does a good job. If you're having trouble getting online, however, here are some places to start looking for help.

Call your Internet service provider (ISP)

How good an option your Internet service provider is depends a great deal on the one you selected. If you selected one of the national ISPs (such as AT&T, IBM, MCI, Sprint, or others), you most likely got a toll-free support telephone number. Despite the fact that it probably didn't make your computer or your modem or the software that's trying to connect it all together, it will probably help you anyway. The reason, of course, is that it's about to make $20 per month from you for the foreseeable future, so it wants to help you get online — and usually does a good job. Although it may take you awhile to get through to an ISP, it's probably worth the wait, especially for the price.

Support from local ISPs can be more spotty. When you're choosing a local ISP, talk to friends about which one they use and whether they like its technical support. Although most local ISPs are technically quite competent, some don't have the resources or inclination to do much front-line technical customer support for the technically unsophisticated (or for you, either). The response you get from a local ISP is a little less predictable. Some are great and go the extra mile that the nationals can't. Others get around to you eventually. Here's a hint: If your provider can't help you get connected, find another one.

Get Windows 98 help

The Windows 98 help file is surprisingly complete when it comes to Dial-Up Networking. It has the added advantage that it can take you directly to some of the procedures you need to perform to get online, such as install a modem or install Dial-Up Networking. To start Windows help, choose the Start⇨Help command and click the Contents tab if it isn't already selected. Help for setting up Dial-Up Networking is hidden in the area of the help file called Using Windows Accessories / Connections to Other Computers. Most topics have at the bottom a link labeled Related Topics that takes you to additional pages of useful information.

A nice feature that has been improved in Windows 98 is *troubleshooters*, a series of questions and recommended actions based on your answers to those questions. Because *troubleshooters* are integrated with Windows, they sometimes take you directly to the dialog box you need to solve your problem. They're available in Help, under Troubleshooting / Windows 98 Troubleshooters. The Dial-Up Networking help is available in the Modem area.

Although the Windows 98 help file is not tremendously detailed, try it before you spend time on the telephone, because it's quick, easy, and *free*.

Call Microsoft — maybe

Microsoft offers 90 days of support for your Windows 98 system, starting from when you first call a support engineer. Try it, at 425-635-7000, but only if you bought your copy of Windows 98 from a store. If Windows 98 came preinstalled on your computer, chances are that you have an *OEM* version — a copy of Windows that was licensed by Microsoft but sold by the company that made your computer. Microsoft would much rather have you call the company that sold you the software than have you call Microsoft directly. Our experience is that Microsoft usually answers your questions, but you never know.

If you're willing to pay, Microsoft supports you after your 90 days are up, for $35 (U.S.) per incident, at 800-936-5700 or 900-555-2000. Our experience with its fee-for-support has been good. Although it hurts to pay, someone there sticks with you until your problem is solved and leaves your case active for 90 days in case the problem reappears in another form. The folks there are also knowledgeable. We rate this option as a good one if you can afford it.

Call the folks who made your computer

If Windows 98 came preinstalled on your computer, Microsoft requires that the computer company support the versions of Windows it sells. This requirement can be a good thing: The company that made your computer should know exactly which components it used and what combination of hardware and software went into your computer. With that knowledge, it should be able to help you zero in on the problems you're having.

In reality, as for ISPs, the quality of the support you get varies from company to company. We've found that the major brands do a surprisingly creditable job of supporting the Windows systems they sell.

Call your friends

If you have friends on the Internet, you're in luck, especially if they're running Windows 98 (or even Windows 95, which isn't all that different). It's even better if they're using the same ISP as you. Check out how they have their computer set up and see whether you can relate their setup to yours. You may find just the one check box or setting that's different, and that could be just what you need. If it doesn't help, at least you have someone's shoulder to cry on.

Getting your Windows 98 system on the Internet shouldn't be all that difficult, although sometimes it is. Between the information in Part I of this book and a little help from your friends, however, we're confident that you're there. Now that you're dialing in and out, you're ready to get some useful (or at least some fun) work done.

Part II
Mail and Gossip

The 5th Wave — By Rich Tennant

"You'd better come out here — I've got someone who wants to run a banner ad on our Web site."

In this part . . .

*I*t seems like every day we hear about some amazing
new thing that someone has figured out how to do on
the Internet. But most people spend most of their time on
the Internet talking to other people. Although e-mail is the
Rodney Dangerfield I-don't-get-no-respect use for the
Internet, it's where most of the useful work happens. We
tell you everything you need to know to get started with
e-mail on the Internet. Then you can get fancy and join
mailing lists and discussion groups and watch all your
free time evaporate.

Chapter 5

All about E-Mail

*E*lectronic mail, or *e-mail,* is without a doubt the most-used Internet service, even though doesn't it get as much press as the World Wide Web. E-mail is much older than the Web, and more people use it. Every system on the Net supports some sort of mail service, which means that you can send e-mail to and receive e-mail from millions of people around the world.

Because mail, much more than any other Internet service, is connected to many non-Internet systems, you can exchange mail with lots of people who don't otherwise have access to the Internet, in addition to all the people who *are* on the Net (see Chapter 10 for help in finding people's e-mail addresses).

This chapter introduces you to all the jargon and ideas around e-mail and then walks you through the use of three popular e-mail programs: Outlook Express, Netscape Messenger, and Eudora.

Addresses, Domains, and Mailboxes

Everyone with e-mail access to the Net has an *e-mail address,* which is the cyberspace equivalent of a postal address or a phone number. When you send an e-mail message, you enter the address or addresses of the recipients so that the computer knows to whom to send it.

Before you do much mailing, you have to figure out your electronic-mail address so that you can give it to people who want to get in touch with you. You also have to figure out some of their addresses so that you can write to them. (If you have no friends or plan to send only anonymous hate mail, you can skip this section.)

Internet mail addresses have two parts, separated by an @ (the *at* sign). The part before the @ is the *mailbox,* which is (roughly speaking) your personal name, and the part after that is the *domain,* usually the name of your Internet service provider (or ISP), such as `aol.com` or `sover.net`. In other words, addresses look like this:

```
username@domain
```

What's in a username?

The mailbox is usually your *username,* the name your provider assigns to your account. If you're lucky, you get to choose your username; in other cases, providers have standardized the naming conventions, and you get what you get. Some usernames are just first names, just last names, initials, first name and last initial, first initial and last name, or anything else, including *made-up* names. Over the years, for example, John has had the usernames `john`, `john1`, `jrl`, `jlevine`, `jlevine3` (must have been at least three `jlevines` there), and even `q0246`; Carol has been `carol`, `carolb`, `cbaroudi`, and `carol377` (the provider threw in a random number); and Margy tries to stick with `margy` but has ended up with `margy1` or `73727,2305` on occasion. A few systems assign names such as `usd31516`. Ugh.

For example, you can write to the President of the United States at `president@whitehouse.gov`. The President's mailbox is `president`, and the domain that stores his mailbox is `whitehouse.gov` — reasonable enough.

Back when many fewer e-mail users were around and most users of any particular system knew each other directly, figuring out who had what username wasn't all that difficult. These days, because that process is becoming much more of a problem, many organizations are creating consistent mailbox names for all users, most often by using the user's first and last names with a dot between them. In this type of scheme, your mailbox name may be something like `elvis.presley@bluesuede.org`, even though your username is something else. (If your name isn't Elvis Presley, adjust this example suitably. On the other hand, if your name *is* Elvis Presley, please contact us immediately. We know some people who are looking for you.)

Having several names for the same mailbox is no problem, so the new, longer, consistent usernames are invariably created in addition to — rather than instead of — the traditional short nicknames.

Is e-mail really private?

Relatively, but not totally. Any recipient of your mail may forward it to other people. Some mail addresses are really mailing lists that redistribute messages to many other people. In one famous case, a mistaken mail address sent a message to tens of thousands of readers. It began, "Darling, at last we have a way to send messages that is completely private."

If you send mail from work or to someone at work, your mail is not private. You and your friend may work for companies of the highest integrity whose employees would never dream of reading private e-mail. When push comes to shove, however, and someone is accusing your company of leaking confidential information and the corporate lawyer says, "Examine the e-mail," someone reads all the e-mail. (This situation happened to a friend of ours who was none too pleased to find that all his intimate correspondence with his fiancée had been read.) Some lawyers even claim that companies have a duty to read their employees' e-mail! E-mail you send and receive is stored on your disk, and most companies back up their disks regularly. Reading your e-mail is very easy for someone who really wants to, unless you encrypt it.

The usual rule is not to send anything you wouldn't want to see posted next to the water cooler or perhaps scribbled next to a pay phone. The latest e-mail systems are beginning to include encryption features that make the privacy situation somewhat better so that anyone who doesn't know the keyword used to scramble a message can't decode it.

The most common tools for encrypted mail are known as PEM (privacy-enhanced mail) and PGP (pretty good privacy). PGP is one of the most widely used encryption programs, both in the United States and abroad. Many experts think that it's so strong that even the U.S. National Security Agency can't crack it. We don't know about that; if the NSA wants to read your mail, however, you have more complicated problems than we can help you solve.

PEM capability is included in versions of Outlook Express sold in the United States and Canada. PEM is not as widely used as PGP, and PEM requires that you buy something called Digital ID from a third company.

PGP is available for free on the Net. You can buy a commercial version that has more features. The latest versions of PGP plug in to popular e-mail programs, including Outlook Express and Eudora, for easy, seamless operation. To find more information about privacy and security issues, including how to get started with PGP, point your web browser to http://net.gurus.com/pgp.

What's in a domain name?

The domain name for Internet service providers in the United States usually ends with three letters (called the *zone* or *top-level domain*) that give you a clue to what kind of place it is:

✔ *Commercial* organizations end with .com, which includes both providers such as America Online (AOL) and CompuServe and many companies that aren't public providers but that are commercial entities, such as amrcorp.com (AMR Corporation, better known as American Airlines), creamery.com (Egg Farm Dairy in New York state, which makes really good French-style soft cheeses), and iecc.com (the Invincible Electronic Calculator Company).

✔ Educational institutions end with .edu (such as yale.edu).

✔ Networking organizations, like ISPs, end with .net.

✔ U.S. government sites end with .gov.

✔ U.S. military sites end with .mil.

✔ Organizations that don't fall into any of those categories, like nonprofits, end with .org.

Outside the United States, domains often end with a country code, such as .fr for France or .zm for Zambia. See our Web site, at http://net.gurus.com/countries, for a listing of country codes. Just to confuse things even more, some domains in the United States end in .us, preceded by a town and a two-letter state code; for example, the city of Cambridge, Massachusetts, is at ci.cambridge.ma.us.

New domains are being registered at a ferocious rate, many thousands per month. New zones are scheduled to be added in 1998 too, as listed in Table 5-1, in an attempt to accommodate the glut.

Table 5-1	New Domains
Zone	*Description*
.firm	Business
.store	Business offering goods to purchase
.web	Organization emphasizing activities related to the World Wide Web
.arts	Organization emphasizing cultural and entertainment activities
.rec	Organization emphasizing recreation and entertainment activities
.info	Organization providing information services
.nom	Individual or personal names

The situation with domains is, to put it politely, fluid. At the time we write this book, the domains in Table 5-1 are scheduled to be activated but aren't yet, and the agreement under which Network Solutions — the registrar for `.com`, `.org.`, `.net`, and `.edu` — operated was about to expire. Visit our Web site to find out the current scoop:

```
http://net.gurus.com/domains/
```

Address tips

If you're sending a message to another user in your domain (the same machine or group of machines), you can leave out the domain part altogether when you type the address. If you and a friend both use AOL, for example, you can leave out the `@aol.com` part of the address when you're writing to each other.

If you don't know what your e-mail address is, a good approach is to send yourself a message and use your login name as the mailbox name. Then examine the return address on the message. Or you can send a message to Internet For Dummies Mail Central, at `internet98@gurus.com`, and a friendly robot will send back a message with your address. (While you're at it, tell us whether you like this book, because we authors see that mail too.) Chapter 10 has more suggestions for finding e-mail addresses.

Where Mail Lives

When e-mail messages come hurtling across the Internet, they need a place to wait until someone is ready to read them. Similarly, when you write a message, you need a mailbox — not unlike the box down at the corner in which you stick your envelopes — for mailing messages. The Internet has two kinds of mail storage containers — more officially called *mail servers.*

When your mail arrives, unless you're one of the lucky (or rich) few whose computers have a permanent Internet connection, the mail doesn't get delivered to your computer automatically. Mail gets delivered instead to an *incoming mail server* (also known as a *POP server,* for Post Office Protocol, or *POP3,* for the version of that protocol), which is sort of like your local post office. To get your mail, you have to go and get it. Actually, your *mail* program has to go and get it.

For you to be able to send mail, your mail program has to take mail to the post office — your *outgoing mail server* (or *SMTP server,* for Simple Mail Transfer Protocol). It's sort of like having a post office box rather than home delivery — you have to pick it up at the post office and also deliver your outgoing mail there.

Every Internet service provider (or ISP) runs a POP server and an SMTP server for the use of its customers. When your mail program picks up the mail, it sucks your mail from your provider's POP server to your PC at top speed. After you have downloaded your mail to your own computer, you can disconnect, which is a good idea if your provider charges by the hour. Then you can read and respond to your mail while the meter isn't running — while you're *offline*. When you're ready to send your responses or new messages, you can reconnect and transmit your outgoing mail to the SMTP server, again at top network speed.

More E-Mail Programs Than You Can Shake a Stick At

Depending on what kind of account you have, you use a different program to get your mail. They all do more or less the same thing because they're all mail programs, after all — they let you read, write, reply, forward, print, and save e-mail messages.

PPP or cable Internet accounts

You can use any Winsock-compatible e-mail program, and countless programs exist. You've got your freeware, you've got your shareware, and you've got your commercial stuff. The good news is that Windows 98 comes with a serviceable e-mail program called Outlook Express. For variety, we also describe Eudora, a solid e-mail program that many of us like, and one version (Eudora Light) is free. Netscape Messenger, which comes with Netscape Communicator, is okay too. Pegasus is another excellent, free e-mail program for this type of Internet account, available from the Net. Because Windows 98 comes with Outlook Express, we concentrate on it for the remainder of this chapter, with short explanations of Eudora and Netscape Messenger.

America Online (AOL) or CompuServe

The access software you use to connect to your account includes an easy-to-use e-mail program. Most of the general information in this chapter applies also to AOL and CompuServe.

As of early 1998, neither CompuServe nor America Online has either an incoming or outgoing mail server. This omission means that you can't use an e-mail program to send or receive mail by using an AOL or CompuServe account. Instead, you have to use the AOL or CompuServe program to read and send your mail. Forget about using Outlook Express or Eudora as your mail program. These services may install mail servers soon, however — if you have an AOL or CompuServe account, ask someone there.

On both AOL and CompuServe, go to the keyword **mail** to read and send mail. If you have an AOL account, your e-mail address is your screen name followed by @aol.com. If your screen name were SteveCase, for example, your e-mail address would be SteveCase@aol.com.

If you have a CompuServe account, you have a CompuServe ID that looks like this: 71234,567 (your numbers will differ). To turn this number into an Internet address, change the comma to a period and add @compuserve.com to the end, like this: 71234.567@compuserve.com. You can register for a name too, if you would rather have a more memorable e-mail address. Go to the keyword **register**.

Free e-mail accounts

At least one service, Juno Online, gives you free dial-up accounts for e-mail only. The price you pay is having advertisements appear on-screen as you read your messages. (It's free, providing, of course, that the phone call your computer makes is not a toll call.) In the United States, call 800-654-JUNO to ask for a software disk (which you do have to pay for) or download Juno from the Web (from http://www.juno.com) which really is free, or get it from a friend. If you use Juno, you have to use its e-mail software (otherwise, the advertisements aren't displayed). You can't use the programs we describe here.

Web-based mail

A few systems offer free e-mail accounts you can access through the Web. The best known are Hotmail, at http://www.hotmail.com, and Yahoo Mail, at http://mail.yahoo.com. Web-based free e-mail service can be handy if you have several family members on one Internet account or if you want a separate account to get private e-mail at work.

LAN and other mail

If you're connected in some other way, you probably have a different mail program. For example, you may be using a PC in your company's Local Area Network that runs cc:Mail, Lotus Notes, or Microsoft Mail and has a mail-only link to the outside world. We don't describe Local Area Network mail programs here, but don't stop reading.

Regardless of which type of mail you're using, the basics of reading, sending, addressing, and filing mail work in pretty much the same way. It's worth looking through this chapter even if you're not using any of the mail programs we describe here.

What Your E-Mail Program Needs to Know

Write your e-mail address in Table 5-2 and on the Cheat Sheet in the front of this book (and then tear it out and tape it to the wall near your computer). Capitalization never matters in domains and rarely matters in mailbox names. To make it easy on your eyes, therefore, most of the domain and mailbox names in this book are shown in lowercase.

If you're using a PPP or cable account, you have to tell your e-mail program the name of your incoming (POP) and outgoing (SMTP) mail servers. Write the names of your mail servers in Table 5-2 and on the Cheat Sheet (it's hanging on your wall, right?). If you don't know what to write, ask your service provider.

Table 5-2   Information Your E-Mail Program Needs to Know

Information	*Description*	*Example*
Your e-mail address	Your username followed by an @ and the domain name.	`internet98@gurus.com`
Your e-mail password	The password for your e-mail mailbox (usually the same as the password for your account). Don't write it here! It's a secret!	`9tcf598`
Your incoming (POP3) mail server	The name of the computer that receives your e-mail messages (get this name from your Internet provider).	`mail.gurus.com`
Your outgoing (SMTP) mail server	The name of the computer that distributes your outgoing mail to the rest of the Internet (often the same as the POP3 server).	`mail.gurus.com`

Sending and Receiving Mail with Outlook Express

Because Outlook Express comes for free with Windows 98, it's a good place to start.

Running Outlook Express the first time

The first time you run Outlook Express, it asks questions about who you are and how you want to collect your mail. Follow these steps:

1. **Start Outlook Express. You don't have to connect to your ISP (yet), although it's okay if you're already connected.**

   Click the Outlook Express icon, or choose it from the Start⇨Programs⇨ Internet Explorer menu. A Wizard asks you where to store your messages. It suggests the C:\Windows\Application Data\Microsoft\Outlook Express folder.

2. **Click OK.**

   The Outlook Express window appears, as shown in Figure 5-1, featuring a list of folders to the left, the contents of the current folder to the upper right, and the text of the current message to the lower right. (When you start the program, no folder or message is selected, so you don't see much.)

List of folders   Contents of current folder

Figure 5-1:
The Outlook
Express
window
shows a list
of folders, a
list of
messages
in the
current
folder, and
the text of
the
selected
message.

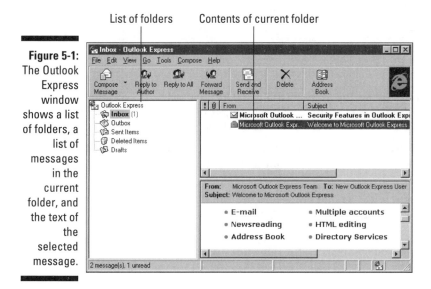

3. **Click the Inbox folder.**

   The first time you open this folder, Outlook Express may run the Internet Connection Wizard to ask you some questions about your e-mail account. If it doesn't, you can assume that it knows everything it needs to know and skip to the following section, "Sending mail with Outlook Express."

4. **Type your name in the Display Name box and click the Next button.**

   Type your actual name, as you want it to appear in the headers of e-mail messages you send. Don't type your e-mail address (yet).

5. **Type your e-mail address in the E-mail Address box and click Next.**

   If you are an obedient reader and filled out Table 5-2, you will find your e-mail address in that table and on the Cheat Sheet too. If you're not sure of your e-mail address, ask your Internet or online service provider. Next, the Internet Connection Wizard asks about e-mail server names, as shown in Figure 5-2.

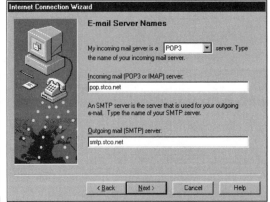

Figure 5-2:
What mail servers do you use for sending and receiving messages?

6. **In the Incoming Mail (POP3 or IMAP) Server box, type the name of your POP server. In the Outgoing Mail (SMTP) Server box, type the name of your SMTP server. Then click Next.**

   Table 5-2 should have the names of these mail servers. The Wizard asks how to log on to the account where you get your mail.

7. **In the POP Account Name box, type your username (the part of your e-mail address that comes before the @). In the Password box, type your account's password. Click Next again.**

   The Wizard asks for a "friendly name" for this account — that is, what name *you* want to use for it in Outlook Express.

8. **In the Internet Mail Account Name box, type the name you want to use for this account. Click Next.**

   Finally, the Wizard wants to be capable of connecting to the Internet automatically when you want to get or send mail, as shown in Figure 5-3.

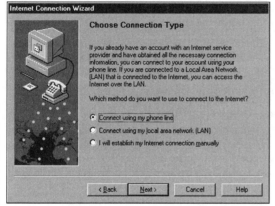

Figure 5-3:
How do you
connect
to the
Internet?

9. **Click the option for how you connect to the Internet, and then click Next.**

   If you dial your account by using your modem, click the option labeled Connect Using My Phone Line. If you connect over a Local Area Network, click the option labeled Connect Using My Local Area Network (LAN). If you would rather that Outlook Express not try to connect you to the Internet and would rather do it yourself, click the option labeled I Will Establish My Internet Connection Manually.

   If you told the Wizard that you dial in to the Internet (in Step 9), it now wants to know which Dial-Up Networking connection to use. The window shows a list of the existing connections.

10. **If you don't yet have a Dial-Up Networking connection set up in Windows 98, click Create a New Dial-Up Connection and skip to Chapter 3 to find out how to proceed. Otherwise, click Use an Existing Dial-Up Connection, and choose the connection from the list. Then click Next.**

    The Wizard congratulates you on a job well done!

11. **Click Finish.**

    You see the Inbox window again. Now Outlook Express knows how to get some incoming mail to put in the Inbox and what to do with mail you create and put in your Outbox.

Outlook Express can send and receive mail from more than one Internet account; choose Tools➪Accounts to tell it about other accounts.

Sending mail with Outlook Express

After Outlook Express knows all about your Internet account, here's how to send mail:

1. **Start Outlook Express by clicking the Outlook Express icon or choosing it from the Start➪Programs➪Internet Explorer menu.**

   You see the Outlook Express window (refer to Figure 5-1).

2. **Click the Inbox folder.**

   Actually, you can click any of the folders on the list.

3. **Click the Compose Message button (the leftmost button on the toolbar), press Ctrl+N, or choose Compose➪New Message from the menu bar.**

   You see a New Message window, with boxes to fill in to address the message, as shown in Figure 5-4.

Figure 5-4: Writing a message with Outlook Express.

4. **In the To box, type the address to which to send the message, and then press Tab.**

   Don't press Enter unless you want to add another line to the To box so that you can type an additional address to which to send the message.

If you click the little Rolodex-style card icon at the left end of the To box, you see the Select Recipients window; it's part of the Outlook Express address book, described in Chapter 6.

For your first e-mail message, you may want to write to us (because we will send you back a message confirming what your e-mail address is) or to yourself (if you know what your e-mail address is).

5. **If you want to send a copy of the message to someone, type that person's address in the Cc box. Another tab takes you to the Bcc box. Then press Tab again or click in the Subject line.**

   Bccs, or *blind carbon copies,* are copies sent to people without putting their names on the message so that the other recipients can't tell.

6. **In the Subject box, type a succinct summary of the message. Then press Tab again.**

   The cursor should be blinking in the message area, the large, empty box where the actual message goes.

7. **In the large, empty box, type the text of the message.**

   When you have typed your message, you can press F7 to check its spelling or choose Tools⇨Spelling from the menu.

8. **To send the message, click the Send button (the leftmost button on the toolbar), press Alt+S (not Ctrl+S, for some strange reason), or choose File⇨Send Message from the menu.**

   Outlook Express sticks the message in your Outbox folder, waiting to be sent. If you're connected to your Internet service provider, Outlook Express sends the message, and you can skip Steps 9 and 10.

9. **Connect to your ISP if you're not already connected.**

   To send the message, you have to climb on the Net.

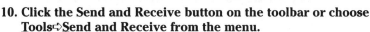

10. **Click the Send and Receive button on the toolbar or choose Tools⇨Send and Receive from the menu.**

    Your message is on its way.

After you have sent a piece of e-mail, you have no way to cancel it!

Reading mail with Outlook Express

If you begin sending e-mail (and in most cases even if you don't), you begin receiving it. The arrival of e-mail is always exciting, even when you get 200 messages a day. Here's how to get your mail:

Send and Receive

1. **Run Outlook Express and connect to your Internet service provider.**

2. **Click the Send and Receive button on the toolbar or choose Tools⇨ Send and Receive from the menu.**

   Outlook Express downloads your incoming mail on your computer and stashes the messages in your Inbox folder. See the list of folders on the left side of the Outlook Express window? You can choose which folder full of mail to look at.

3. **Click the Inbox folder if it's not already selected.**

   The box in the upper-right part of the window lists one line for each message in your Inbox, showing the senders and subjects of each message. The box in the bottom-right part of the window shows the text of the message you select.

4. **Click a message on the list of messages to see the text of the message at the bottom of the Outlook Express window. Or double-click the message header to see the message in a new, big window.**

   If you see a message in its own window, click the Close button, choose File⇨Close from the menu, or press Alt+F4 to get rid of the window.

You can delete, reply to, forward, or print a message after you have seen it. (Chapter 6 tells how to do these tasks.)

If you're happy using Outlook Express, skip the section about Eudora (another e-mail program) a few paragraphs from here, and read about e-mail etiquette. If you don't find Outlook Express to your liking, read on.

Why your parents had dirty hands

The term *carbon copy* should be familiar to those of you who were born before 1960 and remember the ancient practice of putting sheets of carbon-coated paper between sheets of regular paper to make extra copies when using a typewriter. (Please don't ask us what a typewriter is.) In e-mail, a carbon copy — some people now call it a *courtesy copy* — is simply a copy of the message you send. All recipients, on both the To and Cc lines, see who's getting this message. A *blind carbon copy* (Bcc) is a copy sent to a person without putting the person's name on the message so that the other recipients can't tell.

Bcc are best avoided in most cases. The classic situation is when you mail a complaint to your boss with a Bcc to the boss's boss. The big boss, who has her secretary print all her e-mail, sends a copy to your boss and you are in hot water (assuming that your boss has a clue about Bccs). Bccs *are* handy for mailing lists, to keep everyone from getting a long list of all the recipients.

Sending and Receiving Mail with Netscape Messenger

Netscape Navigator is the most popular Web browsing program (you learn about it in Chapter 8). The Netscape folks added a good mail program called Netscape Messenger. This section describes the version of Netscape Messenger that comes with the Netscape Communicator 4 package. We don't think that Netscape Messenger is as good as Outlook Express or Eudora, although if you use Netscape Navigator as your Web browser, you may prefer to use Netscape Messenger.

To run Netscape Messenger, click the Netscape icon on your desktop or choose Start⇨Programs⇨Netscape Communicator⇨Netscape Messenger menu. If you are already running Netscape Navigator, choose the Communicator⇨Messenger Mail box command or click the Mailbox icon (the little picture of an inbox in the lower-right corner of the Netscape Navigator window). Either way, you see the Netscape Folder window, as shown in Figure 5-5.

To tell Netscape Messenger who you are and how to get you mail, choose the Edit⇨Preferences command to display the Preferences dialog box. Click the Identity category in the Categories list to tell Netscape your name and e-mail address. Click the Mail Server category to type your POP mail server and SMTP mail server names. Click OK when you're done.

The top part of the Netscape Folder window shows a list of the messages in the folder you are looking at (you start looking at the Inbox window). The bottom part of the window shows the text of the selected message.

To get your mail, click the Get Msg icon on the toolbar. Netscape may ask you for your password.

To read your mail, make sure that the selected folder is the Inbox folder — the folder name appears in a box just below the left end of the toolbar. If it doesn't say Inbox, click the downward-pointing triangle button at the end of the box to choose the Inbox folder. Then click a message on the list of messages — the text appears in the bottom half of the window.

When you want to send a message, click the New Msg icon on the toolbar. In the Composition window that appears, fill in the To and Subject boxes, and then type the text of the message in the large box. Click the Send button when you're done.

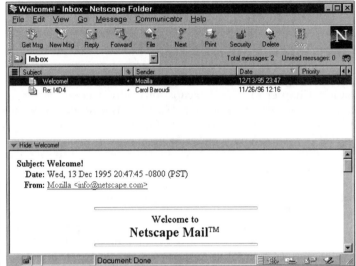

Figure 5-5:
Netscape
does mail
too.

Sending and Receiving Mail with Eudora

Eudora is a popular e-mail program that runs under Windows 98, Windows 95, Windows 3.1, the Mac, and who knows what other systems. Eudora is popular for three reasons: It's easy to use, it's powerful, and it's cheap. You can get a limited version (Eudora Light) for free, and an enhanced commercial version (Eudora Pro) is available for as little as $49. The examples in this book use Eudora Light, and the professional version looks even better. This section describes Version 4.0.

Getting Eudora

You can buy Eudora Pro in any software store. You can also download Eudora Light or Eudora Pro from the Eudora Web site, at `http://www.eudora.com`, or Eudora Light from software libraries like TUCOWS, at `http://www.tucows.com`. Chapter 12 tells how to download and install programs.

Setting up Eudora

The first time you run Eudora (either the Light or Pro version), you have to tell it all about yourself, your e-mail address, and your Internet account. Here's how:

1. **Start Eudora.**

   Click the Eudora icon on the desktop or on the Start⇨Programs menu. You should see an introductory "splash" window that goes away after a few seconds and then an Options window which contains all the settings that control Eudora. If you don't see the Options window, choose the Tools⇨Options command from the menu.

2. **Click the Getting Started icon on the left side of the Options window.**

   This step lets you enter the minimum info needed to get going.

3. **Fill in the Real Name, Return Address, Mail Server, and Login Name boxes with your actual name, your e-mail address, the name of your provider's mail computer, and your login name (probably the same as the part of your address before the @), respectively.**

4. **Click the Sending Mail icon.**

   You see boxes for various mail options. The Return Address box already contains your e-mail address.

5. **In the SMTP Server box, type the name of your SMTP mail server (refer to Table 5-2).**

   You can leave the other boxes blank.

6. **If you want Eudora to automatically connect to the Internet when you tell it to send or receive mail, scroll way down the list of icons until you find the Advanced Network icon, and click it.**

   You see a bunch of scary-looking time-out settings, which we recommend that you leave alone.

7. **Click the Automatically Dial & Hang Up This Connection check box. Choose a Dial-Up Networking connection from the Entry box, and type your username in the Username box. If you want Eudora to remember your password so that you don't have to type it each time you log in, click the Save Password box too.**

   You're done — that's all that Eudora really needs to know about you.

8. **Click OK.**

   The Options box goes away.

Sending mail with Eudora

Here's how to run Eudora and send some mail:

1. **Start Eudora if it's not already running, by clicking the Eudora icon on the desktop or on the Start⇨Programs menu.**

2. **To send a message, click the New Message button (the button with the sparkly paper and pencil) on the toolbar. Or choose Message⊅New Message from the menu. (If you can remember shortcut keys, you can also press Ctrl+N.)**

Eudora pops up a new message window, with spaces in which you type the address, subject, and text of a message, as shown in Figure 5-6.

3. **On the To line, type the recipient's address (internet98@gurus.com, for example).**

For your first e-mail message, you may want to write to us (because we will send you back a message confirming what your e-mail address is) or to yourself (if you know what your e-mail address is).

4. **Press Tab to skip past the From line (which is already filled in) to the Subject line, and then type a subject.**

Make the subject line short and specific.

5. **Press Tab a few more times to skip the Cc and Bcc lines (or type the addresses of people who should get carbon copies and blind carbon copies of your message).**

Blind carbon copies are copies sent to people without Eudora's putting their names on the message so that the other recipients can't tell.

6. **Press Tab to move to the large blank area, and then type your message.**

7. **To send the message, click the Send or Queue button in the upper-right corner of the message window (what the button says depends on how Eudora is set up).**

If the button is marked Send, as soon as you click it, Eudora tries to send the message and displays a little status window that contains incomprehensible status messages. If, on the other hand, the button is marked Queue, your message is stashed in your outbox, to be sent later.

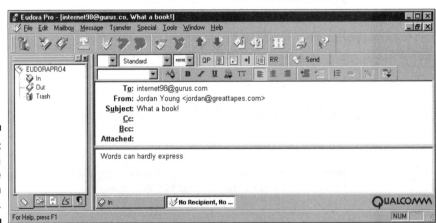

Figure 5-6:
Writing a
message
with
Eudora.

One reason to have a Queue button is that you have a dial-up Internet connection so that your computer isn't connected to the Net all the time. Rather than dial and hang up for each message you compose, you can wait until you have queued a few messages and then send them all at one time.

8. **If your computer isn't already connected, dial up and connect to your provider.**

   If you configured Eudora in the preceding section to connect to the Internet automatically, you may be able to skip this step. Eudora tries to connect automatically when you send messages (see Step 9).

9. **Switch back to Eudora, and choose File⇨Send Queued Messages (Ctrl+T for the lazy) from the menu to transmit all the messages you have queued up.**

Even if you leave your computer connected while you write your mail messages, it's not a bad idea to set Eudora to queue the mail and not send it until you tell it to. (Choose Tools⇨Options from the Eudora menu, click the Sending Mail icon, and be sure that Immediate Send isn't checked.) That way, you get a few minutes after you write each message to ponder whether you really want to send it. Even though we have been using e-mail for almost 20 years, we still throw away many of the messages we have written before we send them.

After you have sent a piece of e-mail, you have no way to cancel it!

Reading mail with Eudora

One seriously cool feature of Eudora is that you can do much of what you do with mail while you're not connected to your account. On the other hand, when you really do want to check your mail, you have to be connected. Eudora can figure out that you're not connected and dial in for you (which, in our experience, doesn't always work).

If you don't have a full-time Net connection, follow these steps to get your mail:

1. **Make your Net connection, if you're not already connected.**

   If you configured Eudora in the preceding section to connect to the Internet automatically, you may be able to skip this step. Eudora tries to connect automatically when you retrieve messages (see Step 3).

2. **Start up Eudora, if she's not already running.**

3. **If Eudora doesn't retrieve mail automatically, click the Check Mail button on the toolbar (the button with the envelope and in-basket) or choose File⇨Check Mail (or press Ctrl+M) to retrieve your mail.**

   If you have a full-time Net connection, Eudora probably is set up to retrieve your mail automatically, in which case you only have to start Eudora and she gets your mail. (If you leave Eudora running, even hidden at the bottom of your screen as an icon, she automatically checks for new mail every once in awhile.)

   If you have a sound card, you hear a little song (that reminds us of Mexican jumping beans) to announce new mail. If you don't have any mail, you don't get any sound effects, although you do see a nice picture of a letter with a big, red X through it. The mail appears in your inbox, a window that Eudora labels In, listing a one-line header for each message.

4. **To see a message, double-click the line or click the line and press Enter.**

   To stop looking at a message, click the Close button for the window or press Ctrl+W or Ctrl+F4.

You can do much more to messages, which we discuss in Chapter 6.

Where Are the Etiquette Ladies?

Sadly, the Great Ladies of Etiquette, such as Emily Post and Amy Vanderbilt, died before the invention of e-mail. Here's what they may have suggested about what to say and, more important, what *not* to say in electronic mail.

E-mail is a funny hybrid, something between a phone call (or voice mail) and a letter. On one hand, it's quick and usually informal; on the other hand, because e-mail is written rather than spoken, you don't see a person's facial expressions or hear her tone of voice.

A few words of advice:

- ✔ When you send a message, watch your tone of voice.

- ✔ Don't use all capital letters — it looks like you're SHOUTING.

- ✔ If someone sends you an incredibly obnoxious and offensive message, as likely as not it's a mistake or a joke gone awry. In particular, be on the lookout for failed sarcasm.

BTW, what does IMHO mean? RTFM!

E-mail users are often lazy typists, and many abbreviations are common. Here are some of the most widely used:

Abbreviation	What It Means	Abbreviation	What It Means
BTW	By the way	RTFM	Read the manual — you could have and should have looked it up yourself
IANAL	I am not a lawyer, (but. . . .)		
IMHO	In my humble opinion	TIA	Thanks in advance
ROFL	Rolling on floor laughing	TLA	Three-letter acronym
RSN	Real soon now (vaporware)	YMMV	Your mileage may vary

Flame off!

Pointless and excessive outrage in electronic mail is so common that it has a name of its own: *flaming.* Don't flame. It makes you look like a jerk.

When you get a message so offensive that you just *have* to reply, stick it back in your electronic inbox for a while and wait until after lunch. Then, don't flame back. The sender probably didn't realize how the message would look. In about 20 years of using electronic mail, we can testify that we have never, ever, regretted *not* sending an angry message (although we *have* regretted sending a few — ouch).

When you're sending mail, keep in mind that someone reading it will have no idea of what you *intended* to say — just what you *did* say. Subtle sarcasm and irony are almost impossible to use in e-mail and usually come across as annoying or dumb instead. (If you're an extremely superb writer, you can disregard this advice — don't say that we didn't warn you.)

Another possibility to keep in the back of your mind is that it is technically not difficult to forge e-mail return addresses. If you get a totally off-the-wall message from someone that seems out of character for that person, somebody else may have forged it as a prank. (No, we don't tell you how to forge e-mail. How dumb do you think we are?)

Laugh and the world laughs with you

Sometimes it helps to put in a : -) (called a *smiley*), which means, "This is a joke." (Try leaning way over to the left if you don't see why it's a smile.) In some communities, notably CompuServe, <g> or <grin> serves the same purpose. Here's a typical example:

```
People who don't believe that we are all part of a warm,
        caring community who love and support each other
        are no better than rabid dogs and should be
        hunted down and shot. :-)
```

Although smileys sometimes help, if a joke needs a smiley, maybe it wasn't worth making. It may sound as though all your e-mail is supposed to be humorless. It's not that bad; until you have the hang of it, though, limit the humor. You'll be glad that you did.

What's Next?

Now that you know how to use e-mail, you will want to send some messages. See Chapter 10 to find out how to find the e-mail address of someone you know. In Chapter 6, we explain more features of e-mail. Chapter 7 tells you how to find other people to write to and how to get interesting information by e-mail.

The Postmaster is In

Every Internet host that can send or receive mail has a special mail address called postmaster that is guaranteed to get a message to the person responsible for that host. If you send mail to someone and get back strange failure messages, you can try sending a message to the postmaster. If king@bluesuede.org returns an error from bluesuede.org, for example, you may try sending a polite question to postmaster@bluesuede.org. Because the postmaster is usually an overworked volunteer system administrator, it is considered poor form to ask a postmaster for favors much greater than "Does so-and-so have a mailbox on this system?"

Chapter 6
Advanced E-Mail Stuff

* *

In This Chapter

▶ Deleting mail

▶ Responding to mail

▶ Forwarding and filing mail

▶ Spotting and avoiding chain letters

▶ Sending and receiving exotic mail and mail attachments

▶ Exchanging mail with robots and fax machines

▶ Dealing with spam

* *

*O*kay, now you know how to send and receive mail. It's time for some tips and tricks to make you into a real mail aficionado. We tell you about Outlook Express and Netscape Messenger (see Chapter 5 for descriptions of these programs).

After you have seen an e-mail message, you can do a bunch of different things with it (much the same as with paper mail). Here are your usual choices:

✔ Throw it away.

✔ Reply to it.

✔ Forward it to other people.

✔ File it.

Unlike with paper mail, you can do any or all of these things to each message. If you don't tell your mail program what to do to a message, the message either stays in your mailbox for later perusal or gets moved to a "read messages" folder.

If your mail program automatically saves messages in a read-messages, Sent, or Outbox folder, be sure to go through the folder every week or so, or else it becomes enormous and unmanageable.

Here's What We Think: Replying to Mail

You should know a couple of things about replying to mail. It's easy enough to do:

- ✔ In Outlook Express, click the Reply to Author button on the toolbar or press Ctrl+R or choose Compose⇨Reply to Author.
- ✔ In Netscape Messenger, click the Reply button on the toolbar, and then choose Reply to Send from the menu that appears. Or, choose Message⇨Reply or press Ctrl+R.

Is this the party to whom I am replying?

When you reply to a message, most mail programs address the message automagically, using the From address of the message you are replying to. They usually also fill in the Subject field with the letters *Re:* (short for *regarding*) and the Subject field of the message to which you're replying.

Be sure to check to whom the reply is addressed. Look carefully at the To: line your mail program has filled out for you. Is that whom you thought you were addressing? If the reply is addressed to a mailing list, did you really intend to reply to the whole list, or is your message of a more personal nature and may be better addressed to the individual who sent the message? Did you mean to reply to a group? Are all the addresses you think you're replying to included on the To: list? If the To: list isn't correct, you can move the cursor to it and edit it as necessary.

Here's what you just said

Do you want to include the contents of the message to which you're replying? Most e-mail programs begin your reply message with the content of the message to which you're replying. If your mail program does this, be sure to edit the text to just the relevant material. If you don't give some context to people who get a great deal of e-mail, your reply makes no sense. If you're answering a question, include the question in the response. You don't have to include the entire text, although you should give your reader a break. She may have read 50 messages since she sent you mail and may not have a clue what you're talking about unless you remind her. On the other hand, it's annoying to receive a copy of the 70-line message you just sent someone, with a one-line reply saying "I agree!" at the end.

Keeping Track of All Your New Friends

After you begin using e-mail, you quickly find that you have enough regular correspondents that it's a pain to keep track of their e-mail addresses. Fortunately, every popular e-mail program provides an *address book* in which you can save your friends' addresses so that you can send mail to Mom, for example, and have the message automatically addressed to chairman@ exec.hq.giant-corp.com. You can also create address lists so that you can send mail to family, for example, and it goes to Mom, Dad, your brother, both sisters, and your dog, all of whom have e-mail addresses.

All address books let you do the same things: save in your address book the address from a message you have just read, use addresses you have saved, and edit your address book.

The Outlook Express address book

The process of copying a correspondent's address into the address book is easy but obscure: Double-click a message from your correspondent to open that message in its own window. Then double-click the person's name in the From line to open a contact-management window, and click the Add to Address Book button. You can edit the address book entry you're creating if you want, and then click OK.

To display and edit the address book, click the Address Book icon on the Outlook Express toolbar, as shown in Figure 6-1. After you manage to get some entries into your address book, you use them while you're creating a new message by clicking on the To: or Cc: line the little icon that looks like a Rolodex card. In the Select Recipients window that appears, double-click the address book entry or entries you want to use, and then click OK. If you don't know someone's e-mail address, click the Find button to display the Find People window; you can search in your own address book or in various Internet directories, such as Yahoo, Bigfoot, and WhoWhere.

Figure 6-1:
Outlook
Express can
track the
e-mail
addresses
you use.

The Netscape Messenger address book

You can see the Netscape address book by choosing Communicator⇨Address Book from the menu (see Figure 6-2). Click the New Card icon on the toolbar to make a new entry ("card") in your address book. If you've just gotten a message from someone whose address you want to remember, select the message and choose the Message⇨Add to Address Book⇨Sender command.

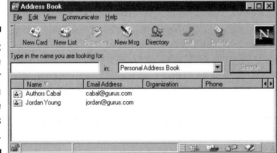

Figure 6-2: Netscape Messenger has a capable address book.

When you are composing a message, click the Address icon on the toolbar. Netscape lets you choose entries from the address book to use in your message.

This One's for You: Forwarding Mail

You can forward e-mail along to someone else. It's easy. It's cheap. Forwarding is one of the best things about electronic mail and at the same time one of the worst. It's good because you can easily pass along messages to people who need to know about them. It's bad because you (not you personally, but, um, people around you — that's it) can just as easily send out floods of messages to recipients who would just as soon not hear *another* press release from the local Ministry of Truth. You have to think a little about whether you will enhance someone's quality of life by forwarding a message to him.

What's usually called *forwarding* a message involves wrapping the message in a new message of your own, sort of like sticking Post-It notes all over a copy of it and mailing the copy and Post-Its to someone else.

Forwarding mail is almost as easy as replying to it:

✔ In Outlook Express, click the Forward message button on the toolbar or press Ctrl+F or choose Compose⇨Forward.

✔ In Netscape Messenger, click the Forward button on the toolbar or press Ctrl+L (since when does *L* stand for *forward?*) or choose Message⇨ Forward.

When you create a forwarded message, Netscape Messenger and Outlook Express provide the forwarded text in the message part of the window. Each line is preceded by the greater-than sign (>). You then get to edit the message and add your own comments. See the following sidebar, "Fast forward," for tips about pruning forwarded mail.

Sometimes, the mail you get may really have been intended for someone else. You probably will want to pass it along as is, without sticking the greater-than character at the beginning of every line, and you should leave the sender and reply-to information intact so that if the new recipient of the mail wants to respond, the response goes to the originator of the mail, not to you just because you passed it on. Some mail programs call this feature *remailing* or *bouncing,* the electronic version of scribbling another address on the outside of an envelope and dropping it back in the mailbox.

For All You Pack Rats: Saving Mail

Saving all your e-mail for later reference is similar to filing away every piece of paper mail you get. (Who knows, the very first letter from Ed McMahon announcing that you may already be a winner could be a valuable collectible by now.) Some of your e-mail is worth saving, just as some of your paper mail is worth saving. (Lots of it *isn't,* of course, but we cover that subject next.)

You can save e-mail in a few different ways:

✔ Save it in a folder full of messages.

✔ Save it in a regular file.

✔ Print it and put it in a file cabinet with paper mail.

The easiest method usually is to stick messages in a folder (a folder is usually no more than a file full of messages with a separator between each message).

People use two general approaches in filing mail: by sender and by topic. Whether you use one or the other or both is mostly a matter of taste.

TIP

Fast forward

Whenever you're forwarding mail, it's generally a good idea to get rid of uninteresting parts. All the glop in the message header is frequently included automatically in the forwarded message, and almost none of it is comprehensible, much less interesting, so get rid of it.

The tricky part is editing the text. If the message is short, a screenful or so, you probably should leave it alone:

```
>Is there a lot of demand for
   fruit pizza?

In answer to your question, I
   checked with our research
   department and found that
   the favorite pizza toppings
   in the 18-34 age group are
   pepperoni, sausage, ham,
   pineapple, olives, peppers,
   mushrooms, hamburger, and
   broccoli. I specifically asked
   about prunes, and they found
   no statistically significant
   response about them.
```

If the message is really long and only part of it is relevant, you should, as a courtesy to the reader, cut it down to the interesting part. We can tell you from experience that people pay much more attention to a concise, one-line e-mail message than they do to 12 pages of quoted stuff followed by a two-line question.

Sometimes it makes sense to edit material even more, particularly to emphasize one specific part. When you do so, of course, be sure not to edit to the point where you put words in the original author's mouth or garble the sense of the message, as in the following reply:

```
>In answer to your question, I
>checked with our research
>department and found that the
>favorite pizza toppings ... and
>they found no statistically
>significant response about
>them.
```

That's an excellent way to make new enemies. Sometimes, it makes sense to paraphrase a little — in that case, put the paraphrased part in square brackets, like this:

```
>[When asked about prunes on
>pizza, research] found no
>statistically significant
>response about them.
```

People disagree about whether paraphrasing to shorten quotes is a good idea. On one hand, if you do it well, it saves everyone time. On the other hand, if you do it badly and someone takes offense, you're in for a week of accusations and apologies that will wipe out whatever time you may have saved. The decision is up to you.

For filing by topic, it's entirely up to you to come up with folder names. The most difficult part is coming up with memorable names. If you're not careful, you end up with four folders with slightly different names, each with a quarter of the messages about a particular topic. Try to come up with names that are obvious, and don't abbreviate. If the topic is accounting, for example, call the folder accounting because if you abbreviate, you will never remember whether it's called acctng, acct, or acntng.

Filing with Outlook Express

To save a message in Outlook Express, you stick it in a folder. You start out with folders named Inbox, Outbox, Sent Items, Deleted Items, and Drafts. To make a new folder, choose File➪Folder➪New Folder from the menu and give the folder a name. You also have to tell Outlook Express which folder should *contain* the folder you're creating — you usually create your folders in the main Outlook Express folder. (Make one called Personal, just to give it a try.) The new folder appears on the list of folders on the left side of the Outlook Express window. Move messages into a folder by clicking a message header and dragging it over to the folder name or choosing Edit➪Move to Folder from the menu. You can see the list of message headers for any folder by clicking the folder name.

You can save the text of a message in a text file by clicking the message and choosing File➪Save As from the menu, clicking in the Save As Type box and choosing Text Files (*.txt), typing a filename, and clicking the Save button.

Filing with Netscape Messenger

To make a new folder, choose File➪New Folder. To move a message into a folder, select the message and choose Message➪File Message from the menu, and then choose the folder name from the menu that appears. To see the messages in a folder, click in the box that displays the current folder name (just below the left end of the toolbar) and choose the folder you want. You can also save a message in a text file by selecting the message and choosing File➪Save As or pressing Ctrl+S.

Recycle Those Electrons: Deleting Mail

When you first begin to get e-mail, the feeling is so exciting that it's difficult to imagine just throwing away the message. Eventually, however, you *have* to know how to get rid of messages, or else your computer will run out of room. Start early. Delete often.

The physical act of throwing away mail is easy enough that you probably have figured out how to do it already. In Outlook Express, click the message and then the Delete button on the toolbar or press the Del key. In Netscape Messenger, click the message and then click the Delete icon on the toolbar.

You can even delete mail without even reading it. If you subscribe to mailing lists, certain topics may not interest you. After you see the subject line, you may want to delete the message without reading it. If you're the type of person who reads every catalog and advertisement sent to you, you may have problems managing junk e-mail too. Consider getting professional help.

I've been working on the chain gang

One of the most obnoxious things you can do with e-mail is to pass around chain letters. Because all mail programs have forwarding commands, with only a few keystrokes you can send a chain letter along to hundreds of other people. Don't do it. Chain letters are cute for about two seconds, and then they're just annoying. After 16 years of using e-mail, we've *never* received a chain letter worth passing along.

A few chain letters just keep coming around and around, despite our best efforts to stamp them out. Find out how to recognize them now and avoid embarrassment later.

The Good Times virus hoax: In late 1994, a chain letter appeared on America Online disguised as a warning that a horrible computer virus capable of erasing your hard disk was being spread by e-mail. The virus allegedly arrived in e-mail messages bearing the words *Good Times.* Well-intentioned individuals quickly sent it to everyone they knew. The chain letter, not the non-existent virus, spread rapidly throughout the Internet. Computer viruses are spread through infected programs that, after they are run, can have malicious effects. E-mail is stored as text — not as a program — that cannot cause damage to your disk unless you give specific commands to run a program. This chain letter shows up under various names; regardless of the title, however, viruses aren't spread by e-mail messages.

Dying boy wants greeting (or business) cards: Not anymore, he doesn't. A decade ago, an English boy named Craig Shergold was hospitalized with a serious brain tumor. Craig wanted to set the world's record for receiving the most greeting cards. Word got out, and Craig received millions of cards and eventually got into the *Guinness Book of World Records.* Then, U.S. TV billionaire John Kluge paid for Craig to fly to the United States for a successful operation. Craig is okay now and doesn't want any more cards. (You can read all about this story on page 24 of the July 29, 1990, edition of the *The New York Times.*) Guinness is so sick of the whole business that it has closed the category — no more records for the most cards are accepted. To help dying children, give the two dollars that a card and stamp would have cost to a children's welfare organization, such as UNICEF.

The modem-tax rumor: In 1987, the U.S. Federal Communications Commission (FCC) proposed changing the rules governing the way online services are billed for their phone connections. The proposal would have had the effect of raising the prices these services charge. Online service customers made their opposition clear immediately and loudly, members of Congress made concerned inquiries, and the proposal was *dropped.* Undated notices about the proposal unfortunately have circulated ever since. If you see yet another modem-tax scare, demand the current FCC docket number because the FCC — as a government bureaucracy — can't blow its nose without making announcements, accepting comments, and so on. No docket means no action, which means that it's the same old rumor. A similar question came up in early 1996, but it's also ancient history now.

Make big bucks with a chain letter: These letters usually have the subject line MAKE.MONEY.FAST, are signed by "Dave Rhodes" or "Christopher Erickson," contain lots of testimonials from people who are now rolling in dough, and tell you to send $5 to the name at the top of the list, put your name at the bottom, and send the message to a zillion other suckers. Some even say, "This isn't a chain letter" (you're supposedly helping to compile a mailing list or sending reports or something — your 100 percent guaranteed tip-off that it's a chain letter). Don't even think about it. These chain letters are extremely illegal even when they say that they aren't, and, besides, they don't even work. (Why send any money? Why not just add your name and send it on? Heck, why not just replace all the names on the list with yours?) Think of them as gullibility viruses. Send a polite note to the sender's postmaster to encourage her to tell users not to send any more chain letters. If you don't believe that they're illegal, see the Postal Service Web site, at `http://www.usps.gov/websites/depart/inspect/chainlet.htm`.

Send e-mail to a publisher so that they give books to children's hospitals: This brief, ill-considered marketing gimmick lasted for a few days in late 1996. Needless to say, they got all the mail they wanted in a few hours after word got around, and now don't want any more.

Send a copy of your child's birth certificate to a P.O. box in Minnesota and get a savings bond: Nobody seems to be quite sure how this one started, but it's completely untrue. If you send anything to the box, the post office sends it back because the box is closed.

Fancy Mail and Getting Attached

Sooner or later, just plain, old, everyday e-mail isn't good enough for you. Someone's gonna send you a picture you just have to see, or you're gonna want to send something cool to your new best friend in Paris. When we talk about sending stuff other than text through the mail, we're talking about using special formats and e-mail programs or helper programs that can read them. Sometimes, the entire message is in a special format such as HTML, which stands for HyperText Markup Language. It's the stuff Web pages are made of (see Chapters 8 and 15), but you can now use it to create mind-blowing e-mail too. Outlook Express and Netscape Messenger let you select fonts; bigger and smaller font sizes; and bold, italics, and other text styles, just as you would in a word processor.

Slinky links

Outlook Express and Netscape Messenger both have a neat feature that turns URLs (Web site addresses) they find in e-mail messages into links to the actual Web site. You no longer have to type these addresses into your Web browser. All you have to do is double-click the highlighted link in the e-mail message and — poof — you're at the Web site. We tell you about the Web and browsers in Chapter 8.

Mail attachments

You can *attach* almost any file stored on your computer's disks to an e-mail message. For example, when we finish writing a chapter of a book, we can attach the word-processing document to an e-mail message to our publisher. When our editor receives the file, she can save the attached file on her hard disk and then open it with her word processor.

Attachments usually come in two flavors:

- ✔ **MIME:** Stands for *m*ultipurpose *I*nternet *m*ail *e*xtensions
- ✔ **Uuencoding:** A method of including information in e-mail; invented back in the days of UNIX-to-UNIX e-mail (hence the *uu* in the name)

The technical details of these methods are totally uninteresting and irrelevant: What matters to you is that your e-mail program must be capable of attaching files by using at least one of these methods and capable of detaching incoming files that other people send you, preferably by using any of these methods.

You can generally send a file as an e-mail attachment by using your regular mail program to compose a regular message and then giving a command to attach a file to the message. You send the message by using the program's usual commands.

When you receive a file that is attached to an e-mail message, your mail program is responsible for noticing the attached file and doing something intelligent with it. Most of the time, your mail program saves the attached file as a separate file in the folder or directory you specify. After the file has been saved, you can use it just like you use any other file.

For example, you can send these types of files as attachments:

- ✔ Pictures, in image files
- ✔ Word-processing documents
- ✔ Sounds, in audio files
- ✔ Movies, in video files
- ✔ Programs, in executable files
- ✔ Compressed files, such as ZIP files

If you receive a message with an attachment that uses a method (MIME, uuencoding, or some other less widely used method) that your mail program doesn't know about, the attached file shows up as a large message in your mailbox. If the attached file contains text, about half the kinds of tarted-up text are readable as is, give or take some ugly punctuation. If the attached file contains sound or pictures, on the other hand, reading the message is hopeless because it just contains binary digitized versions of the images and not any sort of text approximation.

If you get a picture or sound MIME message and your mail program doesn't automatically handle it, clunky but usable methods may exist for saving the message to a file and extracting the contents with separate programs. Consult your Internet service provider's help desk.

Outlook Express attachments

In Outlook Express, you attach a file to a message by choosing Insert⇨ File Attachment from the menu while you're composing a message or click the paper-clip icon on the toolbar. Then select the file to attach. Send the message as usual.

When an incoming message contains an attachment, a paper-clip icon appears in the message on your list of incoming messages and in the message when you view it. Click the paper clip to see the filename — double-click to see the attachment.

Netscape Messenger attachments

Click the Attach button (the fourth button on the toolbar) and then choose File from the menu that appears. Select the file you want to attach and click the Open button. (Why is the button named Open? We can only guess.) The location and filename of the attached file are displayed in the Composition window.

When you receive an attached file, you see an attachment box with information about the file. Click the link (the blue underlined text) on the left side of the box to see the attachment. If the attached file is a picture or some other type of file that Netscape can display, it does so. If Netscape doesn't know how to handle the attached file, it asks you what you want to do with the file.

Robot Mail

Not every mail address has an actual person behind it. Some are mailing lists (which we talk about in Chapter 7), and some are *robots,* programs that automatically reply to messages. Mail robots have become popular as a way to query databases and retrieve files because setting up a connection for electronic mail is much easier than setting up one that handles the more standard file transfer. You send a message to the robot (usually referred to as a *mailbot* or *mail server*), it takes some action based on the contents of your message, and then the robot sends back a response. If you send a message to internet98@gurus.com, for example, you receive a response telling you your e-mail address.

The most common use for mail robots is to get on and off mailing lists. Companies also often use the robots to send back canned responses to requests for information sent to info@whatever.com.

Your Own Personal Mail Manager

After you begin sending e-mail, you probably will find that you receive quite a bit of it, particularly if you put yourself on some mailing lists (see Chapter 7). Your incoming mail soon becomes a trickle, and then a stream, and then a torrent, and pretty soon you can't walk past your keyboard without getting soaking wet, metaphorically speaking.

Fortunately, most mail systems provide ways for you to manage the flow and avoid ruining your clothes (enough of this metaphor already). Here are some tips for handling the deluge:

- ✔ If most of your messages come from mailing lists, you should check to see whether the lists are available instead as *Usenet* newsgroups. Usenet newsreading programs (including Outlook Express and Netscape Messenger, conveniently enough) generally enable you to look through messages and find the interesting ones more quickly than your mail program does and to automatically sort the messages so that you can quickly read or ignore an entire *thread* (conversation) of messages about a particular topic. Your system manager can usually arrange to make particularly chatty mailing lists look like Usenet newsgroups. At our site, we handle about 40 mailing lists that way.

- ✔ Outlook Express has the Inbox Assistant, which can sort your mail automatically. Some other mail programs have similar filtering features.

All this automatic-sorting nonsense may seem like overkill, and if you get only five or ten messages a day, it is. After the mail really gets flowing, however, dealing with it takes much more of your time than it used to. Keep those automated tools in mind — if not for now, for later.

Can the Spam

Pink tender morsel,
Glistening with salty gel.
What the hell is it?

      — Spam haiku, found on the Internet

More and more often, it seems, we get unsolicited e-mail from some organization or person we don't know. The word *spam* (the brand name of that tasty pork product from Hormel) on the Internet now means thousands (or millions) of copies of the same piece of unwanted e-mail, sent to either individual e-mail accounts or Internet newsgroups. It's also known as *junk e-mail* or *unsolicited commercial e-mail* (UCE). The message usually consists of unsavory advertising for get-rich-quick schemes or pornographic Web sites — something you may not want to see and something you definitely don't want your children to see. The message is *spam,* the practice is *spamming,* and the person sending the spam is a *spammer.*

Why call it spam?

The meat? Nobody knows. Oh, you mean the unwanted e-mail? It came from the Monty Python skit in which a group of Vikings sing *Spammity-Spam, wonderful Spam* repeatedly in a march tempo, drowning out all other discourse.

Is it so bad?

You may think that spam, like junk mail, is just a nuisance we have to live with. It's different from junk mail, however, in several ways. First is the cost factor. Unlike receiving junk mail, you, the recipient, pay much more than the sender does to deliver the message. Paper junk mail costs something like 25 to 50 cents an envelope to mail, and nothing to receive. Sending e-mail is cheap: A spammer can send thousands of messages an hour from a PC and a dial-up connection, so it costs the mailer just a tiny fraction of a cent to mail. The time and disk space you use to download e-mail from spammers, though, is costing you money. After that, it costs you time to read (at least the subject line) and dispose of the mail. If spam volume continues to grow at its alarming pace, pretty soon e-mail will prove to be useless because the real e-mail is buried under the junk.

Not only do all of us as e-mail users have to bear a cost, but this volume of e-mail also strains the resources of mail servers and the entire Internet. Think of all the disk space and communication capacity occupied by millions of useless e-mail messages! Internet service providers have to pass along the added costs to its users. America Online has been reported to estimate that of the 20 million pieces of e-mail its mail servers handle daily, about one-third is spam.

Then you have to consider the issue of content. The stuff these spams advertise is generally fraudulent, dishonest, or pornographic. Many of the offers are for get-rich-quick schemes. No honest business would attempt to advertise by broadcasting on the Internet because of the immense bad publicity it would bring on itself.

Many spams include a line that instructs you how to get off their lists, something like "Send us a message with the word REMOVE in it." Why should you have to waste your time to get off the list? In addition, doing so usually doesn't work — some people report getting *more* spam after responding to a removal address. By responding, you've confirmed that you are a warm body who reads your e-mail.

Can I do something?

The Internet tries to be self-policing; the community of people who make up the users and inventors of this marvelous medium don't want the Internet to fall under the control of the government, commercial interests, or gangsters. The Internet grew from a need for the easy and free flow of information, and everyone using it should strive to keep it that way.

Check out these Web sites for information about spam and how to fight it, both technically and legally:

```
http://www.cauce.org
http://spam.abuse.net
http://www.abuse.net
```

Chapter 7

The World According to E-Mail: Electronic Mailing Lists

*N*ow that you know all about how to send and receive mail, only one thing stands between you and a rich, fulfilling, mail-blessed life: You may not know many people with whom you can exchange mail. Fortunately, you can get yourself on lots of mailing lists, which ensures that you arrive every morning to a mailbox with 400 new messages. (Maybe you should start out with only one or two lists.)

Mailing lists are simple. The list has its own special e-mail address, and anything someone sends to that address is sent to all the people on the list. Because these people in turn often respond to the messages, the result is a running conversation among a large group of people.

Different lists have different styles. Some are relatively formal, hewing closely to the official topic of the list. Others tend to go flying off into outer space, topicwise. You have to read them for a while to be able to tell which list works which way.

Mailing lists fall into three categories:

✔ **Discussion:** Every subscriber can post a message. These lists lead to freewheeling discussions and can include a certain number of off-topic messages.

✔ **Moderated:** A moderator reviews each message before it gets distributed. The moderator can stop unrelated, redundant, or clueless postings from wasting everyone's time.

✔ **Announcement-only:** Only the moderator posts messages. Announcement mailing lists work well for publishing an online newsletter, for example.

Signing On to and Getting Off Mailing Lists

The way you get on or off a mailing list is also simple: You send a mail message. Two general schools of mailing-list management exist: the *manual* and the *automatic*. Manual management is the more traditional way: Your message is read by a human being who updates the files to put people on or take them off the list. The advantage of manual management is that you get personal service; the disadvantage is that the list maintainer may not get around to servicing you for quite a while if more pressing business (such as her real job) intervenes.

These days, lists are commonly maintained automatically, which saves human attention for times when things are fouled up. The most widely used automatic mailing managers are families of programs known as LISTSERV, Majordomo, and ListProc, which get their own sections later in this chapter.

The human touch

To get on or off a manually managed list, you send a nice note to the human being who manages the list. Manual lists follow a widely observed convention regarding list manager addresses. Suppose that you want to join a list for fans of James Buchanan (the 15th president of the United States and the only one who never married, in case you slept through that part of history class), and the list's name is buchanan-lovers@gurus.com. The list manager's address is almost certainly buchanan-lovers-request@gurus.com. In other words, just add -request to the list's address to get the manager's address. Because the list is maintained by hand, your request to be added or dropped doesn't have to take any particular form, as long as it's polite. Please add me to the buchanan-lovers list does quite well. When you decide that you have had all the Buchanan you can stand, another message saying Please remove me from the buchanan-lovers list works equally well.

Messages to `-request` addresses are read and handled by human beings who sometimes eat, sleep, and work regular jobs as well as maintain mailing lists. Therefore, these people don't necessarily read your request the moment it arrives. It can take a day or so to be added to or removed from a list, and, after you ask to be removed, you usually get a few more messages before they remove you. If it takes longer than you want, be patient. *Don't* send cranky follow-ups — they just cheese off the list maintainer.

Look before you leap

Here's a handy tip: After you subscribe to a list, don't send anything to it until you have been reading it for a week. Trust us — the list has been getting along without your insights since it began, and it can get along without them for one more week.

This method gives you a chance to learn the sorts of topics that people really discuss, the tone of the list, and so on. It also gives you a fair idea about which topics people are tired of. The classic newcomer gaffe is to subscribe to a list and immediately send a message asking a dumb question that isn't really germane to the topic and that was beaten to death three days earlier. Bide your time, and don't let this situation happen to you.

The number-two newcomer gaffe is to send a message directly to the list asking to subscribe or unsubscribe. This type of message should go to the list manager or to a LISTSERV, Majordomo, or ListProc address, where the list maintainer (human or robotic) can handle it, *not* to the list itself, where all the other subscribers can see that you screwed up.

To summarize: The first message you send, to join a list, should go to a *something-* `request` or `LISTSERV` or `majordomo` or `listproc` address, *not* to the list itself. After you have joined the list and read it for a while, *then* you can send messages to the list.

Here's another thing not to do: Unless you're expressly invited to do so, don't send attachments to mailing lists. Many e-mail programs can't handle attachments, and many people don't have the program they would need to open the attachment anyway. If you have a file you want to distribute on a mailing list, send a message inviting people interested in getting the file to e-mail you privately.

One last thing not to do: If you don't like what another person is posting (for example, some newbie is posting blank messages or "unsubscribe me" messages or is ranting interminably about a topic), don't waste everyone's time by posting a response on the list. The only thing stupider than a stupid posting is a response complaining about it. Instead, e-mail the person *privately* and tell him to stop, or e-mail the list manager and ask that person to intervene.

LISTSERV, the tyrannosaur of mail managers

Because maintaining lots of mailing lists is a great deal of work, people who used an older network called BITNET came up with a program to automate the process. They called their program *LISTSERV,* and it originally ran on great big IBM mainframe computers. (The IBM mainframe types have an inordinate fondness for eight-letter uppercase names, EVEN THOUGH TO MOST OF US IT SEEMS LIKE SHOUTING.) BITNET is history now, and anyone with an Internet address can use LISTSERV, which these days has grown to the point that it is an all-singing, all-dancing mailing-list program with about 15 zillion features and options, almost none of which you care about.

Although LISTSERV is a little clunky to use, it has the huge advantage of being able to easily handle enormous mailing lists that contain thousands of members, something that makes many of the regular Internet mail programs choke. (LISTSERV can send mail to 1,000 addresses in about five minutes, for example, whereas that task would take the regular Internet `sendmail` program more than an hour.)

You put yourself on and off a LISTSERV mailing list by sending mail to `LISTSERV@`*some.machine.or.other*, where *some.machine.or.other* is the name of the particular machine on which the mailing list lives. This address — the address that includes "LISTSERV" as the username — is called the *administrative* address for the list. You send all administrative commands, such as commands to get on or off the list, to the administrative address.

Because LISTSERV list managers are computer programs, they're rather simpleminded, and you have to speak to them clearly and distinctly, using standardized commands.

TIP

Too many messages give computers heartburn!

Some mailing lists are *digested.* No, they're not dripping with digital gastric juices — they're digested more in the sense of *Reader's Digest.* All the messages over a particular period (usually a day or two) are gathered into one big message with a table of contents added at the front. Many people find this method more convenient than getting messages separately, because you can easily look at all the messages on the topic at one time.

Some mail and newsreading programs give you the option of dividing digests back into the individual messages so that you can see them one at a time yet still grouped together. This option is sometimes known as *undigestifying,* or *exploding,* a digest. (First, it's digested, and then it explodes, sort of like a burrito.) Check the specifics of your particular mail program to see whether it has an option for digest-exploding.

Suppose that you want to join a list called SNUFLE-L (LISTSERV mailing lists usually end with -L), which lives at bluesuede.org. To join, send to LISTSERV@bluesuede.org (the administrative address) a message that contains this line in the text of the message (not the subject line):

```
SUB SNUFLE-L Roger Sherman
```

You don't have to add a subject line or anything else to this message — it's better not to, so as not to confuse the LISTSERV program. SUB is short for subscribe, SNUFLE-L is the name of the list, and anything after that is supposed to be your real name. (You can put whatever you want there, but keep in mind that it shows up in the return address of anything you send to the list.) You don't have to tell LISTSERV your e-mail address, which it can read from the automatically generated headers at the top of your message.

Shortly afterward, you should get back two messages:

- ✔ A chatty, machine-generated welcoming message telling you that you have joined the list, along with a description of some commands you can use to fiddle with your mailing-list membership. Sometimes, this message includes a request to confirm that you received this message. Follow the instructions by replying to this message with the single word *OK* in the body of the message. This trick helps lists ensure that they aren't mailing into the void and that it was indeed you who asked to put your name on that list. If you don't provide this confirmation, you don't get on the list.

- ✔ An incredibly boring message telling you that the IBM mainframe ran a program to handle your request and reporting the exact number of milliseconds of computer time and number of disk operations the request took. Whoopee. (It's sobering to think that somewhere there are people who find these messages interesting.)

Keep the chatty, informative welcome message that tells you about all the commands you can use when you're dealing with the list. For one thing, it tells you how to get *off* the mailing list if it's not to your liking. We have in our mail program a folder called Mailing Lists in which we store the welcome messages from all the mailing lists we join.

After you're subscribed, to send a message to this list, mail to the list name at the same machine — in this case, SNUFLE-L@bluesuede.org. This address is called the *list address* (creatively enough), and it's *only* for messages to be distributed to the entire list. Be sure to provide something descriptive in the Subject: line for the multitudes who will benefit from your pearls of wisdom. Within a matter of minutes, people from all over the world will read your message.

To get off a list, you again write to LISTSERV@*some.machine.or.other*, this time sending this line in the text of the message (not the subject line):

```
SIGNOFF SNUFLE-L
```

or whatever the list name is. You don't have to give your name again because after you're off the list, LISTSERV has no more interest in you and forgets that you ever existed.

Some lists are more difficult than others to get on and off. Usually, you ask to get on a list, and you're on the list. In some cases, however, the list isn't open to all comers, and the human list owner screens requests to join the list, in which case you may get some messages from the list owner to discuss your request to join.

To contact the actual human being who runs a particular list, the mail address is OWNER- followed by the list name (OWNER-SNUFLE-L, for example). The owner can do all sorts of things to lists that mere mortals can't do. In particular, the owner can fix screwed-up names on the list or add a name that for some reason the automatic method doesn't handle. You have to appeal for manual intervention if your mail system doesn't put your correct network mail address on the From: line of your messages, as sometimes happens when your local mail system isn't set up quite right or if you no longer use the address from which you subscribed.

Make LISTSERV do stuff

The people who maintain the LISTSERV program have added so many bells and whistles to it that it would take an entire book to describe them all, and, frankly, they're not that interesting. Here are a few stupid LISTSERV tricks. For each one, you send a message to LISTSERV@*some.machine.or.other* to talk to the LISTSERV program. You can send several commands in the same message if you want to do two or three tricks at one time:

✔ **Temporarily stop mail:** Sometimes, you're going to be away for a week or two, and you don't want to get a bunch of mailing-list mail in the meantime. Because you're planning to come back, though, you don't want to take yourself off all the lists either. To stop mail temporarily from the SNUFLE-L mailing list, send this message:

```
SET SNUFLE-L NOMAIL
```

The list stops sending you messages. To turn the mail back on, send this message:

```
SET SNUFLE-L MAIL
```

✔ **Get messages as a digest:** If you're getting a large number of messages from a list and would rather get them all at one time as a daily digest, send this message:

```
SET SNUFLE-L DIGEST
```

Although not all lists can be digested (again, if you've read the sidebars earlier in this chapter, think of burritos), the indigestible ones let you know and don't take offense. If you later want individual messages again:

```
SET SNUFLE-L NODIGEST
```

✔ **Find out who's on a list:** To find out who subscribes to a list, send this message:

```
REVIEW SNUFLE-L
```

Some lists can be reviewed only by people on the list and others not at all. Because some lists are enormous, be prepared to get back an enormous message listing thousands of subscribers.

✔ **Get or not get your own mail:** When you send mail to a LISTSERV list of which you're a member, the list usually sends you a copy of your own message to confirm that it got there okay. Some people find this process needlessly redundant. ("Your message has been sent. You will be receiving it shortly." Huh?) To avoid getting copies of your own messages, send this message:

```
SET SNUFLE-L NOACK
```

To resume getting copies of your own messages, send this one:

```
SET SNUFLE-L ACK
```

✔ **Get files:** Most LISTSERV servers have a library of files available, usually documents contributed by the mailing-list members. To find out which files are available, send

```
INDEX
```

To have LISTSERV send you a particular file by e-mail, send this message:

```
GET listname filename
```

where *listname* is the name of the list and *filename* is the name of a file from the INDEX command. For example, to get the article about Social Security number security from the LISTSERV that hosts the privacy forum, send this message:

```
GET privacy prc.ssn-10 to LISTSERV@vortex.com
```

✔ **Find out which lists are available:** To find out which LISTSERV mailing lists are available on a particular host, send this message:

```
LIST
```

Note: Keep in mind that just because a list exists doesn't necessarily mean that you can subscribe to it. It never hurts to try.

✔ **Get LISTSERV to do other things:** Lots of other commands lurk in LISTSERV, most of which apply only to people on IBM mainframes. If you're one of these people or if you're just nosy, send a message containing this line:

```
HELP
```

You receive a helpful response that lists other commands.

Majordomo at your service, Madam

Another widely used mailing-list manager is *Majordomo*. It started out as a LISTSERV wanna-be for UNIX workstations but has evolved into a system that works quite well. Because of its wanna-be origins, Majordomo commands are almost but (pretend to be surprised now) not quite the same as their LISTSERV equivalents.

The administrative address for Majordomo lists (the address to which you send commands), as you may expect, is majordomo@*some.machine. or.other.* Majordomo lists tend to have long and expressive names. One of our favorites is called explosive-cargo, a funny weekly column written by a guy in Boston who is in real life a computer technical writer. To subscribe, because the list is maintained on host world.std.com, send this message to Majordomo@world.std.com:

```
subscribe explosive-cargo
```

Note: Unlike with LISTSERV, you *don't* put your real name in the subscribe command. Like LISTSERV, Majordomo may send back a confirmation question to make sure that it was you who wanted to subscribe.

To unsubscribe:

```
unsubscribe explosive-cargo
```

After you have subscribed, you can send a message to everyone on the mailing list by addressing it to the list address — *listname@some. machine.or.other.* (You can't post messages to explosive-cargo because it's an announcements-only list: Only the guy in Boston who runs it is allowed to post messages.)

Majordomo does stuff too

Not to be outdone by LISTSERV, Majordomo has its own set of not particularly useful commands (as with LISTSERV, you can send in a single message as many of these as you want):

- ✔ To find out which lists at a Majordomo system you're subscribed to:

  ```
  which
  ```

- ✔ To find all the lists managed by a Majordomo system:

  ```
  lists
  ```

- ✔ Majordomo also can keep files related to its lists. To find the names of the files for a particular list:

  ```
  index name-of-list
  ```

- ✔ To tell Majordomo to send you one of the files by e-mail:

  ```
  get name-of-list name-of-file
  ```

- ✔ To find out the rest of the goofy things Majordomo can do:

  ```
  help
  ```

- ✔ If you want to contact the human manager of a Majordomo system because you can't get off a list you want to leave or otherwise have an insoluble problem, send a polite message to owner-majordomo@ hostname. Remember that because humans eat, sleep, and have real jobs, you may not get an answer for a day or two.

ListProc — yet another list manager

Although ListProc is not as widely used as LISTSERV and Majordomo, its popularity is increasing because it is easier to install than LISTSERV, cheaper, and almost as powerful.

To subscribe to a ListProc mailing list, you send this message to the administrative address for the list, listproc@some-computer:

```
subscribe listname yourname
```

To subscribe to the (hypothetical) chickens mailing list at gurus.com, for example, you send this message to listproc@gurus.com:

```
subscribe chickens George Washington
```

(assuming that you were named after the same person that the first President of the United States was).

To get off the mailing list, send this message to the same address:

```
signoff listname
```

You don't have to provide your name — the ListProc program should already know it.

After you have subscribed to the list, you can send messages to everyone on the list by addressing e-mail to the list address; `listname@some-computer` — `chickens@gurus.com`, for example. (Don't try it — no such mailing list exists!)

If you want to get your messages in daily or weekly groups rather than one at a time, send this message:

```
set listname mail digest
```

To switch back to getting messages one at a time, send this command:

```
set listname mail ack
```

To find out other things ListProc can do, send the message `help` to `listproc@whatever`, where `whatever` is the name of the computer on which the ListProc mailing list lives.

They made them different just to annoy you!

Because LISTSERV, ListProc, and Majordomo work in sort of the same way, even experienced mailing-list mavens get their commands confused. Here are the important differences:

✔ The address for LISTSERV is `LISTSERV@hostname`, the address for Majordomo is `majordomo@hostname`, and the address for ListProc is `listproc@hostname`.

✔ To subscribe to a LISTSERV or ListProc list, send `sub` or `subscribe` followed by the list name followed by your real name. To subscribe to a Majordomo list, just send `subscribe` and the list name.

Sending your first message

Okay, you're signed up on a mailing list. Now what? First, as we say a few pages back, wait a week or so to see what sort of messages arrive from the list — that way, you can get an idea of what you should or should not send to it. When you think that you have seen enough to avoid embarrassing yourself, try sending something in. That's easy: You mail a message to the list address, which is the same as the name of the list — buchanan-lovers@gurus.com or snufle-1@bluesuede.org or whatever. Keep in mind that because hundreds or thousands of people will be reading your pearls of wisdom, you should at least try to spell things correctly. (You may have thought that this advice is obvious, but you would be sadly mistaken.) On popular lists, you may begin to get back responses within a few minutes of sending a message.

Some lists encourage new subscribers to send in a message introducing themselves and saying briefly what their interests are. Others don't. Don't send anything until you have something to say.

After you watch the flow of messages on a list for a while, all this stuff becomes obvious.

Some mailing lists have rules about who is allowed to send messages, meaning that just because you're on the list doesn't automatically mean that any messages you send appear on the list. Some lists are *moderated:* Any message you send in gets sent to a human *moderator,* who decides what goes to the list and what doesn't. Although this process may sound sort of fascist, in practice the arrangement makes a list about 50 times more interesting than it would be otherwise because a good moderator can filter out the boring and irrelevant messages and keep the list on track. Indeed, the people who complain the loudest about moderator censorship are usually the ones whose messages most deserve to be filtered out.

Another rule that sometimes causes trouble is that many lists allow messages to be sent only from people whose addresses appear on the list. This rule becomes a pain if your mailing address changes. Suppose that you get a well-organized new mail administrator and your official e-mail address changes from jj@shamu.pol.bluesuede.org to John.Jay@bluesuede.org, although your old address still works. You may find that some lists begin *bouncing* your messages (sending them back to you rather than to the list) because they don't understand that John.Jay@bluesuede.org, the name under which you now send messages, is the same as jj@shamu.pol.bluesuede.org, the name under which you originally subscribed to the list. Worse, LISTSERV doesn't let you take yourself off the list, for the same reason. To resolve this mess, you have to write to the human list managers of any lists in which this problem arises and ask them to fix the problem by hand.

Reply Like a Pro

Often, you receive an interesting message from a list and want to respond to it. When you send your answer, does it go *just* to the person who sent the original message, or does it go to the *entire list?* It depends, mostly on how the list owner set up the software that handles the list. About half the list owners set things up so that replies automatically go to just the person who sent the original message, on the theory that your response is likely to be of interest only to the original author. The other half set things up so that replies go to the entire list, on the theory that the list is a running public discussion. In messages coming from the list, the mailing-list software automatically sets the `Reply-To:` header line to the address to which replies should be sent.

Fortunately, you're in charge. When you start to create a reply, your mail program should show you the address to which it's replying. If you don't like the address it's using, change the address. Check the `To:` and `Cc:` fields to make sure that you're sending your message where you want.

While you're fixing the recipient's address, you may also want to fix the `Subject:` line. After a few rounds of replies to replies to replies, the topic of discussion often wanders away from the original topic, and it's a good idea to change the subject to better describe what is really under discussion.

Some Lists to Whet Your Appetite

Thousands of lists reside on the Internet — so many, in fact, that entire *books* have been written that just enumerate all the *lists.* These addresses change relatively frequently, and we keep finding new and interesting lists. For our latest list of lists, check out our Web update, at `http://net.gurus.com/lists`. For a complete list of lists — thousands exist — check out one of the mailing-list directory sites, such as the Liszt (bad pun) site, at `http://www.liszt.com`.

If you don't have access to the Web, send e-mail to `lists@gurus.com`, and we'll send you back our current list of recommended lists. If you have a favorite list you want to share, send us mail at `list-suggestions@gurus.com`.

Part III
Windows 98 Web-Whacking

The 5th Wave   By Rich Tennant

"Face it Vinnie — you're gonna have a hard time getting people to subscribe online with a credit card to a newsletter called 'Felons Interactive'!"

In this part . . .

The World Wide Web is the part of the Internet that gets all the publicity. The Web is so popular that more and more of what people do on the Internet, they're doing through the World Wide Web nowadays. In this part, we give you everything you need to know to surf the Web. Because so much stuff is out there, finding what you're looking for can be a real trick, so we've included a chapter about how to do that. Finally, Windows 98 introduces a whole new way to surf the Web: channels. We tell you what they are, what's wrong with them, and how to use them.

Chapter 8

Windows 98 Meets the World Wide Web

*P*eople are talking about *the Web* today at least as much as they're talking about *the Net*. Although the World Wide Web and the Internet are not the same thing, they are related. The World Wide Web (which we call the Web because we're lazy typists) lives "on top of" the Internet. The Internet's network is at the core of the Web, although the Web itself is something different.

So what is it already? The Web is in some ways sort of a cross between libraries, television, computer networks, and telephones — it's all of the above and none of the above.

The Web is a huge collection of "pages" of information connected to each other around the globe. Each page can be a combination of text, pictures, audio clips, video clips, animations, and other stuff. (We're vague about naming the other stuff because they add new types of other stuff every day.) What makes Web pages interesting is that they contain *hyperlinks* (usually called just *links* because the Net already has plenty of hype). Each link points to another Web page, and, when you click a link, your browser program fetches the page the link connects to. (Your *browser* is the program that lets you view the Web — we talk about browsers in a couple of pages.)

Each page your browser displays for you can have more links that take you to other places. Web pages can be linked to other pages anywhere in the world so that when you browse the Web, you can look at pages from Singapore to Calgary, from Sydney to Buenos Aires — you're only seconds away from any site, anywhere in the world.

Where did the Web come from?

The World Wide Web was invented in 1989 at the European Particle Physics Lab in Geneva, Switzerland, an unlikely spot for a revolution in computing. The inventor is a British researcher named Tim Berners-Lee, who is now the director of the World Wide Web Consortium (W3), the organization that sets standards and loosely oversees the development of the Web. Tim is terrifically smart and hard-working and is the nicest guy you would ever want to meet. (Margy met him through Sunday school — is that wholesome or what?)

Tim invented *HTTP (HyperText Transport Protocol)*, the way Web browsers communicate with Web servers; *HTML (HyperText Markup Language)*, the language in which Web pages are written; and *URLs (Uniform Resource Locators)*, the codes used to identify Web pages and most other information on the Net. He envisioned the Web as a way for everyone to both publish and read information on the Net, and early Web browsers had editors that enabled you to create Web pages almost as easily as you could read them, a feature that has recently come back into vogue (see Chapter 15).

For more information about the development of the Web and the work of the World Wide Web Consortium, visit its Web site, at `http://www.w3.org`.

This system of interlinked documents is known as *hypertext*. Figure 8-1 shows a Web page: Each underlined phrase is a link to another Web page. Hypertext is one of those simple ideas that turns out to have a much bigger effect than you would think.

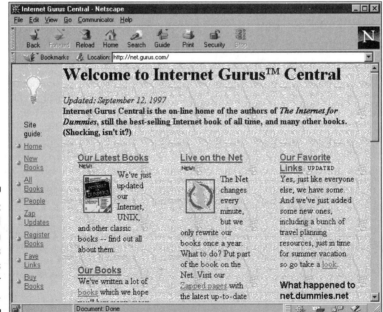

Figure 8-1: Underlined phrases on web pages are links to other pages.

The father of hypertext

John writes:

The term and concept of hypertext were invented around 1969 by Ted Nelson, a famous computer visionary who has been thinking about the relationship between computers and literature for at least 30 years now — starting back when most people would have considered it stupid to think that such a relationship could exist. Twenty years ago, he claimed that people would have computers in their pockets with leatherette cases and racing stripes. (I haven't seen any racing stripes yet, but otherwise he was dead-on.)

Back in 1970, Ted told me that we all would have little computers with inexpensive screens on our desks with superwhizzo graphical hypertext systems. "Naah," I said. "For hypertext, you want a mainframe with gobs of memory and a high-resolution screen." We were both right, of course, because what we have on our desks in 1998 are little computers that are faster than 1970s mainframes and that have more memory and better screens.

Various hypertext projects have come and gone over the years, including one at Brown University (of which Ted was a part) and one

at the Stanford Research Institute (which was arguably the most influential project in computing history because it invented screen windows and mice).

Ted's own hypertext system, Project Xanadu, has been in the works for about 20 years, under a variety of financing and management setups, with many of the same people slogging along and making it work. The project addresses many issues that other systems don't. In particular, Ted figured out how to pay authors for their work in a hypertext system, even when one document has pieces linked from others and the ensuing document consists almost entirely of a compendium of pieces of other documents. For a decade, I have been hearing every year that Xanadu, and now a smaller Xanadu Light, which takes advantage of a great deal of existing software, hits the streets the next year. This year, I hope that they're right.

Margy adds:

Now that the World Wide Web has brought a limited version of hypertext to the masses, Ted is hoping to build a Xanadu-like system on the Web. Stay tuned for developments!

All Hyped Up and Someplace to Go

If you can get a handle on the fundamental structure of the Web, you can use it better and think about all the other ways it can be used. Linked pages of information — hypertext — connects information in ways that make it easy to find — in theory. In traditional libraries (both the kinds with books and the kinds in computers), information is organized in a relatively arbitrary way, such as alphabetical order or the Dewey decimal system. This order reflects nothing about the relationships among different pieces of information. In the world of hypertext, information is organized in relationship to other information. The relationships between different pieces of information are, in fact, often much more valuable than the pieces themselves.

Hypertext also enables the same set of information to be arranged in multiple ways at the same time. In a conventional library, a book can be on only one shelf at a time; a book about mental health, for example, is shelved under medicine or psychology, and it can't be in both places at one time. Hypertext is not as limited, and it's no problem to have links to the same document from both medical topics and psychological topics, for example.

Suppose that you're interested in what influenced a particular historical person. You can begin by looking at her basic biographical information: where and when she was born, the names of her parents, her religion, and other basic stuff like that. Then you can expand on each fact by finding out what else was happening at that time in her part of the world, what was happening in other parts of the world, and what influence her religion may have had on her. You draw a picture by pulling together all these aspects and understanding their connections — a picture that's hard to draw from just lists of names and dates.

A hypertext system allows people to create connections between pieces of information that enable you to find related information easily. As you draw connections between the pieces of information, you can begin to envision the web created by the links between the pieces. What's so remarkable about the Web is that it connects pieces of information from all around the *planet,* on different machines and in different databases, all pretty much seamlessly (a feat you would be hard pressed to match with a card catalog). You may think of it as an extremely large but friendly alien centipede made of information.

The other important thing about the Web is that the information in it is searchable. In about ten seconds, for example, you can get a list of all the Web pages that contain the words *domestic poultry* or your name or the name of a book you want to find out about. You can follow links to see each page on the list, to see which pages contain the information you want.

What's in a Name?

You have to know about one more basic concept before hitting the Web. Every Web page has an address, a code by which it can be found and the name that gets attached to it so that browsers can find it. Great figures in the world of software engineering (Tim again) named this name *URL,* or *Uniform Resource Locator.* Every Web page has a URL. Strings of characters that begin with `http://` or `www.` are URLs. Some people pronounce each letter ("U-R-L,"), and some think that it's a word (pronounced "earl") — it's your choice. Now you know enough to go browsing.

The master plan for the 21st century

The 20th century was when the Scientific Revolution came of age, for better or worse. The 21st century will be about the Information Revolution — led by the World Wide Web. The Web will link together all the information in the known universe, starting with all the stuff on the Internet and heading up from there. (This statement may be a slight exaggeration, although we don't think so.)

One of the keys to global domination is to give everything (at least everything that could be available on the Web) a name, and in particular a consistent name so that no matter what kind of thing a hypertext link refers to, a Web browser can find it and know what to do with it.

Look at this typical URL, the one for the Web page that was shown in Figure 9-1:

```
http://net.gurus.com/index.phtml
```

The first thing in a URL, the word before the colon, is the *scheme,* which describes the way a browser can get to the resource. Although ten schemes are defined, the most common by far is *HTTP,* the *Hypertext Transfer Protocol* that is the Web's native transfer technique. (Don't confuse HTTP, which is the way pages are sent over the Net, with HTML, which is the way the pages are coded internally. We get to that in Chapter 15.)

Although the details of the rest of the URL depend on the scheme, most schemes use a consistent syntax. Following the colon are two slashes (always forward slashes, never reverse slashes) and the name of the host computer on which the resource lives; in this case, `net.gurus.com`. Often, the hostname starts with `www`. Can you guess what `www` stands for? (No fair peeking at the chapter title.) Next comes another slash and a *path,* which gives the name of the resource on that host; in this case, a file named `index.phtml`.

Web URLs allow a few other optional parts. They can include a *port number,* which specifies, roughly speaking, which of several programs running on that host computer should handle the request. The port number goes after a colon after the hostname, like this:

```
http://net.gurus.com:80/
    index.phtml
```

Because the standard `http` port number is 80, if that's the port you want (it usually is), you can leave it out. Finally, a Web URL can have a *search part* at the end, following a question mark, like this:

```
http://net.gurus.com:80/
    index.phtml?chickens
```

Although not all pages can have search parts, in those that do, they tell the host, uh, what to search for. (You almost never type a search part yourself — they're usually constructed for you from fill-in fields on Web pages.)

Three other useful URL schemes are `mailto`, `ftp`, and `file`. A `mailto` URL looks like this:

```
mailto:internet98@gurus.com
```

That is, it's an e-mail address. Clicking a `mailto` URL runs the Outlook Express program or whatever you've designated as your default mail program. (Outlook Express is described in Chapters 5 and 6 .) Mailto URLs are most commonly used for sending comments to the owner of a page.

A URL that starts with `ftp` lets you download files from an FTP server on the Internet (see Chapter 12 for information about FTP servers). An `ftp` URL looks like this:

```
ftp://ftp.loc.gov/pub/thomas/
    c104/s652.enr.txt
```

(continued)

(continued)

The part after the two slashes is the name of the FTP server (`ftp.loc.gov`, in this case). The rest of the URL is the pathname of the file you want to download.

The `file` URL specifies a file on your computer. The URL looks like this:

`file://C|/www/index.htm`

On a Windows computer, this line indicates a Web page stored in the file C:\www\index.htm.

The colon turns into a vertical bar (because colons in URLs mean something else), and the reverse slashes turn into forward slashes. File URLs are useful mostly for looking at graphics files with gif and jpg filename extensions and for looking at a Web page you just wrote and stuck in a file on your disk.

Browsing Around

To check out the Web for yourself, you need a *browser,* the software that gets Web pages and displays them on your screen. Fortunately, you already have one — Windows 98 usually comes with a copy of Internet Explorer. (Though, if the U.S. Department of Justice has its way, you may have a choice of other browsers as well.) If you want to get a copy of Netscape Communicator, see the section "Getting and Installing Microsoft Internet Explorer or Netscape Navigator and Communicator," near the end of this chapter.

If you use America Online or CompuServe software, almost everything we say about Internet Explorer also applies.

So where is this browser we've been talking about so much? If you're using Internet Explorer, you find it in several places on your computer. From the Start menu, you can choose Programs⇨Internet Explorer⇨Internet Explorer. On the taskbar, just beside the Start button is a little area with some icons in it, including the Microsoft Internet Explorer *e* — clicking it starts Internet Explorer. On your desktop, near the upper-left corner, is probably a larger Internet Explorer *e.* Clicking that starts Internet Explorer too.

If Netscape Navigator or Communicator is installed on your computer, it shows up in almost as many places. Try choosing Start⇨Programs⇨ Netscape⇨Navigator or looking for a Netscape Navigator or Communicator icon on your desktop.

However you got there, and whichever browser you're using, as soon as you get your computer connected to the Internet, you're ready to surf the Web. If you follow our recommendations in Chapter 4, your computer dials out whenever it needs to. If not, you may have put your dial-up networking connection on your desktop or on your Start menu. Now would be a good time to start it up. If you still can't find your Dial-Up Networking connection, try choosing Start⇨Programs⇨Internet Explorer⇨Dial-Up Networking. You see a window that should contain your Dial-Up Networking connection.

Surfing the Web with Windows 98

When you start Netscape, you see a screen similar to the one that was shown in Figure 8-1. The Internet Explorer window looks like the one shown in Figure 8-2. Which Web page your browser displays depends on how the browser is set up; many providers arrange to have a browser display their home page. Because Microsoft and Netscape have a fondness for displaying their own Web pages when your browser starts up, you may find yourself looking at them. Netscape is even working at making its page a Web "destination," with news summaries and links to other interesting places.

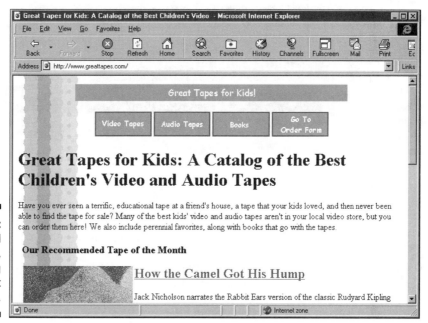

Figure 8-2:
Your typical
Web page,
using
Internet
Explorer.

Anatomy of a browser window

Figure 8-3 illustrates the Navigator and Internet Explorer browser windows, indicating the important parts you really should know about. Here's the rundown:

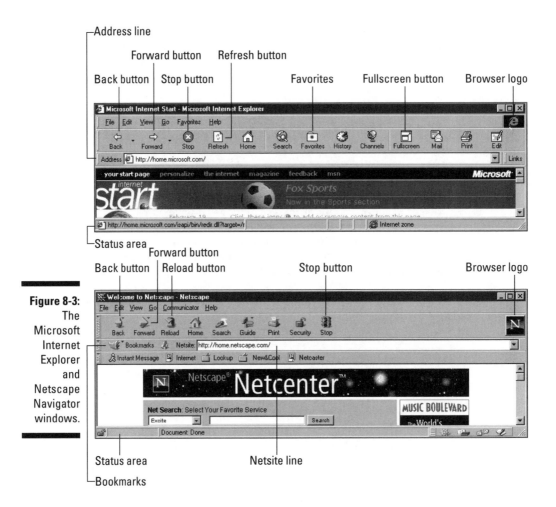

Figure 8-3:
The
Microsoft
Internet
Explorer
and
Netscape
Navigator
windows.

✔ **Address/Netsite line:** The Address line contains the *Uniform Resource Locator,* or *URL,* for the current page. (Netscape labels this box Netsite.) Remember that URLs are an important part of Web lore because they're the secret codes that name all the pages on the Web. For details, see the sidebar "The master plan for the 21st century," earlier in this chapter. *Remember:* To type a URL in the Address or Netsite box, you first must click in the box so that either the address is highlighted (white text on a dark background) or a blinking cursor indicates where your typed characters will go. This process is not as obvious as it may seem. Figure 8-4 illustrates the difference between browsers that are ready to listen to the address you type and browsers that aren't.

These browsers don't care what you type!

These browsers are ready to listen to the address you type!

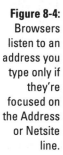

Figure 8-4:
Browsers
listen to an
address you
type only if
they're
focused on
the Address
or Netsite
line.

✔ **Back button:** Web browsers remember pages you visited recently, so if you click a link and decide that you're not so crazy about the new page, you can easily go back to the preceding one. To go back, click the Back button (its icon is an arrow pointing to the left) or press Alt+←. If the Back button is gray, you've gone all the way back to where you began your wandering since you ran your browser today.

✔ **Forward button:** If you've used the Back button to look at a Web page recently on your wanderings around the Web, you can click the Forward button to move forward along that path. Similar to the Back button, if the Forward button is gray, it means that you're as far along your path as you've ever been and you have to tell your browser where you want to go next.

✔ **Refresh/Reload button:** We talk about this button a little later in this chapter, in the section "If at first you don't succeed.," In short, it goes out to the Web and asks for a fresh copy of the Web page you're looking at.

✔ **Stop button:** This button represents the alternative to the saying, "If at first you don't succeed." In other words, give up. If you're tired of waiting for something to arrive from the World Wide Web, you can tell your Web browser to give up waiting and go do something else.

✔ **Favorites and Bookmarks buttons:** These two deserve a section all to themselves, and that's what they get in Chapter 9.

✔ **Fullscreen button:** Only in Internet Explorer, this button removes most of the "Window dressing" from your Internet browser window, leaving only a small version of the toolbar. The rest of your screen is available for the Web page itself. (You can skip ahead and take a peek at Figure 11-4 in Chapter 11 if you want to see how it looks.)

✔ **Status area:** Web pages are made up of many different pieces. When you're in the process of receiving a Web page, the status area tells you what it is that your browser is receiving and perhaps also how far along it is. (Navigator is better about this stuff than Internet Explorer is; IE tends to make unwarrantedly optimistic reports there.) After you've received a page, you may wonder where the links go. Before you actually click a link, the status area tells you where you would go.

✔ **Browser's logo:** The only reason you care about this thing is because it's your indication that your browser thinks that more information is coming. If the little comets are still streaking by the Netscape *N* or the world is still revolving around the Internet Explorer *e,* your browser has not received the "all clear, everything's here." Check out the section "If at first you don't succeed," later in this chapter, if you think that your browser is confused.

Click when ready

The primary skill you need (if we can call something as basic as a single mouse-click a skill) is to find out how to move from page to page on the Web.

It's easy: You just click any link that looks interesting. Underlined blue text and blue-bordered pictures are links. (Although links may be a color other than blue, depending on the look the Web page designer is going for, they're always underlined unless the page is the victim of a truly awful designer.) You can tell when you're pointing to a link because the mouse pointer changes to a little hand. In fact, if you selected the Web style when you configured your Windows 98 desktop (See Chapter 3), opening a Web link is just like opening any icon on your Windows 98 desktop.

If you're not sure whether something is a link, click it anyway because, if it's not, it doesn't hurt anything. Clicking outside a link selects the text you click, or does nothing.

Do you know where your browser has been?

Not only do Web browsers remember pages you visited recently, but Internet Explorer also keeps track of all the places you visited in the past 20 days. For a recap of your surfing experiences, click the History button on the Internet Explorer button bar. We believe that you should be able to surf with privacy. To change the number of days history information is kept (you can set it to zero) or to just clear out the history file, choose View⇨Internet Options to display the Internet Options dialog box. Click the General tab and look at the settings in the History section, near the bottom of the dialog box. Click OK when you're done.

Picture this

Some picture links are *image maps,* such as the big picture shown in the middle of Figure 8-5. In a regular link, it doesn't matter where you click; on an image map, it does. The image map in this figure is typical and has a bunch of obvious places you click for various types of information. (All the 1990 census data except private individual info is online on the Net, by the way, at `http://www.census.gov`.) Some image maps are actual maps — a map of the United States at the Census Bureau, for example, that shows you information about the state you click.

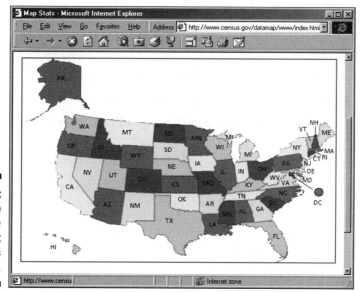

Figure 8-5: Stand up and be counted at the Census Bureau.

As you move the mouse cursor around a Web page, whenever you're pointing at a link, the place you have linked to appears in small type at the bottom of the screen. If the link is an image map, you may see the link followed by a question mark and two numbers that are the X and Y positions of where you are on the map. The numbers don't matter to you (it's up to the Web server to make sense of them); if you see a pair of numbers counting up and down when you move the mouse, however, you know that you're on an image map.

There's no place like home

These days, everyone and his dog has a home page. A *home page* is the main Web page for a person or organization. Chapter 15 shows you how to make one for yourself and your dog. (For an example, check out `http://users.aimnet.com/~carver/cindy.html`.) Companies are advertising their home pages, and people are sending e-mail talking about cool sites. When you see a URL you want to check out, here's what you do:

1. **Click in the Location or Address box, near the top of the Netscape or Internet Explorer window.**

2. **Type the URL in the box.**

   The URL is something like `http://net.gurus.com/`.

3. **Press Enter.**

Many programs, such as Outlook Express and Eudora, automagically highlight any URL they see so that you can click it to send your browser there. If you see a URL in a document that isn't highlighted, however, you can use standard cut-and-paste techniques and avoid retyping:

1. **Highlight the URL in whichever program is showing it.**

2. **Press Ctrl+C to copy the info to the Clipboard.**

3. **Click in the Location box in Netscape or the Address box in Internet Explorer.**

4. **Press Ctrl+V to paste the URL, and then press Enter.**

You can leave the `http://` off the front of URLs when you type them in the Address box. You can even leave the `www` off the front and the `com` off the back — that is, rather than type `http://www.idgbooks.com`, you can just type `idgbooks`. If you don't know a company's URL, it is usually worth typing the company or product name in your browser's Address box before you try other search methods.

One last tip: URLs appear in ads, on the sides of cereal boxes, and in sentences throughout this book. When a URL appears in a sentence, it may be followed by a period, comma, or other punctuation. Don't type the punctuation into your browser! URLs never end with periods or commas.

A few good links to start with

You find out more in Chapter 10 about how to find things on the Web; for now, here's a good way to get started: Go to the Yahoo! page. (Yes, the name of the Web page includes an exclamation point — it's very excitable. But we leave it out for the rest of this book because we find it annoying.) That is, type this URL in the Location or Address box and then press Enter:

```
http://www.yahoo.com
```

You go to the Yahoo page, a directory of millions of Web pages by topic. Just nose around, and you can find something interesting.

For updates to the very book you are holding, go to this URL:

```
http://net.gurus.com
```

Follow the links to the page about our books, and then select the pages for readers of *The Internet For Windows 98 For Dummies*. If we have any late-breaking news about the Internet or updates and corrections to this book, you can find them there. If you find mistakes in this book or have other comments, by the way, please send e-mail to us at internet98@gurus.com.

If at first you don't succeed

Sometimes a Web page gets garbled on the way in or you interrupt it (by clicking the Stop button on the toolbar). Sometimes you receive half a Web page and the rest never shows up. Sometimes you receive the whole thing except for a picture. The Internet is like that: If you've read Chapter 1, you know that the Internet was designed to fail by giving you as much of what you want as it can instead of cutting you off completely. That's what the Stop button and the Refresh/Reload buttons are for: You can tell your browser to get the information on the page again. If your browser still thinks that it's waiting for information (and you disagree), click the Stop button. You know that your browser thinks that more information is out there if the browser's logo in the upper-right corner is still swirling around. After you've clicked the Stop button to tell your browser to give up, in Internet Explorer, click the Refresh button or press F5; in Netscape, click the Reload button or press Ctrl+R. Hope for better luck this time.

Time to quit

Sooner or later, even the most dedicated Web surfer has to stop to eat or attend to other bodily needs. You leave Netscape or Internet Explorer in the same way as you leave any other Windows 98 program: by choosing File⇨Close. You can also click the Close button in the upper-right corner of the window.

Getting and Installing Microsoft Internet Explorer or Netscape Navigator and Communicator

You can download both Netscape Navigator (and its big brother, Communicator) and Microsoft Internet Explorer from the Net. If you have access to any Web browser, try the manufacturers' Web sites:

- **Netscape home page (for Navigator or Communicator):** `http://home.netscape.com`

- **Microsoft home page (for Internet Explorer):** `http://www.microsoft.com/ie`

Several other sites not affiliated with the manufacturers also enable you to download the browser software:

- **TUCOWS (The Ultimate Collection of Internet Software):** `http://www.tucows.com`

  TUCOWS sites are distributed all over the United States (and the world), so you have to pick one that's close to you. After you do, look for a category of software called Win98/95/NT, and then look for browsers.

- **The Consummate Winsock Applications page:** `http://cws.internet.com`

  You can probably find Internet browsers by browsing The Consummate Winsock's 32-bit programs and then looking for Web browsers. You may be able to get directly there by going to `http://cws.internet.com/32www.html`. (Hey, this is the Internet; things change every day, but we're trying to help out here.)

As we explain in Chapter 12, you click a link on a Web page to start the download, tell Windows where to store the downloaded file (in a temporary folder, like C:\Temp or C:\Download), and, when the download is done, run the downloaded file (click or double-click in Windows Explorer or a folder window).

Chapter 9
Working Web Wonders

*I*f you know how to find your way around the Web, you are ready for some comparatively advanced features so that you can start to feel like a Web pro in no time. Try poking around. The best way to find out what you can do is by trying everything. Since you have this book, you could resort to reading it, of course, but why spoil all the fun?

"Where Did I See That?"

You really want to show a friend that exotic cooking page you found with the recipe for chilled snail on crabgrass, but you lost the slip of paper on which you wrote the URL. Fortunately, browsers provide a handy way for you to remember sites and not have to write down those nasty URLs just to have to type them again later.

Although the name varies, the idea is simple: You tell your browser to add to a list the URL of the currently displayed Web page. Later, when you want to go back, you just go to your list and pick out that cool site. Internet Explorer calls these hot spots *favorites;* Netscape calls them *bookmarks*.

Playing favorites in Internet Explorer

Internet Explorer lets you add the current page to your Windows 98 Favorites folder. This Favorites folder is shared with other programs on your computer, however. Other programs also can add things to your Favorites folder, so it's a jumble (in our opinion) of Web pages, files, and other things.

To add the current page to your Favorites folder, choose Favorites⇨Add to Favorites from the menu. To see your Favorites folder, choose Favorites from the menu bar; your favorite Web pages appear right on the menu. Another way to take a look at your favorite sites is to click the Favorites button on the toolbar. The list of Web sites appears on the left side of your Internet Explorer window. To display one of these Web pages, just click the item on the Favorites list. When you want to make the Favorites list go away, click the Favorites button again.

To organize your Favorites folder, choose Favorites⇨Organize Favorites. You see the Organize Favorites dialog box, as shown in Figure 9-1.

Figure 9-1:
Your
favorite
web pages,
word-
processing
files and
other items
all appear
in the
Organize
Favorites
window.

Here are some things you can do to organize your favorite Web sites:

- Change the order of the list by dragging items up or down the list.

- Get rid of them by selecting a Web page and clicking the Delete button.

- Change the names of the Web page on the list by selecting the Web page and clicking the Rename button. You can't change the Web page's name on the Web, of course, but you can change the name that appears on your Favorites list.

✔ Create subfolders in the Favorites folder so that you can store different types of files in different folders. To create a folder, click the Create New Folder button (the button with the yellow folder with a little sparkle, near the upper-right corner of the window). To move an item in the Favorites window into a folder, click the item, click the Move button, and select the folder to move it to. You can see the contents of a folder by double-clicking it.

When you are done organizing your favorite items, click the Close button.

The folders you create in the Organize Favorites window appear on your Favorites menu, and the items you put in the folders appear on submenus. To return to a Web page you've added to your Favorites folder, just choose it from the Favorites menu.

In Windows 98, the Favorites folder usually appears on your Start menu. You can double-click the folder to open it and double-click an item to return to that item. If the item is a Web page, your browser fires up and (if you're connected to the Internet) displays the Web page.

Bookmarking Netscape

The Netscape version of favorites lurks under the Bookmarks menu. To add a bookmark for a Web page displayed in Netscape 4.0, choose Communicator⇨Bookmarks⇨Add Bookmark or press Ctrl+D. You can see your bookmarks as entries on the menu that appears when you click the Bookmarks Quick File button, to the left of the Location box. To go to one of the pages on your bookmark list, just choose its entry from this menu.

If you're like most users, your bookmark menu gets bigger and bigger and crawls down your screen and eventually ends up flopping down on the floor, which is both unattractive and unsanitary. Fortunately, you can smoosh (technical term) your menu into a more tractable form. Choose Communicator⇨Bookmarks⇨Edit Bookmarks or press Ctrl+B to display your Bookmarks window, as shown in Figure 9-2.

Here are things you can do with the Bookmarks window:

✔ Because all these bookmarks are "live," you can go to any of them by clicking them. (You can leave this window open while you move around the Web in your main Netscape window.)

✔ Delete a bookmark by selecting it and pressing the Del key.

✔ Change the order of the bookmarks by dragging them up and down the list.

✔ Rename a bookmark by clicking it and choosing Edit⇨Bookmark Properties from the Bookmarks window menu bar. You can type a comment about the Web page too, if you want.

✔ If your list gets really long and you can't find the Web page you are looking for, choose Edit⇨Find in Bookmarks to search for a word or phrase that appears in a bookmark title, URL, or comment.

✔ You can also add separator lines and submenus to organize your bookmarks and make the individual menus less unwieldy. Submenus look like folders in the Bookmarks window. Choose File⇨New Separator from the Bookmarks window's menu bar to add a separator line. Choose File⇨New Folder to add a new submenu. (Netscape asks you to type the name of the submenu before it creates the folder.) You can then drag the bookmarks, separators, and folders up and down to where you want them in the Bookmarks window. Drag an item to a folder to put it in that folder's submenu, and double-click a folder to display or hide that submenu.

Figure 9-2:
The Netscape Bookmarks window shows the list of web pages you want to come back to.

Because any changes you make in the Bookmarks window are reflected immediately on the Bookmarks menu, it's easy to fiddle with the bookmarks until you get something you like.

When you're done fooling with your bookmarks, choose File⇨Close or press Ctrl+W to close the Bookmarks window.

Netscape 4.0 also has a cool feature that enables you to see which of the items on your bookmark list have been updated since you last looked at them. Open the Bookmarks window as described earlier in this section and then choose View➪Update Bookmarks from the menu bar in the Bookmarks window. A dialog box asks which bookmarks you want to check: all your bookmarks, or just the one (or ones) you selected. Click the Start Checking button. Netscape checks the contents of all the Web pages on your book-marks list to check whether the page has changed since you last looked at it! When Netscape is done checking the Web pages on your bookmarks list, it displays a message telling you how many have changed. The icons in the Bookmarks window reveal which pages have changed: The ones with little sparkles have new material, the ones with question marks are the ones Netscape isn't sure about, and the ones that look normal haven't changed.

Making the Paint Dry Faster

Unless you have a cable modem or a high-speed dedicated connection rather than an ordinary dial-up account, you probably spend a great deal of time wishing that the process of getting to stuff on the Web were much faster. Some people compare Web browsing over a slow modem to watching paint dry. (John has a high-speed dedicated connection and Carol has a cable modem, and they spend a certain amount of time waiting for the Web anyway. Margy, who has a slow modem, has taken up knitting.) This section shows you a handful of tricks you can use to try to speed things up.

Pick a faster place to start

In Internet Explorer: Internet Explorer starts by displaying the Microsoft home page. You can change that start page, or you can tell Internet Explorer to use a blank page. Follow these steps to change your start page:

1. **Display the Web page you want to use as your start page.**

   For example, you may want to start at the Yahoo page, described in Chapter 10, or Internet Gurus Central, at `http://net.gurus.com`.

2. **Choose View➪Internet Options from the menu.**

   You see the Internet Options dialog box.

3. **Find the General tab along the top of the dialog box and click it.**

   If you click the Use Current button, the URL of the current page appears in the Address box. You can also type in the Address box the address of the home page you want Internet Explorer to use or click Use Blank Page.

Choose to start with a blank page or a start page that doesn't have many pictures: By starting with a Web page that loads faster or with no page, you don't have to wait long to start browsing.

In Netscape: When Netscape starts up, it loads the large and attractive Netscape home page. After one or two times, beautiful as the home page is, you may find that you can do without it. You can tell Netscape which Web page to display when you start the program:

1. **Choose <u>E</u>dit⇨P<u>r</u>eferences.**

   You see the Preferences dialog box.

2. **Click the Navigator category.**

   You see a setting called Navigator starts with.

3. **If you want to start with no Web page, click Blank Page. If you want to start with a page you specify, click <u>H</u>ome Page, click in the box below it, and type the name of a page you would rather see (your provider's home page, for example).**

   You also have the option of starting where you left off last time, by clicking Last Page Visited.

4. **Click OK.**

Skip the pix

You can save a great deal of time by skipping the pictures when you're browsing the Web. True, the pages don't look as snazzy, but they load like the wind. If you decide that you want to see the missing pictures after all, you can still do so.

In Internet Explorer: You can tell Internet Explorer not to bother loading images by choosing <u>V</u>iew⇨Internet <u>O</u>ptions from the menu, clicking the Advanced tab, and scrolling down to the Multimedia section. If a check mark appears in the Show Pictures box, click the box to remove the check mark. Then click OK. Where pictures usually appear, you see a little box with three shapes in it. If you want to see a particular picture, right-click the little box and choose Show Picture from the menu that appears.

In Netscape: Choose <u>E</u>dit⇨P<u>r</u>eferences from the menu and then click the Advanced category. Uncheck Auto Load Images. At every place on the page where an image should go, Netscape displays a box with three colored shapes. To see a particular image, right-click the three-shape box and choose Load Image from the menu that appears.

Catch up with your cache

When Internet Explorer or Netscape retrieves a page you have asked to see, it stores the page on your disk. If you ask for the same page again five minutes later, the program doesn't have to retrieve the page again — it can reuse the copy it already has. If you tell the program not to load images, for example, you get a fair number of them anyway because they have already been downloaded.

The space your browser uses to store pages is called its *cache* (pronounced "cash" because it's French and gives your cache more *cachet*). The more space you tell your browser to use for its cache, the more likely it is that a page will appear more quickly the second time you look at it.

In Internet Explorer: To set the size of the Internet Explorer cache, follow these steps:

1. **Choose View⇨Internet Options from the menu.**

   You see the Internet Options dialog box.

2. **Click the General tab.**

3. **Click the Settings button in the Temporary Internet Files box.**

   You see the Settings dialog box, with information about the cache. (Many versions of Internet Explorer never call it a cache — guess they don't speak French.)

4. **Click the slider on the Amount of Disk Space to Use or Maximum Size line and move it to about 40 MB or 10 percent, whichever is less.**

   If you have tons of empty disk space, you can slide it rightward to 80 MB. If you're short on disk space, move it leftward to 1 percent or 2 percent.

5. **Click OK twice.**

In Netscape: To set the size of the Netscape cache, follow these steps:

1. **Choose Edit⇨Preferences from the menu.**

   You see the Preferences dialog box.

2. **Double-click the Advanced category and click the Cache category.**

   The Disk Cache box shows the maximum size of the cache in kilobytes (KB): We like to set Disk Cache to at least 10,000 KB (that is, 10 MB). Set it to a higher number if you have a large hard disk with loads of free space — the more space your cache can occupy, the more often you can load a Web page quickly from the cache rather than slowly from the Net.

3. **Click OK.**

Some of us hardly ever exit from our browsers, which is probably not a good idea for our long-term mental stability. If you are one of us, however, remember that the pages your browser has cached aren't reloaded from the Web (they're taken from your disk) until you reload them. If you want to make sure that you're getting fresh pages, reload pages that you think may have changed since you last visited. Your browser is supposed to check whether a saved page has changed, but because the check sometimes doesn't work perfectly, an occasional Reload command for pages that change frequently, such as stock prices or the weather report, is advisable.

Clear the Deck

Netscape and Internet Explorer have so many buttons, icons, and boxes near the top of the window that not much space is left to display the Web page.

In Internet Explorer: Those folks at Microsoft noticed this problem and, taking a cue from some old word-processing programs, came up with a toolbar button to deal with it. On the Internet Explorer toolbar is a button named Fullscreen; if you can't find it, wander over to Chapter 8 and look at Figure 8-3. When you press this button, everything on your screen disappears, and the whole thing becomes the browser's playground, with the exception of a small toolbar at the top of the screen. This technique is very useful if you're doing some serious surfing for a while and don't want to think about what else might be going on in your computer. Naturally, because the Fullscreen button is one of those on the small toolbar that remains, you can go back to a regular Internet Explorer window.

If that's a little drastic for your tastes, you can selectively remove things from the Internet Explorer window:

- ✔ To get rid of the toolbar (the row of buttons just below the menu), choose <u>V</u>iew➪<u>T</u>oolbars➪<u>S</u>tandard Buttons. Most buttons on the toolbar have keyboard equivalents, some of which we describe in this chapter.

- ✔ To suppress the Address bar and the Address box, choose <u>V</u>iew➪ Toolbars➪<u>A</u>ddress Bar. This action isn't such a great idea because you need that Address box for typing URLs.

- ✔ To get rid of the status bar (the gray bar at the bottom of the Internet Explorer window), choose <u>V</u>iew➪<u>S</u>tatus Bar.

Give the same command again to restore the item you got rid of. Although we prefer to keep these items on our screen most of the time, your tastes may differ, and we have pretty big screens.

In Netscape: You can clear off a little more space in the Netscape window by using commands from the Options or View menu:

✔ To clear off the Location box, choose View➪Hide Location Toolbar. This action isn't such a good idea most of the time because the Location box shows you the URL of the page you're looking at and lets you type a new URL to go to.

✔ To say sayonara to the toolbar (the row of buttons just below the menu), choose View➪Hide Navigation Toolbar. Most people use the Back button all the time, but you won't miss it if you remember that pressing Alt+← does the same thing.

To restore any of the things you just blew away, give the same command again.

Forms, Forms, Forms

Back in the Dark Ages of the Web (that is, in 1993), Web pages were just pages to look at. Because that wasn't anywhere near enough fun nor complicated enough, Web forms were invented. A *form* is sort of like a paper form, with boxes you can fill out and then send in. Techies call the boxes *fields*. Figure 9-3 shows a typical form.

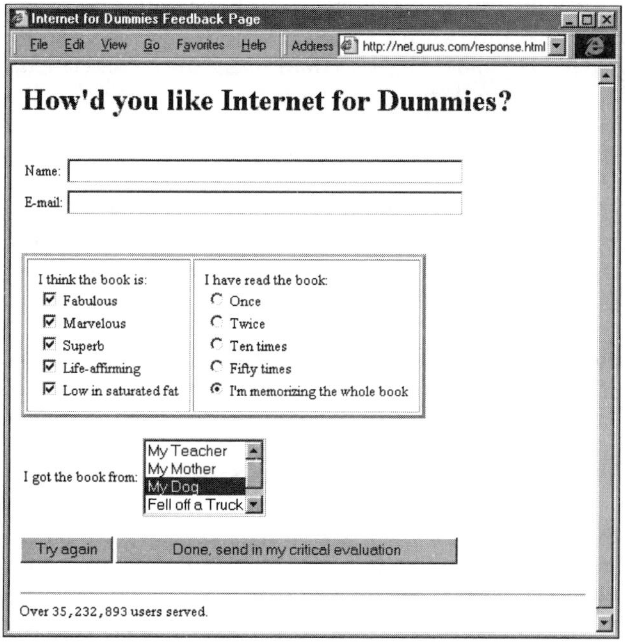

Figure 9-3:
A Web form
(oh, wow!).

The top two lines in the form are fill-in text boxes in which you type, in this case, your name and e-mail address. Under that is a set of *check boxes,* in which you check whichever ones apply (all of them, we hope), and a set of *radio buttons,* which are similar to check boxes except that you can choose only one of them. Under that is a *list box,* in which you can choose one of the possibilities in the box. In most cases, you see more entries than can fit in the box, so you scroll them up and down. Although you can usually choose only one entry, some list boxes let you choose more.

At the bottom of the form are two buttons. The one on the left clears the form fields to their initial state and sends nothing, and the one on the right, known as the *Submit* button, sends the filled-out form back to the Web server for processing.

After the data is sent from the form back to the Web server, it's entirely up to the server how to interpret it.

Save It for a Rainy Day

Frequently, you see something on a Web page that's worth saving for later. Sometimes it's a Web page full of interesting information or a picture or some other type of file. Fortunately, saving stuff is easy.

When you save a Web page, you have to decide whether to save only the text that appears or the entire HTML version of the page, with the format codes. (For a glimpse of HTML, see Chapter 15.) You can also save the pictures that appear on Web pages.

In either Netscape or Internet Explorer, choose File⇨Save As to save the current Web page in a file. You see the standard Save As dialog box, in which you specify the name to save the incoming file. Click in the Save As Type box to determine how to save the page: Choose Plain Text to save only the text of the page, with little notes where pictures occur. Choose HTML or HTML Files to save the entire HTML file. Then click the Save or OK button.

To save an image you see on a Web page, right-click the image (click the image with your right mouse button). Choose Save Image As or Save Picture As from the menu that appears. When you see the Save As dialog box, move to the folder or directory in which you want to save the graphics file, type a filename in the File Name box, and click the Save or OK button.

A note about copyright: Contrary to popular belief, almost all Web pages, along with almost everything else on the Internet, are copyrighted by their authors. If you save a Web page or a picture from a Web page, you don't necessarily have permission to use it any way you want. Before you reuse the text or pictures in any way, send an e-mail message to the site's owner. If an address doesn't appear on the page, write to `webmaster@domain.com`, replacing `domain.com` with the domain name part of the URL of the Web page. For permission to use information on the `http://net.gurus.com/books.html` page, for example, write to `webmaster@gurus.com`.

Touch Your Nose and Rub Your Belly

Netscape and Internet Explorer are known in the trade as *multithreaded* programs. What this term means in practice is that the program can do several things at a time.

If you ask Netscape or Internet Explorer to begin downloading a big file, it displays a small window. The Netscape version of this window displays a "thermometer" showing the download progress; Internet Explorer shows tiny pages flying from one folder to another. Although some people consider watching the thermometer grow or the pages fly entertainment (we do when we're tired enough), you can click back to the main Netscape or Internet Explorer window and continue surfing. You can also have several Web browser windows open at a time. Press Ctrl+N or choose File⇨New⇨Window (in Internet Explorer) or File⇨New⇨Navigator Window (in Netscape 4.0) to create a new window. We find this technique the most useful way to look at two related pages side by side (or overlapping) on-screen.

Doing two or three things at a time in your browser when you have a dial-up Net connection is not unlike squeezing blood from a turnip — there's only so much blood there, no matter how hard you squeeze. In this case, the blood is the amount of data your ISP can pump through your modem. A single download task can keep your modem close to 100 percent busy *if* (and that's a big *IF*) the data you're downloading arrives at your ISP faster than your modem can handle it. Even if it does, if you're viewing a Web page while you're doing a big download, things usually work okay because you spend a fair amount of time looking at what the Web browser is displaying; the download can then run while you think.

What happens more often in this age of Internet traffic jams is that you, your modem, and your ISP are all waiting around for data to trickle its way across the Internet. When that happens, browsing Web pages doesn't make your downloads take any longer. At times like these, it can be handy that Netscape and Internet Explorer let you start two (or more) download tasks at one time. Until you're using up the whole capacity of the line between your modem and your ISP, requesting more Web pages or downloads at the same time doesn't slow you down. (Asking for multiple things at one time creates more load on your ISP and on the high-capacity lines that form the major arteries of the Internet, but not by so much as to make much difference for anyone.)

So how do you find out whether your modem is waiting around for data to arrive from the Internet? If you have an external modem, it's easy. The modem probably has a light labeled RD (for Receive Data) or perhaps just Receive. When you're downloading information from the Internet, the light should be on almost steadily. If it is, your modem is running at full speed. If it isn't, you have joined what has come to be called the World Wide Wait. If you have an internal modem or a PC Card modem, determining how fast data is arriving at your PC can be a little more difficult. You can get a rough idea by double-clicking the dial-up icon (the one with the two little computer screens) near the right end of your taskbar. (We introduce this icon in Chapter 4, in the section about monitoring your Dial-Up Networking connection.)

Double-clicking this icon displays the Communications Statistics dialog box (it's shown over in Chapter 4). If the number of bytes received is counting up in fits and starts, you're probably waiting for the Internet, not for your modem.

Making Treeware (Printing)

To print a page from Internet Explorer or Netscape, just click the Print button on the toolbar, press Ctrl+P, or choose File➪Print. Reformatting the page to print it can take awhile, so patience is a virtue. Fortunately, Netscape and Internet Explorer each display a progress window to keep you apprised of how they're doing.

Keep Your Cookie Crumbs Off My Computer

Back in Chapter 1, we mention cookies — not the kind you eat, but the kind Web sites put on your computer so that they can identify you and remember something about you. We also mention there that many of us have different feelings about cookies: Some of us don't care about them, and some of us view them as an unconscionable invasion of privacy. You get to decide for yourself. Both Internet Explorer and Netscape Navigator let you control whether and when cookies are stored on your computer.

In Internet Explorer, choose View➪Internet Options to display the Internet Options dialog box. The Advanced tab contains a *long* list of settings that control how Internet Explorer works. Click the scroll bar to scroll about halfway down the list. The heading with a little lock on it labeled Security has a subsection with a little Caution symbol labeled Cookies. Choose whichever option you're comfortable with: Always Accept Cookies (for those of us who don't care what computers remember about us), Prompt Before Accepting Cookies (for the truly discriminating — you get to decide on a case-by-case basis whether the site you're looking at gets to put a cookie on your computer), or Disable All Cookie Use. Most Web sites still work if you disable cookies, although they may spend a certain amount of time nagging you about who you are and asking whether they've ever heard of you.

The situation is similar in Netscape Navigator. You choose the Edit➪ Preferences Advanced command to display a Preferences dialog box with a list of option categories on the left and settings associated with those options on the right. Click Advanced, the last of the major headings; you see some settings (similar to those in Internet Explorer) on the right side of the dialog box: Accept All Cookies, Accept Only Cookies That Get Sent Back to the Originating Server (unlike Internet Explorer, Navigator is willing to keep track of which cookie belongs to which Web site), or Disable Cookies.

Additionally, Navigator is willing to warn you whenever it's about to accept a cookie, no matter where it gets sent back to. If you want to know, check the box labeled Warn Me before Accepting a Cookie.

Plug In to What's Happening

As Netscape has evolved from an unknown newcomer in the Web biz to the big gorilla on the block, it has gained a few new features. Lots and lots of features. Lots and lots and lots of features. Netscape already had about as many features as any single human could comprehend, but just in case someone somewhere understood the whole thing, you can now extend Netscape capabilities with *plug-ins,* or add-on programs that glue themselves to Netscape and add even more features.

Not to be outdone, each version of Internet Explorer tries to match the Netscape features. In addition to using plug-ins, you can also extend the already excessive Internet Explorer capabilities by using things called *ActiveX* controls (formerly called OCX controls, formerly called VBX controls, but they keep changing the name as soon as people start to figure out what they are).

Web pages with pictures are old hat. Now, Web pages have to have pictures that sing and dance or ticker-style messages that move across the page or video clips. Every month, new types of information appear on the Web.

What's a Web browser to do with all these new kinds of information? Get the plug-in program that handles that kind of information and glue it to Netscape or Internet Explorer. You *Star Trek* fans can think of plug-ins as parasitic life-forms that attach themselves to your browser and enhance its intelligence.

Popular plug-ins

Here are some useful plug-ins:

> ✔ **RealPlayer:** Plays sound files as you download them (other programs have to wait until the entire file has downloaded before beginning to play). Microsoft NetShow does much the same thing.

- ✔ **QuickTime:** Plays video files and VDOLive, which plays video files as you download them
- ✔ **Shockwave:** Plays both audio and video files in addition to other types of animation
- ✔ **iChat:** Lets you use your Web browser to participate in online chats
- ✔ **Netscape Live3D, WIRL, Liquid Reality, and other VR plug-ins:** Let you move around inside 3-D "virtual reality" worlds on Web pages

Using plug-ins

Some of us try to ignore plug-ins as much as possible. It's not that we have anything against them — it's just that we don't particularly care whose bits of computer code are running in our browser to make someone else's Web site look right. Most Web sites that require a plug-in or ActiveX control either automatically download it for you or provide a link close at hand that will download it for you. Your browser may try to let you know that you're about to run someone else's computer code and advise that you engage in safe computing; as long as you stay in the nice neighborhoods on the Web, however, you shouldn't have to worry much.

If you want to make sure that your browser is fully equipped with plug-ins from reputable sources, you can find Netscape plug-ins and Internet Explorer ActiveX controls at TUCOWS (`http://www.tucows.com`), the Consummate Winsock Applications page (`http://cws.internet.com`), the Netscape Web site (`http://home.netscape.com`), and other reputable sources of software on the Web. That way, when you're surfing an unknown Web site, your browser doesn't have to download any new computer code.

After you have downloaded a plug-in from the Net, run it (double-click its filename in My Computer or Windows Explorer) to install it. Depending on what the plug-in does, you follow different steps to try it out. Here are some examples:

- ✔ **RealPlayer:** Go to the `http://www.realaudio.com` Web page for a list of sites that handle RealAudio sound files. Our favorite site is the National Public Radio Web site (`http://www.npr.org`), where you can hear recent NPR radio stories, and John's site, at `http://iecc.com`, where you can listen to his radio show.
- ✔ **iChat:** Go to the iChat Web site, at `http://www.ichat.com`, to join chats with other iChat users or to participate in Internet Relay Chat (IRC) conversations. (See Chapter 13 for more information about IRC.)

Chapter 10

Finding Stuff on the Net

· ·

· ·

"*O*kay, all this great stuff is out there on the Net. How do I find it?" That's an excellent question. Thanks for asking that question. Questions like that are what makes this country strong and vibrant. We salute you and say, "Keep asking questions!" Next question, please.

Oh, you want an *answer* to your question. Fortunately, quite a bit of (technical term follows) stuff-finding stuff is on the Net. More particularly, indexes and directories of much of the interesting material are available on the Net.

The Net has different types of indexes and directories for different types of material. Because the indexes tend to be organized, unfortunately, by the type of Internet service they provide rather than by the nature of the material, you find Web resources in one place, e-mail resources in another place, and so on. You can search in dozens of hundreds of different ways, depending on what you're looking for and how you prefer to search. (John has remarked that his ideal restaurant has only one item on the menu, but that it's just what he wants. The Internet is about as far from that ideal as you can possibly imagine.)

To provide a smidgen of structure to this discussion, we describe several different sorts of searches:

✔ **Topics:** Places, things, ideas — anything you want to find out more about

✔ **Companies:** Organizations that you think have a Web site or other Net presence

✔ **People:** Actual human beings whom you want to contact or spy on

✔ **Goods and services:** Stuff to buy, from mortgages to mouthwash

To find topics, we use the various online indexes and directories, such as Yahoo! and AltaVista. (Yes, that's Yahoo! with an exclamation point. It's a nice trademark, and we're sure that the Yahoo! people paid lots! of money for market research about it, but we! think that it's hard to read, so from here on we leave it out! 'Nuff said.) To find companies, we also use *WHOIS*, the main directory of Internet domains. To find people, however, we use directories of people, which are (fortunately) different from directories of Web pages. Wondering what we're talking about? Read on for an explanation!

The Five-Minute Guide to Searching

When we're looking for topics on the Net, we always begin with one of the Web guides (indexes and directories) discussed in this section.

You use them all in more or less the same way:

1. **Start your Web browser, such as Netscape or Internet Explorer.**
2. **Pick a directory or index you like, and tell your browser to go to the index or directory's home page.**

    We list the URLs (page names) of the home pages later in this section.

    After you get there, you can choose between two approaches.

Index, directory — what's the difference?

When we talk about a *directory,* we mean a listing that's divided into named categories and the entries assigned to categories partly or entirely by humans. You look things up by finding a category you want and seeing what it contains. In this book, we would think of the table of contents as a directory.

An *index,* on the other hand, simply collects all the items, extracts keywords from them (by taking all the words except for *the, and,* and the like), and makes a big list. You search the index by specifying some words that seem likely, and it finds all the entries which contain that word. The index in the back of this book is more like an index.

Each has its advantages and disadvantages. Directories are organized so that when you find a category of interest, all the items in that category are likely to be related to what you want. Indexes, on the other hand, don't know what the words mean. If you look for program, for example, an index finds computer programs, educational programs, theater programs, and anything else that contains the word. Because indexes can be created largely or completely automatically, indexes on the Net tend to contain many more entries and to be updated more often than directories, which need human catalogers.

Some overlap exists between indexes and directories — Yahoo, the best known Web page directory, lets you search by keyword, and many of the indexes divide their entries into general categories that let you limit the search.

3a. If a Search box is available, type some keywords in the box and click Search.

This is the "index" approach, to look for topic areas that match your keywords.

After a perhaps long delay (the Web is big), an index page is returned with links to pages that match your keywords. The list of links may be way too long to deal with — like 300,000 of them.

3b. If you see a list of links to topic areas, click a topic area of interest.

In the "directory" approach, you begin at a general topic and get more and more specific. Each page has links to pages that get more and more specific until they link to actual pages that are likely to be of interest.

After some clicking around to get the hang of it, you find all sorts of good stuff.

You hear a great deal of talk around the Web about search engines. *Search engines* is a fancy way to say stuff-finding stuff. All the directories and indexes we're about to describe are in the broad category called search engines, so don't get upset by some high-falutin'-sounding terms.

Searching in Depth

So much for the theory of searching for stuff on the Net. Now for some practice. (Theory and practice are much further apart in practice than they are in theory.) We use our two favorite search systems for examples: Yahoo, which is a directory, and AltaVista, which is an index.

Just for you: The Gurus search page

You may feel a wee bit overwhelmed with all the search directories and indexes we discuss in this chapter. If it makes you feel any better, so do we.

To make a little sense of all this stuff, we made ourselves a search page that connects to all the directories and indexes we use so that we get one-stop searching. You can use it too.

Give it a try, at

`http://net.gurus.com/search/`

In the not unlikely event that new search systems are created or some of the existing ones have moved or died, this page gives you our latest greatest list.

Yahoo

You can find stuff in Yahoo in two ways. The easier way is just to click from category to category until you find something you like.

We start our Yahoo visit at its home page, at `http://www.yahoo.com` (at least the page name doesn't use an exclamation point), which looks like Figure 10-1. A whole bunch of categories and subcategories are listed. You can click any of them to see another page that has yet more subcategories and links to actual Web pages. You can click a link to a page if you see one you like or on a sub-subcategory, and so on.

At the top of each Yahoo page is the list of categories, subcategories, and so on, separated by colons, that lead to that page. If you want to back up a few levels and look at different subcategories, just click the place on that list to which you want to back up. After a little clicking up and down, it's second nature. Many pages appear in more than one place in the directory because they fall into more than one category. An advantage of a Web page directory over a card catalog in a library is that although a book can be in only one place on the shelf in the library, Web pages can have as many links referring to them as they want.

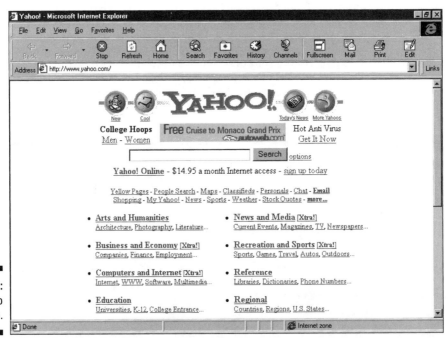

Figure 10-1:
Ready to
Yahoo.

Although all the categories in the Yahoo list have plenty of subcategories under them, some have many more than others. If you're looking for a business-related page, it helps to know that Yahoo sticks just about everything commercial under the category Business and Economy, as shown in Figure 10-2. If you were looking for Internet for Dummies Central, for example (which we think people should look for several times a day, at least), you could click your way to it from the Yahoo home page by clicking Business and Economy, clicking Companies on that page, and then clicking Books, then Computers, and then Internet; on that page, you link to pages with lots of Internet books, including ours.

If you know in general but not in detail what you're looking for, clicking up and down through the Yahoo directory pages is a good way to narrow your search and find pages of interest.

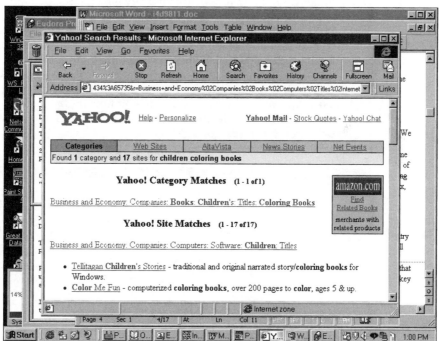

Figure 10-2:
A store-
house of
commercial
information
at Yahoo.

More Yahoo

"Click Business and Economy, click Companies on that page, and then click Books, then Computers, and then Internet"? "How the heck did they know which categories to click?" you're doubtless asking. We admit it. We cheated.

Yahoo also lets you search its index by keyword, which is the best way to use it if you have some idea of the title of the page you're looking for. Every Yahoo screen has near the top a search box in which you can type words you want to find in the Yahoo entry for pages of interest. For example, we typed `internet dummies books`, clicked the Search button next to the type-in box, and got the answer shown in Figure 10-3, with one entry for our Web site and one book by Dan Gookin, who also has written the occasional *...For Dummies* book.

Above each entry Yahoo finds, it reports the category in which it found the entry. Even if the entry isn't quite right, if you click the category, you find other related titles, and some of them may well do the trick.

If Yahoo finds hundreds of pages or categories, you should refine your search. One way to do that is to add extra words to make more specific what you're looking for. If you're looking for a key lime pie recipe (John sent out a good one on the Net about ten years ago) and you search for `baking`, you get 71 fairly random pages; if you search for `key lime pie`, however, you get three pages, one of which is on the page labeled Entertainment:Food and Eating:Recipes:Pie, which has links to lots of tasty pie recipes.

You can click Options, next to the Search button, to get to the slightly more advanced Yahoo search page. It lets you limit how far back you want to see pages (three years is the default), and you can tell it to look for either all the words or any of the words you typed.

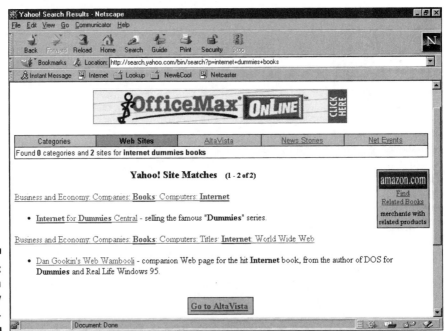

Figure 10-3:
Zeroing in on quality literature.

It's also a cheese grater

Although Yahoo is primarily a directory of resources available on the Web, it has other databases available, each with a link you can click just under the box in which you would enter search terms:

- **Yellow Pages:** A business directory (but not our favorite — see the section "Looking for Businesses," later in this chapter)

- **People Search:** Finds addresses and phone numbers, like a white pages directory (see the "Person to Person" section, later in this chapter)

- **Maps:** Gets a more or less accurate map of a street address you type

- **Classifieds:** Lets you read and submit ads for automobiles, apartments, computers, and jobs

- **Personals:** Lets you read and submit ads for dates in all combinations

- **Chat:** Gets you into online chat through the Web

- **Email:** Free Web-based e-mail service

- **My Yahoo:** A customized starting page just for you, with headlines, sports scores, and other news based on your preferences

- **Today's News, Stock Quotes, and Sports Scores:** News from Reuters

AltaVista

If you examine Figure 10-3 carefully, you notice a link to AltaVista at the bottom. Yahoo and we agree that AltaVista is the best index on the Net.

AltaVista has a little robot named Scooter that spends its time merrily visiting Web pages all over the Net and reporting back what she saw. AltaVista makes a humongous index of which words occurred in which pages; when you search AltaVista, it picks pages from the index that contain the words you asked for.

AltaVista is an index, not a directory. The good news is that it has about ten times as many pages as Yahoo; the bad news is that finding the one you want can be difficult. Regardless of what you ask for, you probably will get 15,000 pages on your first try. After you refine your request a little, however, you can usually get the number of pages down to a somewhat more manageable number.

Using AltaVista, or any index, effectively is an exercise in remote-control mind reading because you have to guess words that will appear on the pages you're looking for. Sometimes, that's easy — if you're looking for recipes for key lime pie, `key lime pie` is a good set of search words because you know the name of what you're looking for. On the other hand, if you have forgotten that the capital of Germany is Berlin, it's hard to tease a useful page out of AltaVista because you don't know what words to look for. (If you try `Germany capital`, you find stuff about investment banking.)

Now that we have you all discouraged, try some AltaVista searches. Direct your browser to `http://altavista.digital.com` (notice the `digital` in there because it's brought to you by Digital Equipment Corporation, the large computer maker recently bought by Compaq). You see a screen like the one shown in Figure 10-4.

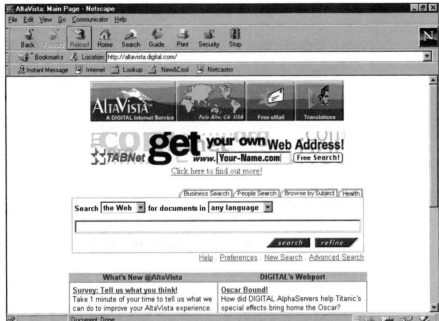

Figure 10-4:
AltaVista, ready to roll.

Type some search terms, and AltaVista finds the pages that best match your terms. That's "best match," not "match" — if it can't match all the terms, it finds pages that match as well as possible. AltaVista ignores words that occur too often to be usable as index terms, both the obvious ones such as `and`, `the`, and `of` and terms such as `internet` and `mail`. These rules can sound somewhat discouraging, but in fact it's still not hard to tease useful results from AltaVista. You just have to think up good search terms. Try that key lime pie example, by typing **key lime pie** and pressing the Search button.

Your results may not look exactly like Figure 10-5 because we told AltaVista to display the results in Compact form rather than Standard form (by clicking the *Preferences* button before searching) so that the example would fit on this page. All the pages it found do, in fact, have something to do with key lime pie, and the first page on that list has a pretty good recipe. Notice that it found about 500,000 matches. Although that's probably more than you wanted to look at, you should at least look at the next couple of screens of matches if the first screen doesn't have what you want. At the bottom of the AltaVista screen are page numbers; click Next to go to the next page.

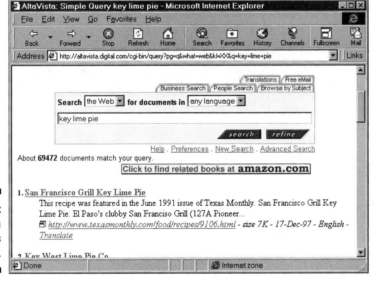

Figure 10-5:
A plethora
of pages
of pie.

AltaVista hints

AltaVista, unlike Yahoo, makes it easy to refine your search more exactly to target the pages you want to find. After each search, your search terms appear in a box at the top of the page so that you can change them and try again. Here are some tips on how you may want to change your terms:

- ✔ Type most search words in lowercase. Type proper names with a single capital letter, such as `Elvis`. Don't type any words in all capital letters.

- ✔ If two or more words should appear together, put quotes around them, as in `"Elvis Presley"`. As a matter of fact, if you do that with the pie search ("key lime pie") because, after all, that is what the pie is called, you get a nice 3,000 matches rather than half a million.

- ✔ Use + and – to indicate words that must either appear or not appear, such as `+Elvis +Costello -Presley` if you're looking for the modern Elvis, not the classic one.

404, why oh why?

More often than we want to admit, when you click a link that Yahoo or one of its competitors found, you get, rather than get the promised page, a message such as 404 Not Found. What did you do wrong? Nothing. Web pages come and go and move around with great velocity, and the various search systems do a lousy job, frankly, of cleaning out links to old, dead pages that have gone away.

The automated indexes, such as AltaVista and Lycos, are better in this regard than the manual directories, such as Yahoo. The

automated ones have software robots that revisit all the indexed pages every once in a while and note whether they still exist; even so, many lonely months can pass between robot visits, and a great deal can happen to a page in the meantime.

It's just part of life on the online frontier — the high-tech equivalent of riding your horse along the trail in the old West and noticing that there sure are a lot of bleached-white cattle skulls lying around.

Yahoo and AltaVista — what a pair!

It occurs to us that a rather effective way to search the Web is to look in the Yahoo directory and then, if you don't find what you want, try AltaVista. Because great minds (or maybe tiny minds) think alike, the Yahoo and AltaVista people got together to make it easy to do just that.

If you rescrutinize Figure 10-3, which shows the result of a Yahoo search, notice — at both the top and bottom of the page — the AltaVista links we mentioned a couple of pages back. (Those Yahoo people aren't subtle. Considering what they call themselves, however, are you surprised?) Click either of those links, and you flip into an AltaVista-in-Yahoo page that shows the results of an AltaVista search using the same terms you just used for a Yahoo search. Although the pages of links look a little different from the "native" AltaVista pages because they're aesthetically designed to match the Yahoo pages, the search finds the same pages either way.

AltaVista away

AltaVista has a few other options that can be handy:

 ✔ Rather than search Web pages, you can search Usenet, the giant collection of Internet newsgroups (online discussion groups). Simply click the box that says Search the Web and flip to Search Usenet. If a topic has been discussed recently on Usenet, this technique is the best way to find the messages about that topic.

✔ You can choose how detailed a report you want to get, in Compact or Detailed form, on the Preferences page. The Compact option gives you a single line per item found; Detailed, about three lines per item. AltaVista normally uses Standard form, which tells it to use Compact if you're doing a Usenet search or Detailed if you're doing a Web search.

Because the compact report is much smaller, it loads faster. If you have a slow dial-up Net connection, Compact form makes searching much snappier, at the cost of not being able to tell quite so easily what's in each item found. If you're searching for a particular page or Usenet item that you will recognize when you see it, Compact form is definitely quicker.

✔ You can limit your search to documents in a specific language. No sense in finding pages in a language you can't read.

It's all free — just like TV

You may be wondering who pays for all these wonderful search systems. All of them are supported by advertising. On every page of Yahoo, Lycos, and most other search systems, you see lots and lots of ads. In theory, the advertising pays the costs. In reality, the independent advertising-supported search systems Excite, Infoseek, Lycos, and Yahoo have all lost pots of money. (In this case, a pot is sized in millions of bucks.) Fortunately for all of them, because they issued stock to the public at the height of the 1996 Internet investment craze, each has plenty of cash to burn up while they try to figure out how to turn a profit. WebCrawler belongs to AOL, which lost 500 pots in 1996–97, though it's hard to tell how much of that was the fault of WebCrawler.

The exception used to be AltaVista, originally a research project to see just how fast the Alpha line of workstations at Digital Equipment Corporation were. The new line turned out to be extremely fast, blowing the socks off most of the competition. Because DEC knew a good thing when it saw it, it turned AltaVista into a product line that it licenses to other search systems (such as Yahoo and CNET, Inc.) and that companies can use to create their own internal indexes. Some folks thought that DEC might issue stock in its AltaVista Internet Software division as well (if the Excite, Infoseek, Lycos, and Yahoo guys can raise all that money, you may as well get in on the party); as of early 1998, it hadn't done so yet, although it has cashed in on its popularity by accepting ads.

Some people think that a big "bubble" is occurring in the search biz and that we can expect some of the search systems to run out of money and shut down or merge with others. Visit http://net.gurus.com/search/ for the latest up- or down-dates.

Wait — There's More

After you have surfed around Yahoo and AltaVista for a while, you may want to check out the competition as well.

WebCrawler

http://www.webcrawler.com

WebCrawler is an automated indexer that crawls around the Web cataloging and indexing every page it comes across — again, sort of like AltaVista. Although America Online (AOL) owns WebCrawler, anyone can use it. It's a reasonable alternative to AltaVista.

Infoseek

http://www.infoseek.com

Infoseek is an index similar to AltaVista rather than a directory: You give it some keywords to look for, and it finds the pages that match the best. It also has a directory of useful Web pages. It can search the Web, Usenet, Reuters news, and a few other odds and ends.

Excite

http://www.excite.com

Excite is primarily an index, like AltaVista, with a "concept search," which is supposed to find relevant pages even if you don't type exactly the same words the pages use. We don't find that the Excite concept search helps much, but perhaps we were too wordy to start with. Excite also has sections with reviews of Web pages, city directories, white pages, and more.

HotBot

http://www.hotbot.com

HotBot is yet another index, like AltaVista. It's affiliated with *Wired* magazine and uses — in classic *Wired* style — bright, clashing colors that make your head hurt. If you can deal with that (try sunglasses), it's not a bad index.

Lycos

`http://www.lycos.com`

Lycos is a largely automated index, sort of like AltaVista. It began as a project at Carnegie-Mellon University and has also gone commercial. It also has a directory called Top 5% of Web Sites. Although Lycos was one of the earliest Web search systems, AltaVista has, at this point, honestly, a better index and Yahoo has a better directory. Lycos also has headline news and local pages for some cities around the United States.

Northern Light

`http://www.northernlight.com`

This site contains an automated index of both the Web and its Special Collection, articles from various sources for which you must pay, usually a dollar or two, if you decide to read them. If you would rather stick with the (free) Web, you can choose to do so. The Northern Light searches also automatically categorize the pages they find, displaying a listings of "folders" you can choose among. We have, on occasion, found useful information in Northern Light and nowhere else.

Other Web guides

Lots of other Web guides are available, including many specialized guides put together for particular interests (Femina, for example, is a feminist guide, at `http://www.femina.com`).

Yahoo has a directory of other guides: Starting at the Yahoo page (`http://www.yahoo.com`), choose WWW (which appears under Computers) and then Searching the Web.

Looking for Businesses

If you are looking for the Web site of a company or organization, try typing its name in the address box of your browser. Many firms have a URL that looks like `www.companyname.com`, and your browser fills in the `www.`, and `.com` parts.

The second way to search for companies is to search for the company name as a topic. If you're looking for the Egg Farm Dairy, for example, search for `Egg Farm Dairy` in Yahoo, AltaVista, or any of the other search systems. (You'll find it, too. We like the Muscoot cheese.)

After you have done that, a few other places are worth checking for business-related info.

WHOIS is a wiz

`http://www.internic.net/wp/whois.html`

Every registered Internet domain has a listed owner and contacts. The WHOIS facility lets you look up domains and contacts. Although some separate WHOIS programs exist, you can do just as well for most purposes by visiting the InterNIC WHOIS Web page.

On that page, you get to choose which WHOIS server to use and what to search for. WHOIS has two servers, one for U.S. military addresses and one for everyone else. By default, it uses both, which usually works okay.

In the Search strings box, enter the name of the company or contact person or network in which you're interested and click Search. With luck, you get back one entry that matches. More likely, you get back a list of all the matches. When we searched for IBM.COM, here's part of what we got:

```
International Business Machines (IBM-DOM)  IBM.COM
International Business Machines (IBM4-HST) IBM.COM
129.34.139.30
To single out one record, look it up with "!xxx", where xxx
          is the handle, shown in parenthesis following
          the name, which comes first.
```

Two possible matches are listed: the IBM.COM domain and the single computer that happens to be called IBM.COM. Each has a code in parentheses, which is a link to more information about that match. The *DOM* in *IBM-DOM* suggests that this might be the official IBM domain, so click it to get a more concrete answer with the full name of the company and the e-mail address of the person responsible for the domain.

In a company as large as IBM, the domain contact is doubtless a technical network specialist; in small companies, however, it's usually someone who can answer short, polite questions, such as "What's the e-mail address of your sales department?" or "Does Jim Smith still work there?"

Hoover is not a vacuum cleaner

`http://www.hoovers.com`

Although WHOIS tells you about a company's connection to the Internet, it doesn't tell you much about the company itself. Hoover's is a business information company that has been publishing paper business directories for quite a while. Now it's on the Net as well. Its Web site offers free company capsules, stock prices, and other company info. If you sign up for its paid service, it offers considerably more. Even the free stuff is quite useful.

Your tax dollars at work — EDGAR

```
http://edgar.sec.gov (government)
http://www.edgar-online.com (private)
```

The U.S. Securities and Exchange Commission (SEC), the people who regulate stock and bond markets, has a system called EDGAR that collects all the financial material which publicly traded companies have to file with the government. Although most of this stuff is dry and financial, if you can read financial statements, you can find all sorts of interesting information, such as Bill Gates' salary.

The government EDGAR site is run directly by the SEC, and the private site, EDGAR ONLINE, is run by an independent company, Cybernet Data Systems, Inc. Although the two sites have pretty much the same information, the private site offers free, limited access and charges a modest price (about $5 per month) for more complete access and automatic e-mail updates when a company in which you're interested files EDGAR documents. Because EDGAR ONLINE has partner arrangements with several other companies, including Hoover's, if you check on a company in Hoover's and then click the EDGAR link to get to EDGAR ONLINE, you can often get documents not directly available from the EDGAR ONLINE home page. If you use EDGAR ONLINE often, however, pay the five bucks.

A bounty of business directories

Tons of business information is available on the Net. Here are a few places to begin.

Companies Online

`http://www.CompaniesOnline.com`

Companies Online is a joint project between Dun & Bradstreet and Lycos. You enter the name of a company in which you're interested, and this site tells you about it.

Inc. magazine

```
http://www.inc.com
http://www.inc.com/500
```

Inc. magazine concentrates on small, fast-growing companies. Each year, its Inc. 500 features the 500 companies it likes the best. Many hot little companies are listed here, with contact information.

Yellow Pages

```
http://www.bigyellow.com
http://yp.gte.net
http://www.switchboard.com
http://www.abii.com (click American Yellow Pages)
```

Quite a few yellow pages business directories, both national and local, are on the Net. The directories in this list are some of the national ones. We like Big Yellow the best (even though it's run by Bell Atlantic, which is otherwise not our favorite telephone company), although they're all worth a look. The American Yellow Pages even offers credit reports, though we can't vouch for its reliability.

Person to Person

Finding people on the Net is surprisingly easy. It's so easy that, indeed, sometimes it's creepy. Two overlapping categories of people finders are available: those that look for people on the Net with e-mail and Web addresses and those that look for people in real life with phone numbers and street addresses.

Call me

A number of directories feature information compiled from telephone white pages all over the world. You don't even have to know what city the person you are seeking lives in (unless he has a common surname like Smith or Jones). Track down that long-lost high school sweetheart! If he hasn't had a listed phone number in the past few years, though, you probably won't find an entry in any of these directories.

On the Net

The process of finding e-mail and Web addresses is somewhat hit-and-miss. Because no online equivalent to the official phone book the telephone company produces has ever existed, directories of e-mail addresses are collected from addresses used in Usenet messages, mailing lists, and other more or less public places on the Net. Because the different directories use different sources, if you don't find someone in one directory, you can try another. Remember that because the e-mail directories are incomplete, there's no substitute for calling someone up and asking, "What's your e-mail address?"

If you're wondering whether someone has a Web page, use AltaVista to search for her name. If you're wondering whether you're famous, use AltaVista to search for your own name and see how many people mention you or link to your Web pages.

Yahoo People Search

    http://www.yahoo.com/search/people

Yahoo has a useful directory that looks up people by name and optionally their address and gives you the full address and phone number. This system is the same as Four11 (described in the following section) but with Yahoo-ish screens.

Four11 (Four-eleven)

    http://www.four11.com

You can search for addresses and phone numbers (the same as with the Yahoo People Search) and e-mail addresses. If you don't like your own listing, you can add, update, or delete it.

American Directory Assistance

    http://www.abii.com/

(Click American Directory Assistance.)

This site is another white pages directory. After you have found the entry you want, you can ask for a graphical street map of the address.

WhoWhere

http://www.whowhere.com

WhoWhere is another e-mail address directory. Although Four11 usually gives better results, some people are listed in WhoWhere who aren't listed in other places.

Canada 411

http://www.canada411.sympatico.ca

Canada 411 is a Canadian telephone book that is complete except for the boring provinces of Alberta and Saskatchewan. Canada 411 is sponsored by most of the major Canadian telephone companies. Aussi disponible en français, eh? (***Note to residents of Alberta and Saskatchewan:*** Advise Telus and Saskatel to prove that you're not boring by joining up and adding their listings. Saskatel has a separate directory at http://www.saskyellowpages.com/ that is still pretty boring but better than nothing.)

Bigfoot

http://www.bigfoot.com

Bigfoot provides a way to search for people in addition to permanent, free e-mail addresses for life. ***Warning:*** After you're listed at Bigfoot, either voluntarily or if they found your name some other way, you have no way to remove the listing, either automatically or manually. We find this situation obnoxious.

Mail, one more time

Mailing lists are another important resource. Most lists (but not all — check before you ask) welcome concrete, politely phrased questions related to the list's topic. See Chapter 7 to find more information about mailing lists, including how to look for lists of particular topics of interest to you.

The hard-boiled egg test

Our friend Doug Hacker claims to be able to find the answer to any factual query on the Net in less time than it takes to hard-boil an egg — about ten minutes. Carol challenged him to find a quote she vaguely knew from the liner notes of a Duke Ellington album, whose title she couldn't remember. He had the complete quote in about an hour but spent less than five minutes himself. How? He found a mailing list about Duke Ellington, subscribed, and asked the question. Several members replied in short order. The more time you spend finding your way around the Net, the more you know where to go for the information you need.

Buying Stuff on the Web

Shopping online makes sense for many of the same reasons that make shopping from mail-order catalogs so popular. You can find stuff online that's not available at a local store, if a local store even exists. The online selection may be better and the prices lower, and online stores are invariably open all night. Although most online stores are in North America, a growing number are in other countries, often with stuff you can't get in North America in any other way.

Online stores are as varied as mail-order stores, and just as good and bad catalogs exist, good and bad stores exist. If you see a reasonable-looking store with something you want and a good price, however, give it a try.

Is it safe to use my credit card?

How do you pay for stuff you buy online? Most often, with a credit card, the same way you pay for anything else. Isn't it incredibly, awfully dangerous to give out your credit card number online, though? Well, no.

Many people seem to be concerned that bad guys with packet sniffers and network analyzers and who-knows-what other kind of high-tech snooping equipment can steal your number as it's traveling over the Net. We have been looking for several years for reports of this situation happening, and, as far as we can tell, none exists. It doesn't happen. For one thing, most online stores arrange to encrypt the message between your computer and the store's server (indicated in your browser by a closed lock icon or unbroken key in the bottom-left corner of the window); for another, trying to pluck the occasional credit card number from the gigabytes of traffic that's flowing every minute on the Net is not so easy, even without encryption.

If you can live with the risk of using your plastic at a restaurant, where you give your physical card with your physical signature to the server who takes it to the back room and does something with it out of your sight, you should be able to live with the risk of sending your number to an online store. We have often said that if we wanted to steal credit card numbers, we wouldn't waste time online — we would go Dumpster diving for credit card receipts and carbons.

If, after this harangue, you still don't want to send your plastic over the Net or you're one of the fiscally responsible holdouts who doesn't do plastic, most online stores are happy to have you call in your number over the phone or send them a check.

Online shopping carts

Stores on the Web work in two general ways: with and without virtual shopping carts. In stores without carts, you either order one item at a time or fill out a big order form with a check box for everything the store offers. In stores with carts, as you look at the items the store has for sale, you can add items to your cart and then visit the virtual checkout line when you're done and provide your payment and delivery information. Until you visit the checkout line, you can add and remove items as many times as you want, just like in the real world — except that when you remove something, you don't have to put it back on the shelf.

Where do I buy an aardvark?

All the serious directories and indices now put shopping information somewhere on their home page to help get your credit card closer to the Web faster. Some are even sponsored by VISA. You can find department stores and catalogs from all over offering every conceivable item (and some inconceivable items). Give it a try.

Speling counts

A major reason that searches fail is that one of the search words is spelled wrong. Check carefully. We once did a search on an embarrassing disease and found the three sites in the world that had misspelled it the same way we did. (Thanks to our friend Jean Armour Polly, for reminding us about this problem.)

Chapter 11

Channel Surfing and Other Unlikely Ways to Use the Web

• •

In This Chapter

▶ Displaying Web pages by using the Active Desktop

▶ Using Web pages as window backgrounds

• •

*M*uch of the appeal of Windows 98 is its integration with the Internet. As you probably have figured out by now, unless your computer is permanently connected to the Internet through a Local Area Network, connecting to the Internet means dialing from Windows 98 to your Internet service provider (interrupting your work), tying up a telephone line (inconvenient), and getting data from the Internet as fast as you can (which usually isn't very fast). All this means that if Windows 98 were really integrated with the Internet, using it would be filled with interruptions, inconvenient, and slow. Fortunately, Windows 98 isn't that integrated with the Internet. Although getting information from the Internet in Windows 98 is easier than in previous versions of Windows and you can do some things in Windows 98 that you couldn't do in previous versions of Windows, all these enhancements are voluntary: You have to go out and decide that you want to turn them on. We talk about some of these Windows Internet integration features in this chapter:

 ✔ You can replace that boring black screen (or that exciting picture you use as wallpaper on your Windows 98 desktop) with a Web page.

 ✔ Perhaps a more interesting feature is that you can display a Web channel on your PC, either in an Internet Explorer (or Netscape Navigator) window or on your desktop itself. A *channel* is a collection of Web pages your PC goes out and gets on whatever schedule you tell it. That way, whenever you want to look at those Web pages, the interruptions, inconvenience, and slow speed are all out of the way, and you can see just the content you're interested in.

✔ Another form of broadcasting to your PC uses live data feeds, in which information flows automatically to your screen. One example is a stock market ticker: You can have the current price of your favorite stock in your face all the time. For live data feeds to work, you have to be online all the time.

Windows 98 comes with several Internet-related "convenience" features because Microsoft wants you to get as much help as possible from the Web rather than bother its real live support engineers. The Internet is also a great mechanism for distributing software updates — improvements to Windows 98. We talk in this chapter about the pros and cons of this approach.

The (Hyper-)Active Desktop

It used to be that a real desktop was a good analogy for your Windows desktop. The desktop was just that: a desktop, on top of which you put things, usually icons that ran programs or windows through which programs communicated to you. Microsoft decided to change your boring old regular desktop into a desktop covered with a mixture of information from your hard disk and from the Internet. To distinguish this new look from the old Internet-free Windows, Microsoft named it the *Active Desktop* — "Active" because it can feed you information from the Internet at any time.

After you clear away all the hype, however, the new Active Desktop is just like the old inactive desktop, except for these three features:

✔ **Web style:** To complete the mixture (confusion?) of your system with the Internet, Microsoft lets you make your Active Desktop act more like a Web page. You can set your desktop to run programs by single-clicking rather than double-clicking and to underline icon names so that they look like the links on Web pages. Both these changes make the Active Desktop feel more like a Web page than the old inactive desktop did.

Many people who were used to previous versions of Windows, however, don't like the changes, so Microsoft lets you have it your way: You can turn the features of the Active Desktop on or off individually. That's why Chapter 3 has a sidebar titled "With a double-click here and a single-click there." We refer to this sidebar in each of the succeeding chapters in this book, to make sure that your Windows 98 desktop is set up the same way ours was when we wrote the instructions. If you've chosen the Web-style desktop (single clicking), the way we suggest in Chapter 3, the icon names on your desktop are underlined, as though they were links on a Web page.

✔ **Putting Web pages on the desktop:** Active Desktop lets you display a whole list of items (usually Web pages) on your desktop; read the next two sections to find out how.

✔ **The channel bar:** The only other difference between viewing your Active Desktop as a Web page and viewing it as a boring old desktop is the presence or absence of the Internet Explorer channel bar, which we talk about in the section "Finding and Crossing the English Channel," later in this chapter.

Putting a tiger in your tank and a Web page on your desktop

Although we whisk you by it rather quickly in Chapter 3, the Display Properties dialog box is the key to seeing Web pages on your desktop. Why would you want to display Web pages on your desktop? We can think of two reasons. One is to display live feeds, such as stock market prices, which requires that you be connected to the Internet all the time. The other is to alert you to changes in Web sites that change every so often. Our favorite example is that of our local performing arts center. Every week or so, it updates its Web site with new performances, and we always forget to check it. With the Active Desktop, the up-to-date Web site can always appear in one corner of our screen and we can browse more deeply if we see something that looks interesting.

Here's the simple way to display a Web page on your desktop:

1. *Right*-click a blank portion of your desktop.

   Depending on how many Web pages and icons you have on your desk, this step can be a difficult trick. For most of us, however, some space on the desktop shows. You know that you're in the right place when nothing is highlighted under your mouse pointer and you're not on top of a Web page. When you right-click the desktop itself, you see a pop-up menu; the first pick on this menu is Active Desktop.

2. Choose <u>A</u>ctive Desktop⇨<u>C</u>ustomize my Desktop from the pop-up menu.

   You see the Display Properties dialog box with a number of tabs in it, as shown in Figure 11-1. Although the Web tab should be selected, if it's not, click the word *Web* to bring it to your screen. The box labeled View My Active Desktop as a Web Page should have a check mark in it; if it doesn't, you haven't followed the instructions in Chapter 3 (shame on you!). This check box controls whether Active Desktop is working on your computer. Turn it on now because you won't be able to see Web pages on your desktop unless this box has a check mark in it.

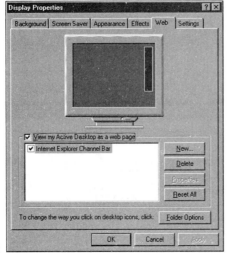

Figure 11-1:
The Active
Desktop
tells you
what it's
planning to
show you.

The box below this check box lists the Web pages to display on your
Active Desktop. Windows 98 comes with one web-page-like-thing
preinstalled. The Internet Explorer channel bar (not to be confused
with the active channels bar *in* Internet Explorer, which we talk about in
the section "Finding and Crossing the English Channel," later in this
chapter) isn't really a Web page, although it behaves like one, so we
ignore the difference.

Right now, ignore the entire thing and tell Windows 98 that you want to
display on your desktop a Web page of your own choosing.

3. Click the New button.

You are greeted by the New Active Desktop Item dialog box. Microsoft
has correctly determined that putting a boring old Web page on your
desktop may not make you immediately appreciate all the time and
effort you may have taken to upgrade to Windows 98. It keeps the
Active Desktop Gallery (a page full of widgets you may want to add to
your desktop) on the Microsoft Web site, just to give you a sense of
what's possible. Right now, skip the gallery and concentrate on putting
a simple Web page on the desktop.

4. Click No to tell Microsoft that you're going it alone.

You see a New Active Desktop Item dialog box with the Location box, in
which you can type the address of the Web page you want to put on
your desktop. You may find it useful to press the Browse button *if* you
have bookmarked the page you want to add to your desktop (in that
case, you may find the page somewhere in your Favorites folder).
Otherwise, warm up those fingers and type the Web address yourself.

5. Click OK when you have the address you want.

Congratulations — you're probably finished. Click OK. The Web page you specified should appear on your desktop. (Don't worry if it doesn't; the rest of this chapter contains lots more information about getting Web pages to appear!)

What exactly have you accomplished? You've taken a Web page (the same kind of Web page you're used to seeing in Internet Explorer or Netscape Navigator) and placed it on your desktop, behind any icons or windows that may be floating there. Windows has gone out to the Internet and gotten a copy of the Web page and stashed it somewhere on your computer so that it can redisplay it without having to connect to the Internet again (avoiding the interruption, inconvenience, and slowness of getting things from the Net directly). Figure 11-2 shows our Windows 98 desktop with the marquee from our performing arts center, the Flynn Theatre. Every morning over coffee, two clicks and no Internet access get us to what's new at the Flynn. We like that!

You can display more than one Web page on your Active Desktop. In fact, the Display Properties dialog box has space for a whole list of Web pages. After you have some Web pages on your desktop, you can drag them around and put each one exactly where you want it (see the section "Moving an Active Desktop item," a little later in this chapter).

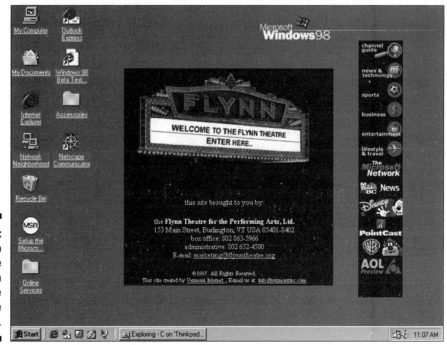

Figure 11-2:
Our desktop
with the
Flynn
Theatre
web page
on it.

Active content for your Active Desktop

With all the work people have been doing on the World Wide Web, you can put a few pretty cool things on your desktop, and more are coming out every day. About every six months, someone comes up with a new technology to distribute fancier and fancier kinds of information over the Web. Just about every week, someone comes up with a new way to use that technology. *Desktop widgets*, which Microsoft offers in its Active Desktop Gallery, are samples of what these technologies can do.

Geekspeak review: A *widget* is a little *thing* that does something. Kinds of widgets include those little toys you sometimes find on people's desks that do strange things and those bizarre tools you find on someone's workbench — the kind whose purpose defies your imagination. *Desktop widgets* are slightly fancy Web pages. The idea of the widgets is to be an information source you can put on your desktop and forget about, sort of like a radio playing in the background. When something catches your attention, you can get more information about it.

To check out desktop widgets, get back to the Display Properties dialog box that was shown in Figure 12-1: Either right-click the desktop and choose Active Desktop⇨Customize My Desktop from the pop-up menu or click the Start button and choose Settings⇨Control Control Panel and click the Display icon. In either case, click the Web tab.

To see the Microsoft gallery of desktop widgets, click the New button to tell Windows 98 to create a new active desktop item. This time, when you see the New Active Desktop Item dialog box, click Yes to tell Microsoft, "Yes, by all means, we would love to see your Active Desktop Gallery."

Quicker than a New York minute, your computer connects to the Internet and Internet Explorer displays a Web page at the Microsoft Web site. The Active Desktop Gallery contains about a dozen widgets, divided into such categories as news, sports, business, and weather, as shown in Figure 11-3.

The flagship example of a Microsoft desktop widget is the stock market ticker. When the Active Desktop Gallery appears, it includes the Microsoft Investor ticker. Along the way, Internet Explorer probably asked whether it could download some programs to your computer to make the ticker work. Although people debate the safety of getting programs off the Internet, we've never had any problem with browser code (Java) from a commercial site such as the one at Microsoft, so we click Yes.

If you like the that stock ticker, you can have it. Hmm, doesn't that sound a little like someone trying to start you on a habit? It's part of the Active Desktop Gallery's News category, so click the News icon to the left of the window. Those old software peddlers give you a list with a few free sample information pages to get you started, including that stock market ticker.

If you click the Microsoft Investor Ticker, the ticker reappears on the right side of your Internet Explorer window. The Add to Active Desktop button, below the ticker, entices you to start your data habit. By all means, feel free to click it — you can always delete the stock ticker program later. As you download the ticker, a dialog box asks you to confirm that you want to download it. A second dialog box asks you to confirm your subscription — click OK in that one too. (We talk more about subscriptions in the section "I want what I want the way I want it when I want it," later in this chapter.) You may see a security alert about accepting programs off the Internet, although we think that that's usually okay too. After you've responded to all these questions, you see the ticker downloading its content for the first time so that you can see it. And then? Nothing. Why? Because it's behind all your windows! Remember that the ticker is on the desktop.

Put your mouse pointer down on the taskbar, on a spot where you're not clicking the names of any of your running programs, and *right*-click. You see a pop-up menu that includes the Minimize All Windows option. Presto! You should see your desktop with the Microsoft Investor Ticker on it.

Figure 11-3:
The
Microsoft
Active
Desktop
Gallery.

Keeping the ticker ticking

If you gaze at the ticker, you notice that it doesn't change much. When was the last time the Dow Jones Industrials spent half an hour at the same point? On the left side of the ticker is a little button labeled Custom. Click this button and you can decide how often the ticker should check for new quotes. As the stock ticker program arrives from Microsoft, it updates every half-hour. Using this dialog box, you can make the program update every minute. This dialog box is unique to the ticker, however, because the ticker is almost unique in needing to give you continuously updated information.

The little box also lets you specify what stock symbols you want to see on your ticker and what news categories you want to see. This task is not unusually complicated for a desktop widget that's so active.

Finally, and most important, the ticker is typical in that you can click any of the stock quotes or headlines as they stream by to see more detailed information about them. Each of the headlines and quotes is in fact a link to additional information.

For information about how to update other active items on your desktop, take a look at the section "I want what I want the way I want it when I want it," later in this chapter.

Care and feeding of your Active Desktop items

So just what is on the Active Desktop, anyway? *Active Desktop items* can be Web pages or widgets from the Microsoft Active Desktop Gallery. Each Active Desktop item appears in a little box: These items aren't traditional windows because everything else on your computer screen (including icons on your desktop) appears on top of them. Desktop items aren't programs either because they don't appear on the taskbar.

Active Desktop items are in very special windows, but windows nonetheless, which act similarly to other windows on your computer. This section tells you how to do windows-ish things to the Web pages and widgets on your Active Desktop.

Changing the size of an Active Desktop item

As you glide your mouse pointer over the edges of an Active Desktop item, two things happen. First, a gray border appears around the Active Desktop item. This *window border* shows you where the edge of the Active Desktop item is. (It may not be obvious if the background of the desktop item is the same color as your desktop.) Second (and you may have to move your mouse pointer slowly over the gray border to see it), the mouse pointer turns into a double-headed arrow. Clicking and dragging the double-headed arrow moves the window border, which changes the size of the Active Desktop item.

Your Active Desktop items may have scroll bars in them if they're too small to display their contents. Although these scroll bars work like regular scroll bars, we find them kind of annoying. Try resizing your Active Desktop windows until they go away.

Moving an Active Desktop item

When your mouse pointer gets near the top of an Active Desktop item, a fat, gray bar appears, similar to the title bar in a regular window. By clicking the bar and dragging it around, you can move the Active Desktop item around on your screen.

Remember that if you move the Active Desktop item over an icon on your desktop, the icons float *over* the desktop item. If you drag one Active Desktop item on top of another, Windows decides which one stays on top (usually the one you're dragging, so if you cover up an item, you have a tricky time finding the buried one).

Microsoft Internet Explorer, Netscape Navigator, the U.S. Department of Justice, and your Windows 98 Active Desktop

We've been careful to point out that everything you can do on the World Wide Web by using Microsoft Internet Explorer, you can also do by using Netscape Navigator. Because Microsoft owns the Windows 98 operating system, the Internet Explorer browser, and the Web site that contains the active desktop widgets we're talking about in this section of this chapter, however, you can probably guess what it did: The Web site asks your browser whether it was written by Microsoft. If your browser says "No," Microsoft refuses to show you its widgets — something like, "If you're his friend, you can't play with our toys." (Sounds like someone flunked out of kindergarten.)

These are the kinds of things the U.S. Department of Justice has been investigating, along with the attorneys general of several states. Chapter 3 has the legal overview. Meanwhile, you the customer must decide which browser you really want to use. Because Microsoft owns the desktop (it is *Microsoft* Windows 98, after all), however, the desktop widgets belong to that company.

Netscape Navigator has a webtop view that works similarly to much of the Microsoft Active Desktop, although that view doesn't have any dancing widgets for you to sample. The webtop gets its own section, "Viewing Channels with Netscape: The webtop," near the end of this chapter.

Hiding an Active Desktop item

In that title bar at the top of the Active Desktop item window, at the right end, you see a familiar X, like the one in a normal window. This X does just what you would expect: It closes the Active Desktop item (the item disappears). You can display it again from the Web tab of the Display Properties dialog box that was shown in Figure 11-1.

You can also hide an Active Desktop item by clicking the little down arrow at the left end of the title bar and choosing Close from the menu that appears.

Finding and Crossing the English Channel

If you've read about Windows 98, you've read about channels. What's the difference between an Active Desktop item and a channel? Not much. An Active Desktop item is a widget that sits on your desktop and does something cute, like the stock ticker. A *channel* is a coordinated set of Web pages that deliver content on their own schedule — channels look much like Web sites. Because Microsoft and Netscape had big plans for channels, people expected that the channel fad may have evolved into something different, although it seems to have cooled. Right now, however, the main difference between a channel and a Web page is the way you look at it. With a Web page, you tell your Internet browser to look at the Web page. With a channel, you select your channel from the channel bar or Netscape Netcaster window. (Read on for a description of both.)

Whether you use the channel bar or Netscape Netcaster, the basic things you have to do to see channel content are the same: Select your channel, and then subscribe to it. You tell Internet Explorer or Netscape Netcaster what content you want it to download and when. You also say how you want to view this information, in a browser window or on your desktop. Both products use different terms, of course, and give you different options. In this section, we take you through the process, first in Internet Explorer and then with Netscape Netcaster and Navigator.

Meet the channel bar

We talk about the channel bar throughout the first three parts of this book because it's the most visible sign of the new Internet features in Windows 98. Now, you finally get a chance to use it. The channel bar comes with your Windows 98 system and contains preview information for some favorite Microsoft Internet channels. The channel bar lets you preview a handful of channels without connecting to the Internet. After you decide that you want to subscribe to a channel or if you decide to peruse the full set of Microsoft channels, you dial out to the Internet as you would for a Web page.

You can move the channel bar around on your desktop just like you can move any other Active Desktop item: Click and drag its title bar.

Displaying channels with Internet Explorer

Figure 11-4 shows what happens when you click the News and Technology button on the channel bar. This rather peculiar-looking screen isn't as different from other screens as it may initially appear. What you're looking at is an Internet Explorer window in full-screen mode. Internet Explorer 4 has a *full-screen mode,* partly as a reaction to the fact that it has so many bells and whistles that not much room is left for the actual Web page you want to see. Another part of the reason for full-screen mode is that it makes channels look new and different. If you press the Full Screen button, as shown in Figure 11-4, Internet Explorer shrinks to a more familiar-looking window.

Internet Explorer has another peculiar behavior when it's displaying channels. If you weren't looking carefully at your screen, you may not have seen the list of channels that appears on the left side of Figure 11-4. The reason is that the list of channels has a habit of gliding off the left side of the Internet Explorer window. To see the list of channels again, click the Channel button on the Internet Explorer toolbar, as shown in Figure 11-4, or just move your mouse pointer over to the left window border to coax the list of channels to come back out.

The list of channels likes to hide so that you can see the other information displayed in the Internet Explorer window. As the text on the left side of the window indicates, the logos in the right part of the screen are links to over-views of each channel. Because these overviews come with Windows 98, you don't have to be connected to the Internet to see them. In most cases, they're just an advertisement for the channel itself. Some require that you insert the Windows 98 CD-ROM to display information about the channel. Each ad also contains an Add Active Channel button.

If you click the Add Active Channel button, your computer connects to the Internet to check out what the channel contains. Windows asks whether you want to subscribe to the channel. You have three choices: No, just keep it in the Channel Bar; Yes, but tell you only when updates occur; and Yes, notify you of updates and download the channel for offline viewing:

- ✔ If you just keep the channel on your channel bar, it works like a regular set of Web pages: You retrieve the information you want from the Internet when you want to see it.

- ✔ If you subscribe but just ask for notification of updates, you get an e-mail message from Internet Explorer every time it notices that the Web site has changed. It doesn't go online to download the Web site to your computer, however.

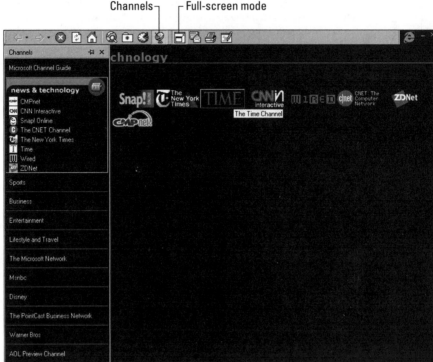

Figure 11-4:
Internet
Explorer
gives you
the channel
overview.

✔ If you ask for updates and downloading, you get the full effect: Based on the publisher's schedule (which you can change; see the section "I want what I want the way I want it when I want it," later in this chapter), Internet Explorer checks the contents of the channel, downloads it, and lets you know about it.

Displaying even more channels with Internet Explorer

The first of the channels listed in the channel bar isn't a channel but is in fact a link to an ever-changing list of channels that Microsoft keeps at its Web site. Because the Microsoft lists have hundreds of channels, the company has organized them into a few categories; click a category and you get a list, similar to the list you get from a Web search engine, of all the channels in the category. You can search for the channel you want or just browse through them a few at a time.

Each channel has an Add Active Channel button somewhere on its screen. If you find a channel you like, you can press the button to have the channel add itself to your channel bar. Then it acts just like the channels Microsoft features on the channel bar.

I want what I want the way I want it when I want it

A couple of tricks can help you get the Active Desktop to display what you really want when you really want it. Here are a few reasons you may want to know about these tricks:

✔ You can tell Internet Explorer how much of the channel's Web site you want it to download. For example, the updates page from our local arts center is two clicks away from the home page that was shown in Figure 11-2. One click gets us past the marquee, and the second gets us to the updated events. If we get just the opening page, then as soon as we click past the marquee, the computer would have to connect to the Internet for more information. (Although we could, of course, just get the page of updated events we're interested in, on a more news-oriented Web site, you may not know where you want to go from the front page; the links to the stories change every day.)

✔ You can control how often the Active Desktop goes out and gets a fresh copy of your Web pages. *Channels* (Web pages that expect to be picked up this way) can tell the desktop how often they want to be updated; regular Web pages get updated just once a day. But you can change that.

✔ You can control the fine points of whether the Active Desktop connects to the Internet just to retrieve your page and whether it does so while you're working.

✔ Your Web page may require that you log on with a username and password.

As usual with Windows, you can do most of this stuff in two ways: the Wizard way and the cast-your-own-spell way. The Subscription Wizard can be hard to find when you need it, though, and really isn't much simpler than doing it yourself. We show you how to do it yourself.

All the do-it-yourself incantations for Active Desktop Web pages start from the Display Properties dialog box that was shown in Figure 11-1. Display the dialog box by right-clicking the desktop and choosing Active Desktop⇨ Customize My Desktop from the pop-up menu; then click the Web tab. (You can also click the Windows 98 Start button and choose Settings⇨Control Control Panel and click the Display icon.)

After you've added Web pages to your Active Desktop, additional items appear on the list on the Web tab of the Display Properties dialog box, under the words *Internet Explorer Channel Bar.* To change the properties of an Active

Desktop item, click the item you want to cast spells over, and click the Properties button. You see the Desktop Item Properties dialog box, with the Subscription tab visible. Figure 11-5 shows the dialog box with all three tabs.

You can also display the properties for an Active Desktop item by displaying its title bar (cruise your mouse pointer over the top of the item and wait for the title bar to appear), clicking the down arrow at the left end of the title bar, and choosing Properties from the menu that appears.

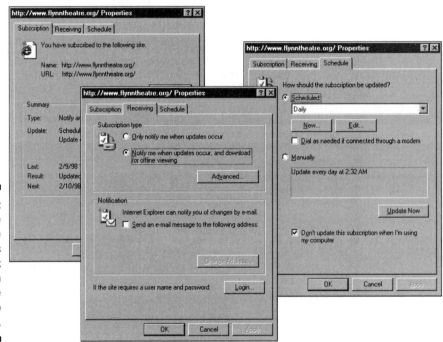

Figure 11-5:
The three tabs in the Properties dialog box for an Active Desktop item.

Hiding and exposing a page you've subscribed to

Look carefully again at Figure 11-1. Each of the Web pages you've put on your desktop has a check box in front of it. You can remove the Web page from your desktop by clearing the check box. You are still subscribed to the Web page; that is, Windows 98 continues to go out and download updates to the Web site according to the schedule you've given it. To be able to see it, however, you have to come back to this dialog box and fill in the check box again.

Providing a password for a Web page on your active desktop

Click the Receiving tab of the Desktop Item Properties dialog box, and then click the Login button. Windows asks you to enter your username and password for the Web pages you want to retrieve. Click OK after you've typed them, and click OK after you're done with the Desktop Item Properties dialog box.

The Wizard of Subscriptions

You can start the Subscription Wizard in two ways. One is from the Add Item to Active Desktop dialog box — that's what you see when you're at the end of the process of adding an item to your Active Desktop. The other way is from Internet Explorer. If you're looking at a Web page and choose Favorites⇨Add to Favorites, the dialog box you see contains a Customize button that starts the Subscription Wizard.

The Subscription Wizard is one of the more simple-minded wizards in Windows 98. It just gives you a slightly simplified version of the three dialog box tabs that are shown in Figure 11-5. If you start the Wizard, look through the instructions there; they should contain all the information you need to make it through the Wizard.

Getting several pages from the same Web site

Click the Receiving tab of the Desktop Item Properties dialog box, and then click the Advanced button. The Advanced Download Options dialog box is shown in Figure 11-6. The setting labeled Download Linked Pages within a Depth of is the one you're looking for. Translated into English, it says "Download all the pages within so many clicks of the home page." Setting this number to two means that we can click the Flynn Theatre's home page to get past the marquee and then click the Updates page we're really interested in, all without connecting to the Internet.

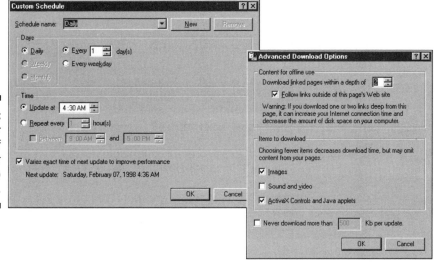

Figure 11-6: The finer points of your desktop web page.

It is probably important that you uncheck the check box labeled Follow Links Outside This Page's Web Site. Otherwise, you could end up downloading a tremendous amount of information from the Internet.

Preventing Windows 98 from automatically updating the Web pages on your Active Desktop

The Active Desktop (in our opinion) is designed for people whose computers are permanently connected to the Internet, usually at a company or school. These people don't really care how often their computers zip out to the Internet to update information. At the other extreme, those people who have only one telephone line they share with their computer probably care a great deal about when their computer picks up the telephone. In consideration of those folks, Windows 98 enables you to update your Web pages only when you want.

On the Schedule tab of the Desktop Item Properties dialog box is the Manually setting. Click this setting if you want the whole dialing and updating process to happen only when you tell it to, with no automatic updates. To update the Web pages on your desktop, you have to run Internet Explorer and then choose Favorites⇨Update All Subscriptions. Although that command connects to the Internet just as though you wanted to see the Web page in the Internet Explorer Web browser, it runs down the list of Web pages on your desktop and updates all of them.

Getting pages daily, weekly, or monthly

Click the Schedule tab of the Desktop Item Properties dialog box to show you when Windows thinks that it should go get the Web pages you just said you were interested in. The exact schedule appears under the Manually setting (which can be a little confusing). You can click in the Scheduled box to choose Daily, Weekly, or Monthly.

If the Windows schedules are not to your liking, you can click the Edit button and look at the Custom Schedule dialog box (also shown in Figure 11-6) and set up your own schedule. Or you can click the New button to create and name your own schedule and get different options depending on whether you click Daily, Weekly, or Monthly first.

We want to point out that the check box labeled Varies Exact Time of Next Update to Improve Performance is present not so much to help you as to help the Internet. Imagine the traffic jam at 4:30 a.m. if all 100 million Windows computers got on the Internet to update their Web pages. Unless the exact time of your update really matters to you, do the rest of us a favor and leave this box checked.

Making sure that Windows 98 can connect by using your modem

Many of those people we talked about a couple of paragraphs ago whose computers are permanently connected to the Internet have laptop computers that are sometimes on the corporate net and sometimes not. When the computers are not on the corporate net, they usually connect to the Internet by telephone, which is much slower. Windows 98 is faced with the question: If it can't get to the Internet by using a Local Area Network, should it try using the telephone?

If you're in a hotel room somewhere, the answer to this question is probably No. If you're at home and the only way your computer *ever* connected to the Internet is over the phone, the answer is probably Yes. That's what the Dial As Needed check box is for (it's on the Schedule tab of the Desktop Item Properties dialog box). Those of us who use only dial-up connections to the Internet should make sure that this box is checked, to enable Windows 98 to make a phone call when necessary. Otherwise, all this scheduling stuff is to no avail because Windows 98 will try to update your Web pages and won't be able to find the Internet. You may see a dialog box from Windows asking whether you're really sure that you want to let Windows dial at will. You are.

Checking out the channels with Netscape Netcaster

Because Netscape and Microsoft are dueling for dominance in the Internet market, both offer channels. What's more, you can't watch a Netscape channel from Microsoft Internet Explorer, and you can't watch a Microsoft channel from Netscape. And, with few exceptions, the channels available from one are not available from the other. *If* you're interested in checking out channels, therefore, it's worth checking them both out.

Netcaster is the program that displays the Netscape version of the channel bar. Netcaster is similar in function to the channel bar, but because it doesn't come with Windows 98, it has to dial out to the Internet almost immediately to show you the channel previews. Figure 11-7 shows what the Netcaster Channel Guide looks like on-screen.

The browser window that's displayed with Netcaster seems unnecessary, especially because Netcaster brings up *another* Netscape browser window to preview channels for you. We usually just close this window by clicking the icon on the title bar just to the left of the words *Netscape Channel.* From the resulting menu, choose Close. Check out the section "Casting your custom net," later in this chapter, for tips on how to make this window go away.

Like Internet Explorer, Netcaster can show or hide the channels itself, but rather than automatically hide the list of channels the way Internet Explorer does, Netcaster gives you a little tab to press to make the channels appear and disappear, as shown in Figure 11-7.

Meet Netscape Netcaster

When you run Netcaster, it appears as a strip on the right side of your screen, as shown in Figure 11-7. The Netcaster window consists of two lists: a list of channels Netscape wants you to peruse (the Channel Finder list) and a list of My Channels (channels you have subscribed to). To switch between the two lists, click the little triangles beside the name of each one. You cannot see both lists at the same time.

At the bottom of the Netcaster window is a small menu with four selections: New, Options, Help, and Exit. Help and Exit do exactly what you may expect. The New option gives you a way to subscribe to a channel without using the Channel Finder, and Options controls both your channels and the behavior of the Netcaster window. In the next section, we take a closer look at subscribing and channel options.

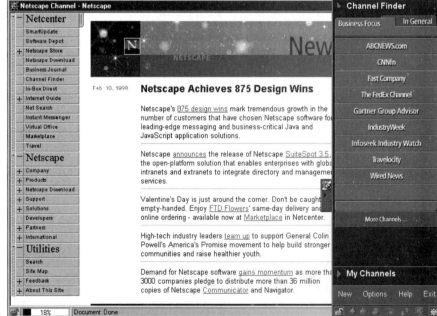

Figure 11-7:
The Netscape Netcaster Channel Guide (and the browser that comes with it).

At the bottom of the Netcaster screen is a row of icons that are not part of the Netcaster screen. They control the behavior of the *webtop,* the Netscape version of the Active Desktop. The webtop deserves its own section, which we give it just ahead.

Subscribing with Netcaster

Clicking a channel in the Channel Finder displays the channel's logo and displays two options directly beneath the logo. You can preview the channel or subscribe to it directly. The previews are single screens that give you an idea of the channel's content, and most of the subscriptions let you look at a couple of screens before you subscribe, so we definitely think that you should just plunge ahead and subscribe. You can always stop before you're fully subscribed, and unsubscribing is easy.

You may be confronted with an unsettling surprise when you go to subscribe to one of the Netscape channels: You have to sign up with Netscape. That wouldn't be so bad if it weren't for the rather intrusive survey Netscape wants you to fill out. It wants your name, street address, and e-mail address — if you're feeling generous, you can tell it all about how you use the Internet. In fairness, Microsoft already knows your e-mail address from when you set up your Internet parameters in Internet Explorer or when you set up Microsoft Outlook. If you registered Windows 98, it knows your street address too. What's annoying about is that Netscape gives no indication what it will do with this information — thoughts of junk mail and e-mail spam do come to mind, however.

What's more, Netscape may not remember who you are from time to time. In that case, you may have to tell it your e-mail address so that it can find you again.

After you've convinced Netscape of your bona fides, the channel you're subscribing to *disappears* and the Channel Properties dialog box appears. In most cases, you can just click OK to accept the Netscape suggestions. After you do, the dialog box disappears. The channel has already disappeared, and Netcaster may have disappeared too! Inspirational, isn't it? You can get the Netcaster window back by pressing the Netcaster button on the taskbar or pressing the little Netcaster tab. When you open up My Channels, you find that the channel you just subscribed to has been added.

You can, of course, customize a little of what goes on with Netcaster. The following section describes how.

Casting your custom net

You can customize two aspects of the Netscape channels from the Options button: how Netcaster itself behaves and how any particular channel behaves.

The Layout tab on the Netcaster Options dialog box lets you put the Netcaster list of channels on the right or left side of the screen and control whether the Netcaster window automatically hides when you go to look at a channel.

Most interesting, however, is the Default Channel. When we first talk about Netcaster (a few pages back), we mention that the program seems to come with a worthless Netscape Navigator window. You can convince it not to open that window by clicking None as your Default Channel.

The Channels tab does two things for you: lets you see a list of channels you have subscribed to and lets you change the properties of those channels. Click a channel and then the Properties button, and you see *another* three-headed dialog box.

The Channel Properties dialog box, with its three tabs, is shown in Figure 11-8. The meaning of these tabs is not too obscure: The General tab gives you a limited selection of update schedules, and the Display tab lets you choose between seeing your channel in a Navigator window and seeing it on your webtop (we talk about the webtop in a minute).

The Cache tab lets you decide how many clicks deep you want to go in the site and how much of your hard disk you want to allow this channel to take up. Generally, the more levels you download, the longer each update takes, but the more stuff you can view without getting on the Internet.

More Netcaster channels

You may not find the original list of channels provided by Netscape to be very interesting. At the bottom of the Channel Finder list is the More Channels button. Clicking this button takes to you a channel at Netscape containing more than a dozen different *categories* of channels. Browse through the tabs and channels. In each category, you can click the name of a channel to see a small description and sample picture of the channel. Some channels have a Preview button, though the previews seldom show much more than you can see in the Channel Finder window. An Add Channel button appears below the sample.

Don't be shy about adding channels; they're easy to remove later.

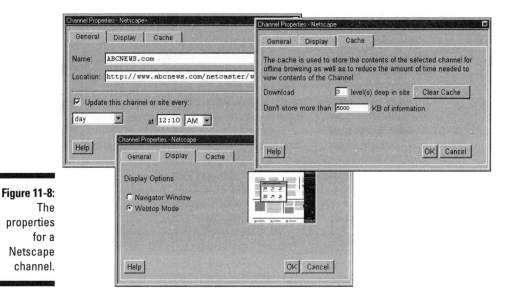

Figure 11-8:
The
properties
for a
Netscape
channel.

Fewer Netcaster channels

To unsubscribe from a channel, go back to the Netcaster window, click the Options button at the bottom of the channels list, and look at the Options dialog box. To delete a channel, click its name and click the Delete button.

Viewing channels with Netscape: The webtop

After you've subscribed to one or more channels, you probably want to look at them. That's easy: In the Netcaster window, click the triangle next to My Channels. You see a list of channels you've subscribed to. Figure 11-9 shows what your list of channels looks like. Channels with green dots beside them have been updated recently. Channels with a little TV beside them are *webtop channels* — they want to take up the entire screen.

Figure 11-9:
What
channels
have you
subscribed
to in
Netcaster?

Most Netscape channels appear in a regular Netscape browser window. You can have channels that take up the entire screen, however, which Netscape calls a webtop; the similarity to the desktop is intentional. Unlike with Internet Explorer, you can see those channels when other things are on the desktop, by clicking some of the icons at the bottom of the Channel Finder window. In fact, as we mention when you first meet Netcaster, those icons aren't really part of the Channel Finder. When you click the Channel Finder's tab to make it shrink or when you're viewing the webtop, they're still there. That's a good thing because they enable you to control what you're seeing on the webtop. Figure 11-10 shows the webtop icons that appear at the bottom of the screen. Here's what they do:

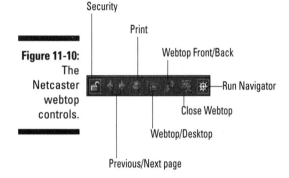

Figure 11-10: The Netcaster webtop controls.

Security

Print

Webtop Front/Back

Run Navigator

Close Webtop

Webtop/Desktop

Previous/Next page

- ✔ **Security:** Tells you whether the site you're visiting supports one of the Internet's schemes for sending and receiving information in ways that others can't look at it.

- ✔ **Previous Page and Next Page:** Work just as they would in a browser, if the webtop page you're looking at has multiple pages.

- ✔ **Print:** Prints. (Surprise!)

- ✔ **Webtop/Desktop:** Toggles between viewing the webtop channel and your Windows 98 desktop.

- ✔ **Webtop Front or Back:** Puts your running programs in front of the webtop or behind it. (Internet Explorer could use a button like this one.)

- ✔ **Close Webtop:** Closes the channel that is being displayed on the webtop.

- ✔ **Run Navigator:** Does just that, in case you decide that you would rather be browsing.

Part IV
Other Stuff You Can Do on the Internet

The 5th Wave   By Rich Tennant

"Just how accurately should my Web site reflect my place of business?"

In this part . . .

Computer geeks enjoy collecting software from the Net. Photographers enjoy collecting pictures from the Net. Collectors enjoy getting catalogs from the Net. No matter what you get from the Net, you have to know how to get it on your computer. That's what downloading is all about. You can also waste (or invest) a tremendous amount of time chatting with people on the Internet. And nobody should be without a home page on the World Wide Web. We show you how to make your own.

Chapter 12

Downloading, Uploading, and Other File-Flinging Fun

• •

In This Chapter

▶ Understanding why people download files from the Net

▶ Downloading using your Web browser

▶ Looking at file-transfer basics

▶ Giving your Web browser FTP URLs to swipe files

▶ Using better file-transfer programs, like WS_FTP

▶ Uploading files to the Net

▶ Installing software you've grabbed from the Net

▶ Getting WinZip to handle zip files

• •

*F*irst, the fancy terminology: *Downloading* means copying files from a
computer that's Up There on the Internet "down" to the computer
you're using. Because the Internet has an amazing number of cool files
available, lots of stuff is available to download. *Uploading* is the reverse —
copying a file from your computer "up" to a computer on the Internet. If
your Internet service provider lets you "publish" Web pages, you upload
your Web pages to your provider's computer to do the publishing. *File
transfer* means to copy files from one system to another — downloading or
uploading. *FTP* stands for File Transfer Protocol, one way that computers
transfer files across the Internet.

In this chapter, we tell you about two ways to download files: using a Web
browser and using an FTP program. The Web is the easiest way to download
files, although you usually can't upload. FTP programs can both download
and upload.

Why Download Files?

Because lots of cool stuff is available out there for free. You can download programs, pictures, sounds, and text to your computer — the process is relatively quick, and the price is right. Much of the Internet software we use with PPP accounts, for example, you can download right from the Internet, and you can also get nice clip art, recipes — you name it!

Why Upload Files?

Well, you may be a crackerjack programmer who has written a wonderful program you want to contribute to one of the many libraries of shareware and freeware on the Internet. The most common reason to upload files, however, is to create or update a Web site; you create the Web pages for your Web site on your computer and then upload them to a Web server, as described in Chapter 15.

Downloading Web Pages

Getting files over the Web is simplicity itself. You probably have been doing it for ages and didn't even know. Every Web page, every icon or image on a Web page, every ornate Web background is a file. Every time you click a link or type a URL to go to a Web page, you're getting at least one file. (If it's a page with a large number of graphics, you're getting a large number of files, one per picture.)

The technical term for the way that files are transferred by using the Web is *HTTP,* or *Hypertext Transport Protocol.* In English, this term means that your browser sends a command across the Internet to the Web server on which a file is stored, asking for the file to be sent to your computer. All you have to do to trigger this type of command is to know where to click. (We crabby old nerds feel that this stuff makes life much too simple, but such is the price of progress.)

Downloading pictures

To download a picture over the Web, first display the picture in your Web browser. When you see on a Web page a picture you want to save on your hard disk, right-click the picture. From the menu that appears, choose Save Image As or Save Picture As. Tell your browser where to save the picture. That's all it takes!

Graphics files have filename extensions that identify what graphics format the file is in. When you download a picture, you can change the name of the file, but *don't* change the extension. Most of the graphics files on Web pages have the extension GIF or JPEG or JPG because these are the types of graphics files that most Web browsers can display.

Just because a picture is now stored on your hard disk doesn't mean that you own it. Most pictures on Web pages are copyrighted. Unless a picture comes from a site that specifically offers pictures as reusable "clip art," you have to get permission to use the picture for commercial purposes or even to upload it to your own noncommercial Web page.

Downloading programs

Downloading a program file over the Web is also easy — you click a link to it, frequently a link that says either Download or the name of the program. Your Web browser stops and asks you what to do with the file. If it's a program (an EXE or COM file) or a zip file, the most reasonable thing for your browser to do is to save it to disk so that you can run it or unzip it later. If it's a zip file and you have WinZip (mentioned later in this chapter) installed, you can also tell the browser to run WinZip directly, by making it the handler program for zip files; we find that method less handy than you may think.

If you're interested in downloading an Internet program, for example, you may go to TUCOWS, The Ultimate Collection of Windows Software, at http://www.tucows.com. After you're at the site, click a link to choose a site near you, choose Windows 95 or Windows 98, and choose the type of program you want to download. TUCOWS displays a Web page like the one shown in Figure 12-1, with a list of programs available for downloading. To download a program file, just click the name of the program, the Download button (if you see one), or any other link that looks like it may download something.

To make absolutely sure that your browser downloads a file for which you have a Web link to the disk, rather than try to run it, display it, or otherwise get clever, hold down the Shift key while you click the link.

Downloading other files

To download other types of files — sound files, video files, whatever — you follow the same steps as for downloading a program. Find a Web page that contains a link to the file you want. For sound clips of news stories, for example, you can try the National Public Radio Web site, at http://www.npr.org. Then click the link for the file you want, and tell your browser where to store it.

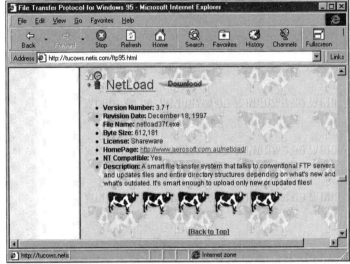

Figure 12-1:
Click the
program
name to
download
the program
file.

File Transfer in Theory and Practice

Being able to download files from the Web is great, although not all files are *available* over the Web. And what if you want to upload a file? You need FTP — File Transfer Protocol.

Transferring a file via FTP requires two participants: an *FTP client program* and an *FTP server program.* The FTP client is the program that we, the Joe Six-Pack Users of the world, run on our computers. The FTP server is the program that runs on the huge mainframe somewhere (or, these days, likely as not, on a PC under someone's desk) and stores tens of thousands of files. The FTP server is similar to an online library of files. The FTP client can *upload* (send) files to the FTP server or, more commonly, *download* (receive) files from the FTP server.

Thousands of publicly accessible FTP servers exist, and they store hundreds of thousands of files. Many of the files are freeware or shareware programs. Some FTP servers are so popular that they can't handle the number of file requests they receive. When FTP servers are inundated, other FTP servers, called *mirrors,* which have copies of the same files, are set up to handle the overflow traffic.

Anonymous downloads

To use an FTP server, you have to log in with a username and password. What happens if you don't have an account on the FTP server machine? No problem, if it's a publicly accessible FTP server. You log in as anonymous and type your e-mail address as your password. Voilà! You have access to lots of files! This method of using public FTP servers is called *anonymous FTP.* There's nothing sleazy about it; public FTP sites expect you to use anonymous FTP to download files.

Text files versus everything else

FTP puts files into two different categories: ASCII and binary. An *ASCII* file is a text file; a *binary* file is anything else. FTP has two modes — ASCII and binary (also called *image* mode) — to transfer the two types of files. When you transfer an ASCII file between different types of computers that store text files differently, ASCII mode automatically adjusts the file during the transfer so that the file is a valid text file when it's stored on the receiving end. (Because Macs, Windows, and UNIX all have slightly different conventions for storing text files, this automatic conversion can save a great deal of hassle.) A binary file is left alone and transferred verbatim.

Choosing an FTP client program

If you want to get files by FTP, you need an FTP client program. Luckily, you have several excellent ways to do so:

- ✔ **Use your Web browser.** Most browsers can handle anonymous FTP for downloading files (no anonymous uploading — you probably didn't want to do that anyway). See the next section, "Downloading Files By Using Your Web Browser."

- ✔ **If you have a PPP account, you can use a Winsock program.** The most popular freeware Windows FTP program is WS_FTP, and you find out how to use it in this chapter (in the section "Downloading with WS_FTP"). WS_FTP can handle both uploading and downloading files by using both anonymous FTP or private accounts on an FTP server.

- ✔ **Use the Windows 98 built-in FTP program.** Yes, Windows 98 comes with an FTP client program, but it's so old-fashioned that we don't suggest you use it.

- ✔ **If you use America Online (AOL) or CompuServe, it's easy to get files via anonymous FTP.** On both services, use the keyword **ftp**.

A few anonymous FTP tips

Some FTP servers limit the number of anonymous users or the times of day that anonymous FTP is allowed. You may be refused access, but don't gripe about it — no law says that the owner of the system has to provide any access.

Don't store *(upload)* files on the FTP server unless the owner invites you to do so. A directory called INCOMING or something similar is usually available in which you can put stuff.

Some FTP servers allow anonymous FTP only from host computers that have names. That is, if you try to FTP anonymously from a host that has a number but no name, these hosts don't let you in. This problem occurs most often with PPP dial-up accounts, which, because they generally offer no services that are useful to other people, don't always have names assigned. If you have this problem, complain to your Internet service provider, who can fix it easily.

Downloading Files By Using Your Web Browser

To get your Web browser to transfer files by using FTP, you use a special kind of URL: an FTP URL. (Don'tcha love these acronyms!) Interestingly, browsers are smart enough to tell which files are ASCII and which are binary. You don't have to worry about it.

The URL of FTP

When you've used your Web browser as a Web browser, you have probably typed URLs that begin with *http*, the abbreviation for the way browsers talk with Web servers (Hypertext Transport Protocol, if you must know). To tell your Web browser to log in to an FTP server, you tell it a different kind of URL — an FTP URL. An FTP server's URL looks like this:

```
ftp://servername/directoryname/filename
```

You can leave out the directory name and filename, if you like, to get the top-level directory of that FTP server. For example, the URL of the Microsoft FTP server (at `ftp.microsoft.com`) is

```
ftp://ftp.microsoft.com/
```

This URL has no filename part: If you omit the filename, the server displays the top-level directory to which you have access.

Downloading from your own private account

Some Web browsers — Netscape Navigator, in particular — can handle more than just anonymous FTP; they can FTP files from sites on which you have to have an account. To download a file from a password-protected FTP server, assuming that you have an account on the server, you can include your account name by typing the account name followed by an at-sign immediately before the FTP server name. If your account name is `zac`, for example, and your password is

`framistan`, you type a URL like this:

`ftp://zac:framistan@ftp.gurus.com`

Because this line puts your otherwise secret password on-screen for everyone to see, don't type this line when untrustworthy folk are present. Netscape but not Internet Explorer lets you leave the password off the URL and lets you type it instead in a box where it's displayed as asterisks, as a password should.

Giving your browser an FTP URL

No matter which Web browser you use, you follow the same general steps to retrieve files via FTP:

1. **Run the Web browser as usual.**

2. **To tell your browser to load the URL of the FTP server, type the FTP URL in the Address, URL, or Netsite box just below the toolbar, and then press Enter.**

   If you use a browser in which you can't type a URL in that box, you must give a command to tell it which URL to go to. Internet Explorer and Netscape Navigator let you choose File⇨Open (or press Ctrl+O) and then type the URL in the dialog box that's displayed.

   The browser logs in to the FTP server and displays its home directory. Each file and directory in the current directory appears as a link. Depending on the Web browser you use, the format may differ from the one shown in this figure.

3. **Click the directory name to move to the directory that contains the file you want.**

   When you click a directory name, you move to that directory and your browser displays its contents.

4. **Click a filename to download the file.**

   If you download a text file or another file your browser knows how to display, the browser displays it after it downloads. If you click the filename Readme.txt, for example, the browser displays the text file. If you want to save the file after you look at it, choose File⇨Save As from the menu and tell your browser the filename to use.

If you download a file your browser doesn't know how to display, such as a program, it usually asks what to do.

5. **If your browser asks what to do with the file, tell it to save the file and choose the directory and filename in which to save it.**

Your browser downloads the file.

Real FTP with WS_FTP

What if you want to upload files? Or what if you want to be able to transfer groups of files or rename files after you transfer them or see the files that are on the FTP server? Your Web browser just doesn't cut the mustard. Face it — you need a *real* FTP program.

If you use a PPP Internet account, you can use any Winsock FTP client program. Many good freeware and shareware FTP programs are available right off the Internet. This section describes how to use our favorite, WS_FTP. Tasty features of WS_FTP include

✔ Scrollable and selectable windows for the names of local and remote files and directories

✔ Clickable buttons for such common operations as connecting and setting binary mode

✔ Connection profiles, which save the hostname, login name, password, and remote host directory of your favorite FTP sites; comes with a bunch of useful profiles already set

---

FTP-ing Web pages

If you maintain a Web site, you use FTP to transfer from your computer to the Web server the Web pages you create or edit. You can use WS_FTP or another FTP program to transfer the pages, although you have to keep track of which Web pages you created, changed, or deleted on your computer and remember to do the same on the Web server computer. The larger your Web site grows, the bigger headache you have.

There's a better way: Use an FTP program designed just for maintaining Web sites. Margy uses NetLoad, a nifty program that can compare the files (by checking file sizes and dates) on your computer and on your Web site to see which files need to be uploaded or deleted. One click of a button, and NetLoad transfers all the necessary files. You can get NetLoad, or one of a number of similar programs, from TUCOWS (at http://www.tucows.com) on the Net.

Downloading WS_FTP

The freeware version of our favorite FTP program, WS_FTP LE (for Limited Edition), is available by (what else!) FTP from a variety of places, including its "home," the United States Military Academy. (And you thought that they were only trained how to fight wars!) You can also download it from the Web. Follow these steps to download WS-FTP LE from the Web:

1. **In My Computer or Windows Explorer, make a folder in which to put WS_FTP.**

2. **Use your Web browser to go to The Ultimate Collection of Winsock Software (TUCOWS), at** `http://www.tucows.com`. **Click the mirror site closest to you, and then click the link for Windows 95 or Windows 98 programs. Then click the link for FTP programs.**

   You see a long list of freeware and shareware FTP clients. Cool!

3. **Scroll down to WS_FTP LE and click the program name. Tell your browser to store the file in the folder you created in Step 1.**

   Your browser downloads the file. It's time to install it.

4. **Unzip the Ws_ftple.zip file.**

   We give you instructions later in this chapter for unzipping a file. You end up with a bunch of files, including the install program, which is named Inst32.exe.

5. **Run the installation program.**

   It asks a bunch of questions, such as whether you agree to the terms for noncommercial use (if you're a home user, you probably do), which directories to use, and which version of the program to use. In each case, the suggested answer is fine.

You're ready to FTP by using WS_FTP!

The big WS_FTP picture

The steps you follow to use WS_FTP (or any other FTP client program) are more complicated than using a browser:

1. **Connect to the Internet.**

2. **Log in to the FTP server by using WS_FTP.**

3. **Move to the directory on the server that contains the files you want to download, or move to the directory to which you want to upload files.**

FTP servers have the same kinds of tree-structured directory structure as Windows. Most FTP servers use pathnames similar to the ones Windows uses, except for forward slashes (/) rather than backslashes (\ ).

4. **Move to the folder on your own computer in which you want to download files or from which you want to upload files.**

5. **Tell the program which type of files (ASCII or binary) you are moving.**

6. **Download or upload the files.**

7. **Log off the FTP server.**

Connecting to an FTP server

Here's how to use the WS_FTP program to connect to an FTP server:

1. **Run the WS_FTP program by double-clicking its icon.**

   You see the Session Profile dialog box, as shown in Figure 12-2. This dialog box lets you enter information about the FTP server you want to connect to. After you have entered this information, WS_FTP saves it so that you can easily connect to the saved FTP server again.

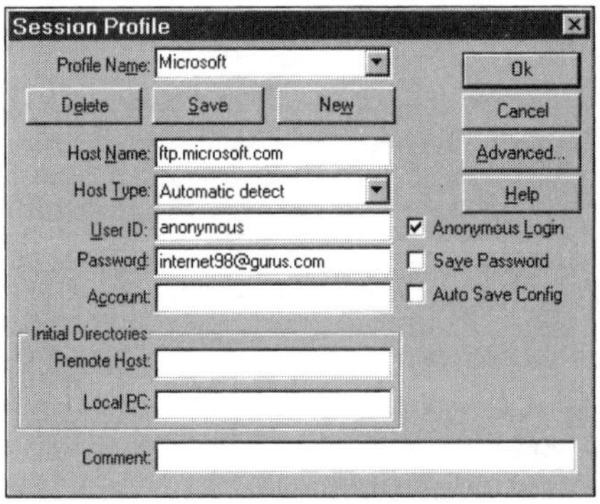

Figure 12-2:
Which FTP
server do
you want to
talk to?

2. **In the Profile Name box, enter the name you want to use for this FTP server.**

   If you want to FTP to rtfm.mit.edu, for example, which contains FAQs for all the Usenet newsgroups, you may enter **Usenet FAQ Central**.

3. **In the Host Name box, enter the name of the FTP server.**

   This name can be a regular Internet name (such as oak.oakland.edu, another useful FTP server) or a numeric address.

4. **Leave the Host Type box set to auto-detect.**

   This step tells WS_FTP to guess which operating system the FTP server is using. It usually guesses right.

5. **If you really have a username on the FTP server, enter your username and password in the User ID and Password boxes.**

   Otherwise, click the Anonymous Login box. WS_FTP asks for your e-mail address, which it uses as your password (the usual thing to do when you FTP anonymously).

6. **Enter your address and click OK.**

   WS_FTP fills in the User ID and Password boxes for you.

   If you want WS_FTP to store the password in the Password box rather than ask you for it every time you connect to the FTP server, click the Save Password box so that it contains an X.

   Leave the Account box blank, unless you have your own account on the FTP server and you know what account name to enter.

7. **In the Initial Directories Remote Host box, enter the directory in which you want to look on the FTP server.**

   Alternatively, you can leave this box blank and look around on your own.

8. **In the Initial Directories Local PC box, enter the folder on your own PC in which you want to store downloaded files.**

9. **Click the Save Config button to save this information.**

10. **Click OK.**

   WS_FTP tries to connect to the FTP server.

"It won't speak to me!"

If you have a problem connecting to the FTP server, messages appear in the two-line box at the bottom of the WS_FTP window. You can scroll the little window up and down to see what happened. For example, `rtfm.mit.edu` is frequently overloaded and doesn't let you log on. When this situation happens, some helpful messages are displayed about other FTP sites that may have the information you want. You can see these messages in this box.

To see the messages the FTP server sent, double-click them. WS_FTP opens a big window so that you can see them better. These messages can be helpful if something isn't working the way you hoped. To close the window, click the Close button.

Local and remote

After you're connected to the FTP server, you see the WS_FTP window, as shown in Figure 12-3. (Some versions of WS_FTP arrange the window a little differently.) WS_FTP displays information about the files on your own computer on the left side of the window (labeled Local System) and the directories and files on the FTP server on the right side (labeled Remote System). On each side are buttons that enable you to change directories (ChgDir), make directories (MkDir), delete directories (RmDir), view files, and so on. Naturally, you don't have permission to delete or change anything on most FTP servers, so don't even try.

To move from directory to directory on the FTP server, choose directory names from the list box on the Remote side. Or you can click the ChDir button and enter the full pathname of the directory to go to.

Here's how to download a file:

1. **Choose ASCII or Binary by clicking the buttons at the bottom of the window.**

   For files that consist entirely of text (like HTML files), choose ASCII. For anything else (like graphics files), choose Binary.

2. **On the Remote System side, move to the directory that contains the file you want to download, and then select the file.**

3. **On the Local System side, move to the folder on your own computer in which you want to store the downloaded file.**

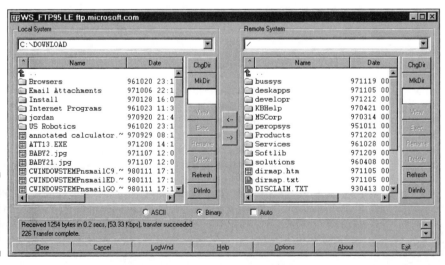

Figure 12-3: Prepare to receive some files!

4. Click the left-pointing arrow button in the middle of the window.

The arrow points from the Remote side to the Local side. (Get it?) WS_FTP downloads the file. For large files, this step can take some time; WS_FTP displays your progress as a percentage completed.

If you want to download several files from the same directory (and all the files are the same type — either text or binary), you can select all the filenames and download them at the same time. Click the first filename. Then Shift+click the last filename to select it and all the filenames in between. Or Ctrl+click to select one additional filename.

"I am outta here!"

To disconnect from the FTP server after you're finished, click the Close button in the bottom-left corner of the WS_FTP window.

Connecting again

To call someone else, click the Connect button. You see the Session Profile window again. Fill in different information and click OK to make the connection.

To call an FTP server you have called before, click Connect. In the FTP Client Connect To window, click the arrow button to the right of the Config Name box. You see a list of the configurations you've entered — choose one and then click OK.

FTP-ing wrong

The most common error inexperienced Internet users make (and *experienced* users, for that matter) is transferring a file in the wrong mode. If you transfer a text file in binary mode from a UNIX system to your Windows 98 system, the file looks something like this:

```
This file
        should have been
                    copied in
                        ASCII mode.
```

Why is it called FTP?

We could say that FTP is short for *file-transfer program* and you probably would believe us, but that would be wrong. It really stands for *File Transfer Protocol.* Way back in 1971, the Internet Powers That Be decided on a *protocol,* a set of conventions for copying files from one place to another on the Net. Then many people wrote programs that implemented the protocol and called them all FTP. Is this clear? Never mind. The geeks among us also use FTP as a verb. The megageeks try to pronounce FTP as a word.

If, on the other hand, you copy something in ASCII mode that isn't a text file, it gets scrambled. Compressed files don't decompress; executable files don't execute (or they crash or hang the machine); images look unimaginably bad. When a file is corrupted, the first thing you should suspect is the wrong mode in FTP.

If you're FTP-ing (Is that a verb? It is now!) files between two computers of the same type, such as from one Windows system to another, you can and should make all your transfers in binary mode. Because a text file or a nontext file doesn't require any conversion, binary mode does the right thing.

Hurry up and wait

The Internet is pretty fast, although not infinitely so. When you're copying stuff between two computers on the same local network, information can move at about 200,000 characters per second. When the two machines are separated by a great deal of intervening Internet, the speed drops — often to 1,000 characters per second or fewer. If you're copying a file that's 500,000 characters long (the size of your typical inspirational GIF image), it takes only a few seconds over a local network, although it can take several minutes over a long-haul connection.

It's often comforting to look at the directory listing before retrieving a file so that you know how big the file is and can have an idea of how long the copy will take. Because programs get inexorably larger, even with faster modems, patience remains the key to successful downloading.

Uploading Is Cool Too

Okay, now you know how to retrieve files from other computers. How about copying the other way? If you write your own Web pages and want to upload them to your Internet service provider's computer, here's how you do it: FTP them to the provider's Web server.

Internet Explorer doesn't handle uploading. You have to use a real FTP program like WS_FTP or Netscape Navigator if you want to use FTP to upload files to your server.

Uploading with Netscape

In Netscape Navigator, you can log in to the Web server as yourself by using an FTP URL that includes your username, like this:

```
ftp://yourid@www.yourprovider.com/
```

Type your login ID in place of *yourid*. (It pops up a box asking you for your password when needed.) Rather than type www.provider.com, type the name of your provider's Web server, which most likely is www followed by the provider's domain name but may also be something like ftp.www.fargle.net. (Ask your provider if this info isn't in the sign-up packet it gave you.)

When you connect to an FTP server by using this method, you see your home Web directory listed on-screen. If you want to upload files to a different directory, click that directory's name so that you see that directory.

After you have the directory you want on-screen, just drag the file to upload it from any other program (such as Windows Explorer or My Computer) into the browser window. Way cool. Netscape Navigator asks whether you really want to upload the file. You can also choose File⇨Upload File from the menu if you find dragging to be a drag.

Uploading with WS_FTP

In WS_FTP, log in as we just described in the preceding section, using your login ID and password. After you have the local and remote directories you want in their respective windows in WS_FTP, just click the local file you want to upload, and then click the right-pointing arrow button pointing to the Remote window.

If you're uploading a Web page to a Web server, be sure to upload the page itself (in ASCII mode because the HTML file that contains the Web page is a text file) along with any graphics files that contain pictures which appear on the page (in binary mode).

After You Download a Program

Using FTP, you can download freeware and shareware programs and install and use them. You need a few well-chosen software tools, including a program to uncompress compressed files. (Useful little programs like this one are called *utilities* in the jargon.)

Installing FTP'd software usually requires three steps:

1. **Using FTP, download the file that contains the software.**

2. **If the software isn't in a self-installing file, it's usually in a compressed format, so uncompress it.**

3. **Run the installation program that comes with it, or at least create an icon for the program.**

By now, you know how to do Step 1, the FTP part. The rest of this chapter describes Steps 2 and 3: uncompressing and installing. Here goes!

Getting WinZip for unzipping

Most software on FTP servers is in a compressed format, to save both storage space on the server and transmission time when you download the file. An increasing amount of software is self-installing — the file is a program that does the necessary uncompressing and installing. Self-installing files end with EXE, and non-self-installing compressed files end with ZIP (and are called *zip files*). To uncompress a self-installing EXE file, just run it — lots of files pop out.

If you download a zip file, you need a program to unzip with it. A guy named Nico Mak wrote a nice little Windows program called WinZip that can both unzip and zip things for you. Other programs work too, like PKZIP and PKUNZIP.

If you already have WinZip (which is also available through the mail or from various shareware outlets), skip ahead to the following section, "Running WinZip." If you have and love PKZIP and PKUNZIP or UNZIP and don't mind running them from an MS-DOS window, you can skip this section too. You can get a Windows version of PKUNZIP, which isn't as nice as WinZip, although some people like it. It works fine.

To get WinZip on the Web, go to `http://www.winzip.com`, a page full of pictures of outer-space-type blobs. Click the blob marked Download Evaluation to get to the download page. On that page, download the Windows 95/ Windows 98 version.

To install WinZip:

1. **Run Winzip95.exe or Winzip98.exe (or whatever the name of the file is that you downloaded).**

2. **Follow the installation instructions WinZip gives you.**

   Although you have a bunch of options, you can accept the suggested defaults for all of them. WinZip installs itself and makes a WinZip icon on your desktop. If it gives you a choice, we prefer the WinZip Classic to the WinZip Wizard interface, so that's what we describe here.

Running WinZip

Give it a try! Click that icon! WinZip looks like Figure 12-4.

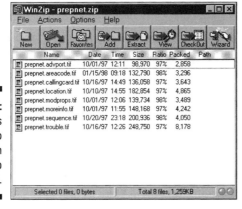

Figure 12-4: WinZip is ready to deal with your zip files.

To open a zip file (which the WinZip folks call an *archive*), click the Open button on the toolbar and choose the directory and filename for the zip file. Poof! WinZip displays a list of the files in the archive, with their dates and sizes.

Unzipping files

Sounds suggestive, we know, although it's not as much fun as it sounds. If you want to use a file from a zip file, after you have opened the zip file, you *extract* it — that is, you ask WinZip to uncompress it and store it in a new file.

To extract a file:

1. **Choose it from the list of files.**

   You can choose a group of files that are listed together by clicking the first one and then Shift+clicking the last one. To select an additional file, Ctrl+click it.

2. **Click the Extract button.**

   A dialog box asks in which directory you want to put the file and whether you want to extract all the files in the archive or just the one you selected.

3. **Select the directory in which to store the unzipped files.**

4. **Click OK.**

   WinZip unzips the file. The zip file is unchanged, and now you have the uncompressed file (or files) also.

Another way to unzip files is to select them in the WinZip window and drag them to a Windows Explorer or My Computer window. (Drag-and-drop can be so convenient sometimes.)

Zipping around

Although WinZip can do a bunch of other things too, such as add files to a zip file and create your own zip file, you don't have to know how to perform these tasks in order to swipe software from the Net, so we skip them. (We bet that you can figure them out, just by looking at the buttons on the WinZip toolbar.)

Windows 6.3 comes with the Internet Browser Support Add-on, which you can also download from the `http://www.winzip.com/ibrowser.htm` Web page. You can tell this add-on to download and open zip files automatically.

Now that you know how to unzip software you get from the Internet, you're ready for the next topic: safe software.

Scanning for viruses

We all know that you practice safe software: You check every new program you get to make sure that it doesn't contain any hidden software viruses that may display obnoxious messages or trash your hard disk. If that's true of you, you can skip this section.

For the rest of you, it's a good idea to run a virus-scanning program. You never know what naughty piece of code you may otherwise unwittingly download to your defenseless computer!

Run a virus checker after you have obtained and run any new piece of software. Although the FTP servers on the Internet make every effort to keep their software archives virus-free, nobody is perfect. Don't get caught by some prankster's idea of a joke!

If you use WinZip, you can configure it to run your virus checker before you even unzip the zip file containing a program. Choose Options➪Program Locations from the menu and type in the Scan program box the pathname of your virus checker program.

Although Windows 98 doesn't come with a virus checker, several commercial ones are available, including the McAfee VirusScan program, which you can download from the McAfee Web site, at `http://www.mcafee.com`. Lots of other virus scanners are available at TUCOWS. Check it out, at `http://www.tucows.com`.

Installing the program you downloaded — finally!

After you have downloaded the software and unzipped it (if it's a zip file), the program is ready to install. To install the program, click its name in Windows Explorer or My Computer. If it's an installation file, it installs the program. In the process, the installation program usually creates an icon for the program. It may also add the program to your Start menu or Programs menu.

Some programs don't come with an installation program — you just get the program itself. To make the program easy to run, you need an icon for it. Here's how to make one:

1. **Run either My Computer or Windows Explorer, and select the program file (the file with the extension .exe or occasionally .com).**

2. **Use your right mouse button to drag the filename out on the desktop or into an open folder on the desktop.**

   An icon for the program appears. (Technically, this icon is called a *shortcut,* and it works great for running a program.)

Configuring the program

Now you can run the program by double-clicking its icon. Hooray!

You may have to tell the program, however, about your Internet address or your computer or who knows what before it can do its job. Refer to the text files, if any, that came with the program or choose Help from the program's menu bar to get more information about how to configure and run your new program.

Finding the Good Stuff

"The world of FTP sounds fine and dandy," you may say, "but what's out there, and where can I find it?" One of the best places to find software is to look at http://www.tucows.com. It has a great collection of FTP sites grouped by platform and category of program.

Also visit our online favorite software page, with our current updated list of greatest hits:

http://net.gurus.com/software

Chapter 13

Online Chatting: How to Make Friends and Influence People

*I*f you like e-mail but get irritated when people don't answer for hours or maybe even days (what? — they have something better to do?) while you sit around looking at your empty mailbox, maybe online chat is for you. *Online chat* lets you communicate instantly with another person who is logged on to the Net anywhere, by typing messages back and forth to each other. It's much faster than regular mail and considerably faster than e-mail. You can chat with several people at one time. And Windows 98 comes with an unbearably cute chat program that even displays your conversation as a comic strip — what more could you ask?

What's Chatting All About?

Online chat is similar to talking on an old-fashioned party line or CB radio. Although you're probably too young to remember, in the infancy of the telephone system, people often didn't have private phone lines; instead, they shared their line with one or more other families, especially in rural America, where stringing telephone lines was expensive. Everyone on the party line could join in any conversation, although, of course, they weren't always welcome to do so. Today, people often arrange conference calls to have several people all talk together.

Chatting is similar to a conference call except that rather than talk, you type on your keyboard what you want to say and read on-screen what other people are saying. Although all the people participating in the chat can be typing at one time, each person's contribution is presented on-screen in order of its receipt, identified by the name of the person who typed it. After you type what you want to say, it appears on the screen of general conversation and is identified by your screen name.

You can chat in two main ways:

✔ **Channels or rooms:** Resemble an ongoing conference call with a bunch of people. After you join a channel, you can read on-screen what people are saying and then add your own comments just by typing them and pressing Enter.

✔ **Direct connection:** A private conversation between you and another person connected to the chat portion of the Internet.

"Is there a room for me?"

Which groups are available when you begin to chat depends on how you're connected to the Internet. If you use America Online (AOL), where the groups are called *rooms,* you chat with other AOL users. If you access the Internet, you talk to other people by using the Internet's IRC (Internet Relay Chat) capability — see the section "Cruising IRC with Microsoft Chat," later in this chapter. Some web sites let you chat by using your browser.

Each room or channel has a name; with luck, the name is an indication of what the chatters there are talking about or what they have in common. Here is a sample chat room conversation:

```
FJD718:  Hi everyone
Buline596:  Hi DavQC
Draw7card:  HIya FJD
Pezaz:   a man that other men don't like LOL
ORNOT2B: not discussing me...pez
Mostlyfun:  {{{{{{{{{{{dav}}}}}}}}}}}}] thanks he is
            hopeless
DavQC:   anyone catch clintons speech?
Draw7card:: Hiya Pez
Snowball33: Hi FJD
FJD718:  hi Draw
Mostlyfun:  Davvvvvvvvvvvvvvvvvvvvvvv ;-)
DavQC:   FJD whats with debra
ORNOT2B: hi paige
Paige282:  Hi everyone
```

```
Snowball33: sorry dav
Harddisc3:  anyone from atlanta area ?
Mostlyfun:  Paige hiya
LadyA3826:  snooooooo Queen
Draw7card:  HIya SNO
DavQC:      Paigeee
```

"I didn't catch your name"

No matter which chat facility you're using, you should know that most people select a *screen name, handle,* or *nickname* to use before they join a group. Other members of the group know you by your screen name, a temporary name often chosen to be unique, colorful, or clever and used as a mask. The choice of a screen name may be good for only the duration of a chat session. If you join a group and have a nice chat with someone named ObiWan, the next time you see that name, you have no guarantee that it's the same person. This anonymity can make chatting a place to be careful. On the other hand, one of the attractions of chatting is meeting new and interesting people. Many warm and wonderful friendships have evolved from a chance meeting in a chat room.

When you join a group and begin chatting, you see the screen names of the people who are already there and a window in which the current conversation goes flying by. If the group is friendly, somebody usually sends you a welcome message because everyone is notified when you join the group.

As in real life, a room full of strangers may include people you don't like much. Because it's possible to be somewhat anonymous on the Internet, some people take advantage of the situation to act boorish, vulgar, crude, or worse. For that reason, don't let your children chat unsupervised. While you're new to chat, you may accidentally visit a number of disgusting places, although you can find out how to avoid them and find rooms that have useful, friendly, and supportive conversations.

Getting Ready to Chat

Your first time in a chat room can seem stupid or daunting. Here are some of the things you can do to get through your first encounters:

- ✔ Remember that when you enter a chat room, a conversation is probably already in progress. You don't know what went on before you entered.
- ✔ Wait a minute or two for a page full of exchanges to appear on-screen so that you can understand some of the context before you start writing.

- Start by following the comments of a single screen name. Then follow the people that person mentions or who reply to that person.

- After you can follow one thread, try picking up another. It takes practice to get the hang of it.

- Some services, such as AOL, let you highlight the messages from one or more screen names. This technique can make things easier to follow.

- You can also indicate screen names to ignore. Messages from these chatters no longer appear on-screen, though other members' replies to them do appear.

- Scroll up to see older messages if you have to, and remember that after you have scrolled up, no new messages appear until you scroll back down.

- If you find one chat room uninteresting, leave it and try another.

Chat etiquette

Chatting etiquette is not that much different from e-mail etiquette, and common sense is your best online guide. Here are some additional chatting tips:

- The first rule of chatting is not to hurt anyone. A real person with real feelings is at the other end of the computer chat connection.

- The second rule is to be cautious. You really have no idea who that other person is. See the following section, "A serious chat about safe chatting."

- Read messages for a while to figure out what is happening before sending a message to a chat group. (Reading what's happening in a chat room or mailing list without saying anything is known as *lurking*, and, contrary to what that word may imply, it's considered perfectly good manners on a chat or e-mail list. When you finally venture to say something, you're *delurking*. People who are delurking for the first time often mention that fact in their message. It tells others that they have been following the conversation and may actually know what has been going on.)

- Keep your messages short and to the point.

- Don't insult people, and don't use foul language.

- Create a profile with information about yourself. Most chat systems have provisions for creating profiles (personal information) that other members can access. We caution people never to give out their last name, phone number, or address. We think that the extra caution is necessary for kids: Insist that kids *not* enter their age, hometown, or school nor their last name, phone number, or address.

✔ Although you don't have to tell everything about yourself in your profile, what you do say should be truthful.

✔ If you want to talk to someone in private, send that person a message saying hi, who you are, and what you want.

✔ If the tone of conversation in one chat room offends you, you can always leave. As in real life, you may run into more people out there you *don't* want to meet than people you *do*.

A serious chat about safe chatting

Here are some guidelines for conducting safe and healthy chats:

✔ Many people in chat groups lie about their occupation, age, locality, and, yes, even gender. Some think that they're just being cute, some are exploring their own fantasies, and some are really sick.

✔ Be careful about revealing information that enables someone to find you personally — such as where you live or work or your phone number. This information includes your last name, phone number, mailing address, and schools your kids attend.

✔ Never give out your password to anyone. No one should ever ask you for it. (We once received a message saying, "There's been a serious threat to security, and we need your password to help determine the problem.") If you ever get a message like that — whenever you're online, in a chat room or anywhere else, inform your provider's staff. No legitimate person will ever ask you for your password.

✔ If your chat service offers profiles and a person without a profile wants to chat with you, be extra cautious.

✔ If you're a child, never, ever meet someone without your parents. Do not give out personal information about yourself or any member of your family, even when you're offered some sort of prize for filling out a form.

✔ If your children use chat, realize that others may try to meet them. Review the guidelines in this list with your kids before they log on.

If you choose to meet an online friend in person, use at least the same caution you would use in meeting someone through a newspaper ad:

✔ Don't arrange a meeting until you have talked to a person a number of times, including conversations at length by telephone over the course of days or weeks. (If you think that someone's single and he won't let you call him at home, think again.)

✔ Meet in a well-lit public place.

  ✔ Bring a friend along, if you can. If not, at least let someone know what you're doing and agree to call that person at a certain time (for example, a half-hour) after the planned meeting time.

  ✔ Arrange to stay in a hotel if you travel a long distance to meet someone. Don't commit yourself to staying at that person's home.

Abbreviations, emoticons, and smileys

Many chat abbreviations are the same as those used in e-mail, as described in Chapter 5. Because chat is live, however, some are unique. We've also listed some common *emoticons* (sometimes called *smileys*) — funky combinations of punctuation used to depict the emotional inflection of the sender. (If at first you don't see what they are, try tilting your head down to the left.) Table 13-1 shows you a short list of chat abbreviations and emoticons.

Table 13-1	Chat Shorthand
Abbreviation	**What It Means**
AFK	Away from keyboard
A/S/L	Age/sex/location (response may be 35/f/LA)
BAK	Back at keyboard
BBIAF	Be back in a flash
BBL	Be back later
BRB	Be right back
BTW	By the way
GMTA	Great minds think alike
IM	Instant message
IMHO	In my humble opinion
IMNSHO	In my not-so-humble opinion
J/K	Just kidding
LTNS	Long time no see
LOL	Laughing out loud
M4M	Men seeking other men
NP	No problem
ROTFL	Rolling on the floor laughing

Abbreviation	*What It Means*
RTFM	Read the fine manual
TOS	Terms of service (the AOL member contract)
TTFN	Ta-ta for now!
WAV	A sound file
WB	Welcome back
WTG	Way to go!
:D	A smile or big grin
:) or :-)	A smile
;)	A wink
{{{{bob}}}}	A hug for Bob
:(or :-(	Frown
:'(	Crying
:~~(	Crying
0:)	Angel
}:>	Devil
:P	Sticking out tongue
:P~~	Drooling
***	Kisses
<——	Action marker (<—eating pizza, for example,)

In addition to the abbreviations in the table, chatters sometimes use simple shorthand abbreviations, as in "If u cn rd ths u r rdy 4 chat."

There's always some jerk

Some people act badly online while hiding behind the anonymity that chat provides. You have four good options and one bad option when this situation happens:

- ✔ Go to another chat room. Some rooms are just nasty. You don't have to hang around.

- ✔ Pay no attention to the troublemaker, and just converse with the other folks.

- ✔ Make offenders disappear from your screen. On AOL, double-click the jerk's screen name in the room list and then click the Ignore box.

✔ Complain to the individual's Internet service provider. This technique is most effective on the value-added services. If you use AOL, see the section "The chat police at your service," later in this chapter.

✔ (The bad option.) Respond in kind, which just gives the offender the attention he (it's usually a he) wants and may get *you* kicked off your service.

Ways to chat

The rest of this chapter describes chatting on America Online (AOL), *Internet Relay Chat (IRC)* — the Internet's original chat service — and using web-based chat services.

Chatting on AOL

Although many online service providers have their own chat services, the AOL service is unique. Its large membership means that thousands of potential chatters are always online. The AOL chat rooms, even the specialized ones, are lively most of the time. Also, because chat is one of the major AOL attractions, AOL has staff members who check on its chat rooms to prevent the boorish, outlandish, and sometimes dangerous behavior that is too often common on unsupervised services like IRC. Although this supervision is by no means perfect, it makes AOL a top choice if you're planning to let your kids chat online.

AOL users can participate in IRC too. AOL has a built-in IRC program (go to keyword **irc**).

Only AOL members can participate in the AOL chat rooms. If you have Internet access through a different service, you can join AOL at a reduced rate. Go to http://www.aol.com and look for the Bring Your Own Access membership option.

Walk on in

You get started chatting in America Online 4.0 by clicking the People icon on the toolbar and choosing People Connection or by typing the keyword **chat**. Then click the Chat Now icon.

You're now in an AOL "lobby room." You see two windows, a larger one in which conversation is taking place and a smaller one that lists the people (screen names) in this room. If you're one of those people who just has to say something whenever you enter a crowded room, type something in the bottom area of the conversation window and click Send. In a few seconds, your comment is displayed in the window.

AOL limits the number of people in most public rooms to 23, so when a room is full and a new user wants to join in, a new (similar) room is automatically created.

Rooms with a view

You probably won't find much conversation of interest in the lobby room you were thrown into when you joined the chatters. Pressing the Find a Chat button shows you the Find a Chat window with a list of the public chat rooms that are available. Two windows are displayed; the left one shows the room categories. When you double-click a category, the right window shows the room names in that category along with the number of current occupants in that room.

The room categories are mostly self-explanatory:

- **Town Square:** Rooms with a restaurant, bar, or coffeehouse flavor
- **Art & Entertainment:** Hollywood, music, book, and trivia themes
- **Friends:** People who like to talk
- **Life:** All sorts of lifestyles and age groups
- **News, Sports, Finance:** What you would expect
- **Places:** Major metropolitan areas
- **Romance:** Boy meets girl, in all combinations
- **Special Interests:** Hobbies, pets, cars, and religion
- **Countries:** Germany, United Kingdom, Canada, France, and Japan

Figure 13-1 shows a chat taking place in the Boston room (it's room number 4 because the first three Boston rooms already had 23 participants). Everything you type in the little box at the bottom, next to the Send button, is part of the conversation. You can either press the Enter key after typing your message or click Send. When you want to leave a room, click List Chats, find another room, and join it. Or you can close the window of the chat room to get out of the AOL People Connection.

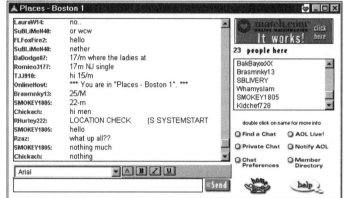

Figure 13-1:
Chatting in
the Boston
room.

People power

If you want to know something about the other occupants of the room, double-click one of their names in the window labeled People Here. A little box pops up that enables you to do one of several things:

- ✔ **Ignore:** If you check this box, no messages from this user are displayed on-screen. This technique is one way to stop receiving messages from annoying people.

- ✔ **Get Profile:** Click this button to retrieve the profile of this user. A *profile* is a list of information a user has supplied about herself. You have no guarantee that a profile has any true facts in it.

- ✔ **Send Message:** Click to send an instant mail message to this user. It's sort of like whispering in his ear. If someone sends you this type of message (an Instant Message, or IM), that message appears in a small window. You can ignore it or respond with a message of your own. The two of you can keep a running conversation going as long as you want.

"Who am I now?"

You're identified by your screen name, the name you used when you signed on to the service. For privacy reasons, many people use a different screen name when they're chatting. AOL lets each account use as many as five different screen names. One of the screen names is the master screen name, which can never be changed. If you want to add or change other screen names, you must log on to AOL under the master screen name. After you've established other screen names and passwords, you can log on to AOL by using the alternative name. Each screen name has a separate mailbox. You can use screen names for either different family members or different personalities: for example, your business self and your private self.

To set your *profile,* the information that other users can see about you when you're chatting, click the Member Directory button under the People Here window or go to keyword PROFILE. A box is displayed in which you can search the AOL membership list for names you may know. In this window is a button labeled My Profile. If you click this button, you can set or modify all your own profile settings.

For members only

In addition to the chat rooms AOL sets up, members can create rooms. Click the Find a Chat button in the lower-right part of the chat window. In the Find a Chat window that appears, click the button labeled Member Chats, and the list of rooms switches over to the member rooms. Anyone can create a member room, and so can you, by clicking the Start Your Own Chat button. These rooms have the same categories as the public rooms — they're usually silly, serious, or kinky.

"Meet me under the sign of the rose"

The names of private rooms, unlike public or member rooms, are not revealed. To join one, you have to know its name; that is, someone must invite you to join. When you click the Enter a Private Chat button in the Find a Chat window, you're asked to name the room you want to join. If it doesn't exist, one is created and you're the sole occupant.

Private rooms enable people to talk more intimately — you face little danger of a stranger popping in. Two (or more) people can agree to create a private room and meet there. Private rooms have a somewhat sleazy reputation: If you get invited to one, you should be careful about guarding your privacy — anyone in a room can save the conversation to a file.

The chat police at your service

Another button under the People Here window is labeled Notify AOL. If you think that someone is violating the AOL terms of service (TOS) by asking you for your password or credit card number, using abusive language, or otherwise behaving badly, you can and should report them to AOL. When you press the Notify AOL button, a window pops up to help you gather all the information you want to report: the chat category and room you were in, the offensive chat dialog pasted into a window, and the offender's screen name, for example.

Because of this policing and the power of AOL to terminate (permanently) the accounts of people who play without the rules, the AOL chat rooms have a deserved reputation for safety and for being a good place to play.

Cruising IRC with Microsoft Chat

IRC (Internet Relay Chat) is available from most Internet service providers (or ISPs). To use IRC, you need an IRC *client program* on your computer. An IRC client program (or just *IRC program* or *chat program*) is another Internet program, like your web browser or e-mail program, and freeware and shareware programs are available for you to download from the Net. Windows 98 comes with an IRC program called Microsoft Chat, although you can use other chat programs (see the sidebar "Alternatives to Microsoft Chat," later in this chapter).

"Serve me some chat"

Microsoft Chat (or any chat program) has to connect to an *IRC server* — an Internet host computer that serves as a switchboard for IRC conversations. Although dozens of IRC servers are available, many are full most of the time and may refuse your connection. You may have to try several servers, or the same one dozens of times, before you can connect.

IRC servers are organized into networks. Although servers within each network talk to each other, servers on one IRC network don't connect to servers on other networks. Someone on EFnet can't talk to someone on Undernet, for example.

The four biggest networks and their home pages are shown in this list (in descending order):

- **EFnet:** http://www.irchelp.org (the original network of servers; has the most users)
- **Undernet:** http://www.undernet.org
- **IRCnet:** http://www.funet.fi/~irc
- **DALNet:** http://www.dal.net

Most people on IRC eventually develop a preference for one network — usually the one where their friends hang out.

Lots of smaller IRC networks exist. Microsoft has its own that appears automatically in the Chat Connection window. Here are some, with the addresses of web pages that have more information about them:

- ✔ **Microsoft:** `http://mschat.msn.com`
- ✔ **Kidsworld:** `http://www.kidsworld.org`
- ✔ **AnotherNet:** `http://www.another.org` (one of our favorites)
- ✔ **StarLink:** `http://www.starlink.org`

When you're choosing a server, pick one that's geographically close to you (to minimize response lag, as explained in the following sidebar, "Splits and lags") and on the IRC network you want. Because each server entry notes its network and location, you can easily choose one near you.

Roaming the channels

The most popular way to use IRC is through *channels*. Most channels have names that start with the # character. Channel names are not case-sensitive. Numbered channels also exist (when you type a channel number, you don't use the # character).

In Microsoft Chat, channels are called *rooms*. Why? Because Microsoft can do anything it wants, that's why.

Thousands of IRC channels are available. Different channels are available on different IRC networks. You can find an annotated list of some of the best by visiting `http://www.funet.fi/~irc/channels.html`. Each channel listed there has its own linked home page that tells you much more about what that channel offers.

Good channels to know about include

- ✔ **#irchelp:** A place to ask questions about IRC

  Check out our web page too, at `http://net.gurus.com/irc/tips.html`, for some tips and tricks and some links to more information about IRC.

- ✔ **#newbies:** All your IRC questions answered
- ✔ **#21plus: and #30plus:** Age-appropriate meeting places
- ✔ **#41plus:** A more mature channel (with many people on it younger than 41)
- ✔ **#teens:** For teenagers — chill and chat
- ✔ **#hottub:** A "rougher" meeting place

✔ **#collective:** The place to report problems on the Microsoft IRC server

✔ **#windows98:** Meeting place for Windows 98 users

✔ **#chat:** A friendly chat channel

✔ **#mirc:** A help channel for mIRC users

You can also try typing # followed by the name of a country or major city.

In the nick of time

Everyone using IRC needs a *nickname*. This name is unique within the network: No two people connected to the same IRC network can use the same nickname at the same time. If you attempt to connect to a network and your chosen nickname is already in use, you cannot join a channel. The name can be the same as the username in your e-mail address, although most people pick a different name.

Nicknames can be as long as nine characters. Because common names are usually already in use, choose something distinctive.

Unlike e-mail addresses, nicknames can change from day to day. Whoever claims a nickname first on an IRC server gets to keep it for as long as she is logged in. Nicknames are good for only a single session on IRC. If you chatted with someone named AlGore yesterday and then run into someone named AlGore today, you have no guarantee that it's the same person. To find out more about the person behind a nickname, double-click his entry in the list of room members.

Splits and lags

Two phenomena, lags and netsplits, are the bane of an IRCer's existence. A *lag* is the delay between the time you type a message and when it appears on other people's screens. Lags foul up conversations. Sometimes, one group of people on a channel is lagged while another group is not, and the first group's messages appear after delays of several minutes. You can check on the amount of time a message takes to get from you to another person and back again by clicking a nickname in the members list and choosing Member⇨Lag Time.

A *netsplit* breaks the connection between IRC servers — the network of connected IRC servers gets split into two smaller networks. A netsplit looks like a bunch of people suddenly leaving your channel and then reappearing en masse sometime later. Although all the people who are connected to the IRC servers in one half of the network can chat among themselves, they can't communicate with the people connected to the IRC servers in the other half. Eventually (after minutes or hours), the two networks reconnect and the netsplit is over.

Installing Microsoft Chat

Because Microsoft Chat is an optional part of Windows 98, it may not be installed on your computer. Try running Chat by clicking the Start button and choosing Programs⇨Internet Explorer⇨Microsoft Chat. If no such command exists, you have to install Chat from your Windows 98 CD-ROM or disks. If the program runs, skip this section — you're ready to chat.

To install Chat, follow these steps:

1. **Close all your other programs, and then click the Start button and choose Settings⇨Control Panel.**

   You see the Windows 98 Control Panel window.

2. **Click or double-click the Add/Remove Programs icon — whatever it takes to display the Add/Remove Programs properties window.**

3. **Click the Windows Setup tab.**

   Windows 98 thinks for a few minutes while it checks to see which programs you've already installed. You see a list of the types of programs that come with Windows 98.

4. **Click Communications on the list of components because Chat is all about communications! Click the Details button to see the list of programs of that type.**

5. **Click the Microsoft Chat program so that a check mark appears in its box, and then click the OK button to return to the Add/Remove Programs Properties Windows Setup dialog box.**

6. **Click the OK button.**

   Windows 98 determines which programs to install and installs them. If Windows says that you have to restart your computer when the installation is complete, click Yes to do so.

Check with your ISP for any additional information you may need in order to use IRC. If you have a direct link to the Internet, ask your system administrator whether the link supports IRC. Many companies block IRC.

Connecting on chat

Start up the Microsoft Chat program by clicking the Start button and choosing Programs⇨Internet Explorer⇨Microsoft Chat. You see the Connect dialog box, as shown in Figure 13-2. Click the Server box and click a server on the list that appears. You can also choose the channel you want to join. Click OK to attempt to connect to the server.

Figure 13-2:
Which IRC
server do
you want to
connect to?

When you get connected, you see the Microsoft Chat window, as shown in Figure 13-3. If you're not in Comic Strip view (we are not making this up), you can choose View⇨Comic Strip to make your window look more like Figure 13-3. The conversation, in comic strip form, appears in the left part of the window. In the upper-right corner is a list of the people in the chat room with their comic strip characters (you can't tell the players without a scorecard!). Scroll this list up and down to see everyone. In the lower-right corner is a gizmo that lets you choose the facial expression of your own character.

At peak times, the servers can be extremely busy. If at first you don't connect, try, try again. If you don't see the Connect dialog box or you want to reconnect later, click the Connect button on the toolbar (the fourth button from the left).

Alternatives to Microsoft Chat

Another good shareware Windows IRC program is mIRC. You can find mIRC, along with others, at shareware web sites, such as TUCOWS (http://www.tucows.com), or at the mIRC home page; it's at (http://www.mirc.co.uk).

For more detailed information about setting up mIRC, point your browser to http://www.mirc.com. You can also find a great deal of useful information about IRC there.

If you want to chat with a friend who does not have Windows 98, she can probably get a suitable IRC client. Microsoft Chat and mIRC also work on older versions of Windows, *Ircle* is a good choice for Macintosh users, and most UNIX systems feature a built-in client, which you start by typing the command **irc** or **ircii**.

Figure 13-3:
Microsoft
Chat in
comic strip
view.

"What's on the channels tonight?"

In Microsoft Chat, the name of the channel (room) you're in appears on the title bar for the window, so you can always tell where you are. To see a list of the available channels on the IRC server to which you're connected, click the Chat Room List button on the toolbar (the 11th button from the left) or choose Room⇨Room List from the menu bar. You see the Chat Room List window, as shown in Figure 13-4.

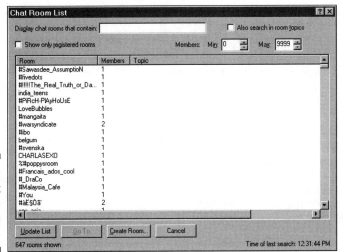

Figure 13-4:
A long list
of available
rooms
(channels).

If you're looking for a particular channel name, type in the Match text box the text you're looking for. If you want to see channels with at least several people on them (rather than the hundreds of channels with one bored, lonely, or lascivious person waiting), type a number in the Min box. Then click Update List. Because the list of channels can be extremely long, you may have to wait a few minutes for the list to be displayed. If you want to see the channels listed in your Channels folder (the list of channels you visit frequently), click the Channels folder icon instead.

"Join me"

If you're looking at the Chat Room List window, join a channel by double-clicking its name. Otherwise, you can join a channel by clicking the Enter Room button on the toolbar (the sixth button from the left) or by choosing Room⇨Enter Room from the menu bar. Then type the name of the channel in the box provided. Don't forget the # before the channel name.

In some chat programs, you can join several channels at a time; Microsoft Chat doesn't let you — although you can fire up several copies of the program and use different channels with each one. You leave a channel by clicking the Leave Room icon on the toolbar (the seventh from the left) or by choosing Room⇨Leave Room.

Telling chat who you are

You can tell Microsoft Chat your preferred nickname so that it doesn't ask you every time you run it. Choose View⇨Options, click the Personal Info tab, and enter your chosen name in the Nickname box.

See ya in the funnies

Plain old text as a conversation tool isn't good enough for Microsoft, which likes to "embrace and extend" existing Internet standards. Microsoft Chat can display a chat room's conversation as panels in a comic strip that your computer draws on the fly. Click the Comics View button on the toolbar (the one with the face), or choose View⇨Comic Strip to try it. You select the character that will represent you by choosing View⇨Options and clicking the Character tab. You can also select one of

several emotions your character will display by using a little wheel in the bottom-right corner of the chat window.

Comic displays are well realized and fun to watch, although they can get confusing when a number of people are in the room. Click the Text View icon or choose View⇨Plain Text if you yearn for a conventional text display of the conversation.

"Whisper in my ear"

To send a private message to someone in on a channel, click her name on the members list and click the Whisper Box icon or choose Member⇨ Whisper Box from the menu bar.

You can set up private conversations with more than one room member. Right-click a person's name in the member list and then click the Whisper Box icon. Repeat this process for each person you want to engage in private chat. If you want several members in the same conversation, select each name and then click the Whisper Box icon.

Trying to manage too many conversations at one time can get you into a heap of trouble.

Own your own channel

Each channel has its own channel operator, or *chanop,* who can control, to some extent, what happens on that channel. In the list of nicknames on a channel, operators' nicknames are preceded by a gavel icon. You can start your own channel and automatically become its chanop by choosing Room⇨ Create Room or clicking the Create Room button on the toolbar (the eighth one from the left).

As with nicknames, whoever asks for a channel name first gets it. You can keep the name for as long as you're logged on as the chanop. You can let other people be chanops for your channel — just make sure that they're people you can trust. A channel exists as long as anyone is on it; when the last person leaves, the channel winks out of existence.

As chanop, you get to use special commands, like setting the room proper- ties by using the Room⇨Room Properties command. The main one is Member⇨Host⇨Kick, which kicks someone off your channel, at least for the three seconds until he rejoins the channel. Kicking someone off is a thrill (although a rather small one), sort of like finding a penny on the sidewalk. People usually get kicked off channels for being rude or by sending so many garbage messages that they make the channel unusable. To kick people out and keep them out, choose Member⇨Host⇨Ban.

Server operators manage entire servers and can kick unruly users off a server permanently.

By invitation only

Three types of channels are available in IRC:

- **Public:** Everyone can see them, and everyone can join.
- **Private:** Although everyone can see them, you can join them only by invitation.
- **Secret:** They don't show up on the usual list of channels, and you can join them only by invitation.

If you're on a private or secret channel, you can invite someone else to join by choosing Member⇨Invite from the menu.

Command performance

You can also control what is happening during your chat session by typing IRC commands. All IRC commands start with the slash character (/). You can type IRC commands in upper- or lowercase or a mixture — IRC doesn't care. If you use Microsoft Chat, many commands are available directly from the toolbar. Other commands don't work at all — Microsoft Chat just displays an error message.

If anyone ever tells you to type in IRC any commands you don't understand, *don't do it — ever*. You can unwittingly give away control of your IRC program and even your computer account to another person. (No, we don't tell you the commands!)

The most important command for you to know gets you out of IRC:

```
/quit
```

The second most important command gives you an online summary of the various IRC commands:

```
/help
```

Here are a few more useful IRC commands:

- **/admin** *server:* Displays information about a server.
- **/away:** Tells IRC that you will be away for a while. You don't have to leave this type of message; if you do, however, it's displayed to anyone who wants to talk to you.

- ✔ **/clear:** Clears your screen.

- ✔ **/join:** *channel:* Joins a channel. It's the old-fashioned way of doing the things we describe in the "Join me" section, earlier in this chapter.

- ✔ **/leave:** Leaves a channel. Typing /part does the same thing.

- ✔ **/me:** Sends a message that describes what you're doing and is used to punctuate your conversation with a description of gestures. If you're Mandrake, for example, and type /me gestures hypnotically, other users see *Mandrake gestures hypnotically on-screen.

- ✔ **/topic** *whatwearetalkingabout:* Sets the topic message for the current channel.

- ✔ **/who** *channel:* Lists all the people on *channel.* If you type /who *, you see displayed the names of the people on the channel you're on.

- ✔ **/whois** *name:* Lists some information about the user *name.* You can use your own name to see what other users can see about you.

- ✔ **/nick** *newname:* Changes your name to *newname.*

- ✔ **/ping** *#channelname:* Gives information about the lag (delay) between you and everyone on that channel.

- ✔ **/msg** *name message:* Sends a private message to *name* (only *name* can see it).

Before typing **/list** to see all the available channels, type

```
/set hold_mode on
```

This phrase keeps the names from flying by so fast on-screen that you can't read them. Don't forget to type /set hold_mode off after you finish reading the list.

You can also limit the number of channels listed by typing

```
/list -min 8
```

Only channels with at least eight people on them are listed when you type this phrase.

Remember: Lines that start with a slash are commands to the IRC program; everything else you type is conversation and gets put in the chat box. You may be a tad embarrassed if you are in #cleanliving and type join #hottub, forgetting the slash.

You're not in Kansas anymore

Compared to AOL, IRC is a lawless frontier. Few rules, if any, exist. If things get really bad, you can try to find out an offender's e-mail address by choosing <u>M</u>ember⇨Get I<u>d</u>entity from the menu or clicking the Get Identity button on the toolbar. You receive some information about that person, including, perhaps, his e-mail address — badguy@jclt.com, for example. You can then send an e-mail complaint to postmaster at the same hostname; in this example, postmaster@jclt.com. Don't expect much help, however.

Microsoft is making some attempt to control its own IRC server; you can report problems to the channel #collective.

Web-Based Chat

Although IRC is still the most popular chat service on the Internet, some sites on the Web let you chat by using the web browser — Internet Explorer or Netscape — you already have. You don't have to download and install any software or learn any arcane commands. The good news is that new Web-based chat sites are appearing all the time. The bad news is that having so many chat sites to choose from may not be such a good thing because each site has relatively few members at any given time, particularly compared to AOL and IRC. Here are a few web sites with chat service you may want to try:

   ✔ **Geocities:** http://www.geocities.com
   ✔ **WBS:** http://pages.wbs.com
   ✔ **Parent's Place:** http://www.parentsplace.com

You can find more Web-based chat sites listed by starting at Yahoo (http://www.yahoo.com) and choosing Computers and Internet, then Internet, then World Wide Web, and then Chat.

Chatting in 3-D Worlds

People are now building three-dimensional worlds on the Internet. In these virtual reality worlds, you see a 3-D landscape on-screen, and your character and others are represented by figures called *avatars* that walk, talk, and gesture. A prime example of these virtual reality environments is AlphaWorld (http://www.worlds.net/alphaworld). Microsoft has its own 3-D chat technology, called *V-chat* (the *V* stands for *virtual*). You can find out more about V-chat and download the latest V-chat software by visiting http://www.microsoft.com/ie/chat.

Chapter 14

Getting Together with NetMeeting

● ●

In This Chapter

▶ Calling people and receiving calls

▶ Videoconferencing with another person

▶ Chatting with a bunch of people

▶ Drawing on the whiteboard to make your point

▶ Co-authoring a document

● ●

*W*hen you use IRC as explained in Chapter 14, you probably think to yourself, "This would be a great way for me to meet with my business associates without having to fly to Cleveland (or Dallas or Chicago or Toronto)." Okay, maybe you don't think that. Using the Internet to improve communication among individuals, however, is what the Internet is all about.

How do you make the jump from social chatting with IRC to an online business meeting? By using NetMeeting, of course. NetMeeting is an audio- and videoconferencing program. It allows you to

✔ Talk to another person through your computer's microphone and hear the person speaking through your computer's speakers.

✔ Meet face-to-face with another person (if both of you have cameras connected to your PCs). Even if you don't have a camera, you can still receive video and see the other person. She just won't be able to see you.

✔ Hold a chat session where a number of people can type messages on the screen.

✔ Send files to other meeting participants. It's a handy way to distribute agendas for the meeting.

✔ Create and edit drawings by using a draw program and an online whiteboard that everyone can see.

✔ Share an application with others and see immediately the editing changes your collaborators make online.

This chapter explains how to do all these things in NetMeeting Version 2.1. We also describe the technical stuff you need to know to get NetMeeting up and running on your PC.

Setting Up NetMeeting

NetMeeting has many features, and to use most of them all you need is your Internet connection. To use audio- or videoconferencing, however, you need some extra hardware on your PC:

- **Audioconferencing**. To talk to another person and hear responses, you need a microphone and speakers connected to your PC. You also need a sound card — a full-duplex sound card works best. Because most newer computers have a full-duplex sound card, you probably don't have to worry about it. If you have an older computer, however, or if you want to see what kind of sound card you have, check the owner's manual for your PC. If you can't locate the sound card information, just go ahead and set up NetMeeting — it won't hurt anything. The worst that happens is that you can't send or receive audio.

- **Videoconferencing**. If you want to transmit your picture to another person, you need a camera installed on your PC. What happens if you don't have a camera? You still see the other person, assuming that a camera is attached to the PC, although he doesn't see you. (Currently, you can do audio- or videoconferencing with one other person, but programs are always changing. As NetMeeting evolves, you'll probably be able to exchange audio and video with more than one person or location. For now, however, you're limited to a one-to-one conversation.)

Whenever you change or upgrade your sound card or drivers, you have to run the Audio Tuning Wizard in NetMeeting. You can access it by choosing Tools⇨Audio Tuning Wizard from the NetMeeting toolbar.

When you've checked out your hardware, you're ready to start NetMeeting. The first time you start NetMeeting, you're asked to fill out some personal information to identify yourself and to indicate the types of audio and video drivers your computer uses.

To start NetMeeting, choose Start⇨Programs⇨Internet Explorer⇨Microsoft NetMeeting. (In addition to using the version of NetMeeting that comes with Windows 98, you can also get NetMeeting by downloading it from the Microsoft web site, at www.microsoft.com/netmeeting. To start your downloaded version of NetMeeting, choose Start⇨Programs⇨Microsoft NetMeeting.)

Your ID, please

When you run NetMeeting, you log on to a server. A number of servers are available; some are hosted by Microsoft, and some are from other companies.

Each server has a directory that shows who is logged on to the server. To call someone, you can either select her name from the directory list or type her e-mail address. Of course, other people can also select your name and call you from the directory list. (To keep yourself from being pestered by people you don't want to talk to, a Do Not Disturb option is available. We go over all this a little later when we tell you how to make calls.)

As part of your setup process for getting NetMeeting up and running, you have to supply the personal information (such as your name, e-mail address, and location) that other people see in the directory. You can also add comments to help people locate you or to indicate what you want to talk about.

NetMeeting is a great tool to use to meet with people you know, although you can also call strangers from the directory list. Even though we focus on using NetMeeting for business meetings, you can also put it to use in your personal life — maybe you want to start an online book discussion club or use it for a brainstorming session while writing song lyrics.

Get started by filling out the NetMeeting start-up screens. (If you already have NetMeeting set up on your computer, skip this section.) To fill out the start-up screens, follow these steps:

1. **Read the introductory remarks on the first screen, and click <u>N</u>ext.**

2. **Make sure that the <u>L</u>og On to a Directory Server When NetMeeting Starts check box is selected. Leave the directory server at** ils.microsoft.com **for now.**

   After you see the NetMeeting window, you can view directory lists from different servers to see who is logged on or log on to a different server. Because ils.microsoft.com is the default server, it gets quite busy. If you have trouble logging on to it, you can always change this setting later from the NetMeeting window.

3. **Fill in your name, e-mail address, location, and comments you want to show in the directory, as shown in Figure 14-1.**

   The directory is like the server's phone book — your listing in the directory identifies you to everyone else on the server. Although comments are optional, they do help identify you and what you're going to talk about in the meeting. Don't worry if you can't think of any pithy comments right now. You can always modify these settings at another time from the NetMeeting Options dialog box (by choosing <u>C</u>all⇨ <u>C</u>hange My Information).

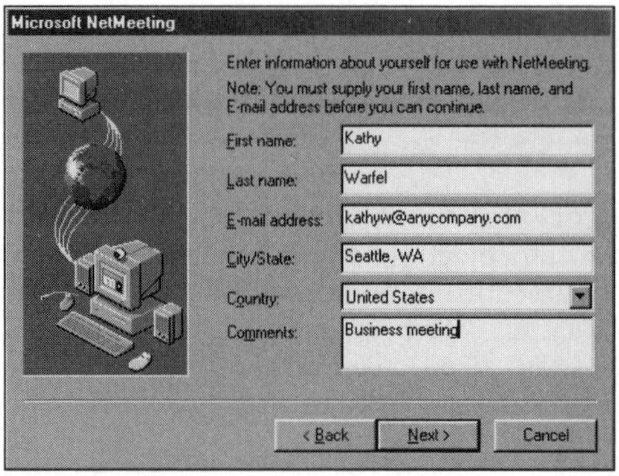

Figure 14-1:
Filling in
personal
information
for the
directory.

Wondering where the nickname goes? If you would rather use a nickname than your real name, enter the nickname in the First name and Last name fields (you must have something in both fields). The information from the First name and Last name fields is displayed on the call recipient's screen when you make a call.

4. **Select the For business use category.**

   Again, you can select any category you want; for the purposes of this chapter, we're concentrating on business meetings.

5. **Select the option that matches your modem speed or connection method.**

   If you're not sure which option to select, accept the default selection for now and go to the next screen.

6. **Click the down arrow and select the video-capture device your computer uses.**

   Again, if you're not sure what to select, leave the default selection as is and go to the next screen.

7. **Verify that you don't have any other programs running on your computer that use audio or video and click Next.**

8. **Click the down arrow and select the Recording device used on your computer. Do the same for the Playback device.**

   You can probably guess what to do if you're not sure what to select. That's right! Leave the default selections and go to the next screen.

9. **Click the Test button to fine-tune your audio.**

   You should hear a drumming noise coming from your speakers. Move the slider bar to adjust the volume.

10. **Click Stop to stop the drumming noise, and click Next.**

11. **Click Finish.**

The NetMeeting window opens and you're finished with the start-up screens!

Getting connected

Depending on how you set up your Internet connection in Chapter 4, you are connected automatically to the Internet when you start NetMeeting or else you have to log on manually. *Hint:* If you see a Dial-Up Connection dialog box prompting you for your username and password, you have to log on manually.

When you get connected to the Internet, you're logged on to the default server you selected on the start-up screen and the directory is displayed, as shown in Figure 14-2. (If you don't see the directory, click the Directory button.)

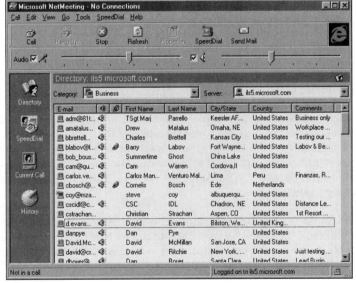

Figure 14-2:
This is it!
The
NetMeeting
window —
your base of
operations
for all things
NetMeeting.

Anatomy of the NetMeeting window

The NetMeeting window contains the usual menu bar and toolbar you're accustomed to seeing. You see how to use these menu options and toolbar buttons as you progress through this chapter. What's unusual about the NetMeeting window are the buttons on the left side of the window and the audio controls.

The buttons on the left side of the window control what information you see in the rest of the NetMeeting window. When you click a button, the information to the right of the buttons changes to display the information you asked for. Here's what the buttons do:

✔ **Directory:** Shows the Directory list — the list of people logged on to the server. A speaker icon next to a name indicates that the person has audio capabilities; a camera icon indicates that the person has video capabilities (the person's computer does, anyway). Your name should appear on the list too.

✔ **SpeedDial:** As you call people and accept calls from others, NetMeeting adds their e-mail addresses to your SpeedDial list. (If you want to turn off this feature, you can set it by choosing Tools⇨Options and clicking the Calling tab.) When you want to place a call, it's much faster to find someone on your SpeedDial list than to search a directory. Clicking the SpeedDial button displays the SpeedDial list, which shows you the status of each person so that you can tell whether she's available.

✔ **Current Call:** Displays the Current Call list — a list of the names of all the people in your current meeting. If you're using videoconferencing, this screen shows the outgoing picture (you) and the incoming picture (the person you're talking to) at the same time on the screen.

✔ **History:** Displays the History list — your NetMeeting log. It shows your activity during your NetMeeting session, including the names of people who have called you, whether you took the call or ignored it, and the time the call was placed.

Near the top of the window are Audio buttons. You see two sections of audio controls — one for your microphone and one for your speakers. When the check boxes next to the microphone icon and the speaker icon are selected, you have full audio capabilities. You should be able to carry on a conversation with the person you've called by speaking into the microphone and listening to the speakers.

If the volume isn't quite right, move the slider bar until volume levels are acceptable. If the person you're talking to has trouble hearing you, for example, increase the volume on your microphone. If you hear only faint sounds from your speakers, increase the volume on your speakers.

NetMeeting has no Hold button, although if you want to stop sending audio momentarily, you can deselect the microphone check box. This feature is handy if you want to confer with someone in your office without the person in NetMeeting hearing you or if you suddenly need to sneeze. When you're ready to resume the conversation in NetMeeting, click the microphone check box again to enable your microphone.

Trying another server

Occasionally, you may get an error message which says that the server is busy, or you may want to look at the directory list for a different server.

Why would you want to do that?

- ✔ If the default server is too busy, you can't use NetMeeting until you log on to a server that's *not* too busy.
- ✔ If you can't find the person you want to call on one directory, you can view another server's directory and then call the person.

To log on to a different server if your default server is busy:

1. **Click the Directory button to access the directory screen.**

2. **Choose <u>C</u>all⇨<u>C</u>hange My Information.**

3. **Click the Calling tab. Click the down-arrow button at the right end of the <u>S</u>erver name box and select a different server from the list that appears.**

   When you click OK to exit the Options dialog box, you log on to the new server. If you get disconnected for some reason, reconnect by choosing <u>C</u>all⇨<u>L</u>og On To. You can always tell which server you're logged on to — the server name is displayed on the right side of the status bar at the bottom of the window.

   The new server you've selected stays in effect until you go back in and change it on the My Information tab. The next time you start NetMeeting, your default server is the new server you selected.

You're not limited to calling people who are on your server. You can be logged on to one server and call someone on a different server. Your name is listed in only one directory, however, and that's the directory of the server you're logged on to. (Or, as your high school English teacher would make you say, the server on to which you're logged. Hmmm, sometimes computer-ese doesn't fit in well with proper English.)

Suppose that you want to call some people but their names don't appear in your directory. They may be logged on to a different server or in a different category. Using the Server and Category fields on the directory screen, you can locate them without logging off your current server.

Here's how to find people on different servers:

1. **Click the Directory button, and then click the down-arrow button at the right end of the Server box. Select a new server from the list that appears.**

   The status bar at the bottom of your NetMeeting window relays everything that's happening. The left side of the status bar shows the directory you've chosen to look at, and the right side of the bar shows the server to which you're connected. The names of the people logged on to the new server are displayed on the screen.

2. **If you still can't find the person you're looking for, repeat Step 1.**

   You can keep trying different servers until you find the person or people you want to call.

   You can also try looking in a different category. Click the down arrow next to the Category box, and select a new category. Options on the category list also enable you to limit the number of names you see in the directory. You can elect to see only people with videocameras, for example, or only people in your country.

To see whether any new people have logged on while you were messing around, click the Refresh button on the toolbar to update the directory list.

Making a Call

To make calling people as convenient as possible, you can use one of many methods because Microsoft couldn't make up its mind about how the NetMeeting program should work. All the methods work the same way and accomplish the same task. Try each method to find the one that's most comfortable for you.

Because audio- and videoconferencing work with you and just one other person, start off by calling one other person. (Whether you're calling one person or ten people, the methods you use to place the call are the same.) In the "Let's Chat" section, later in this chapter, we talk about including lots of people in a meeting.

To call another person in NetMeeting, use one of these methods:

- ✔ Locate in the directory the person you want to call and double-click his name.
- ✔ Click the Call button on the toolbar and type the e-mail address of the person you want to call.

> ✔ Choose Call⇨New Call (or press Ctrl+N) and type the e-mail address of the person you want to call.
>
> ✔ Click the SpeedDial button and double-click a name on your SpeedDial list.

If you watch the status bar, you see the message `Waiting for response` followed by the name of the person you called. A dialog box appears on the recipient's screen telling her that you're calling and asking whether she wants to accept the call or ignore it. When she decides what she wants to do with your call, you are notified. If the recipient accepts your call, you see the Current Call list, and you're ready to start your conversation.

Whenever you want to terminate a call, click the Hang Up button on the toolbar. In most cases, if you placed the call, the other person is also disconnected when you use the Hang Up button.

Talk to me

Assuming that both you and the person you called have microphones and speakers hooked up to your computers, you can start talking as soon as the call is connected. (Remember to look for the speaker icon next to the person's name to check for audio capabilities.)

After your call is accepted, all you have to do to talk to the other person is speak into the microphone! (Think about this: Thousands of dollars worth of computer hardware and software and you've re-created the functions of a $19 telephone! But, wait — it gets better if you start using some of the other NetMeeting features.) The other person's voice is relayed to you through your computer's speakers. During the conversation, you can move the slider bars in the Audio section to adjust the volume.

If you're going to play around with your microphone or speaker volume during a conversation, tell the other person what you're doing before you start experimenting with the volume controls. It's only polite!

Watch what you say

You've probably noticed the small boxes on the right side of the Current Call list. These boxes are your video connections. The first box, labeled My Video, shows your picture. Yes, it's the same picture the person you're talking to receives. The second box shows the other person's name and picture. It's video, not a still picture; when you move, the other caller sees your movements and vice versa.

To start sending video, click the start button (which is the black triangle) at the bottom of the My Video box.

If you want to stop sending video, click the stop button (which is the black square) at the bottom of the My Video box.

You can still keep talking to the other person, whether or not you are sending or receiving video.

The videocamera captures, roughly, your head and shoulders and whatever is in the background. It may be necessary to reposition your camera to hide a messy office. Also, if you got up in the morning and put on only the top half of your business suit (knowing the camera could not see below your shoulders), remember not to stand up during your conversation. You don't want your colleague to see you in your jammies. *A tip within a tip:* You may want to check your video image *before* you call anybody. To do so, make sure that you're not on a call, and then click the start button in the My Video box. This button puts you in Previewing mode, as shown in Figure 14-3, and you can fiddle around with the camera placement and the placement of your chair, for example, before anybody else sees the video. If you work in your bedroom, consider putting a poster of something impressive on the wall behind you.

Figure 14-3:
Previewing
your
outgoing
video
before
anyone else
sees it.

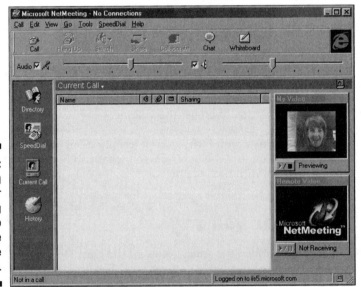

I see you!

Video options are available that let you control whether images are sent and received automatically at the beginning of a call. The default video options are set to start receiving video immediately at the beginning of a call and to wait until you click the start button before sending your video to the other person. These settings mean that all you have to do to see the other person is just look in his video box on the Current Call screen. Figure 14-4 shows the Current Call list when both parties are using video.

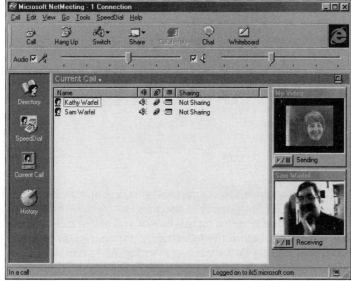

Figure 14-4:
A conversation in which both people are using video.

If the other person's video is not coming through on your screen, click the start button that's at the bottom of his video box or ask the person (via the microphone) whether the camera is working.

You can change the video options by choosing Tools⇨Options, clicking the Video tab, and selecting or unselecting the options in the Sending and receiving video area.

Answering a Call

When someone calls you, a dialog box like the one shown in Figure 14-5 pops up on your screen. All you have to do to answer the call is click the Accept button. If you don't recognize the caller's name or if you don't want to take the call, click the Ignore button.

A list of all incoming calls is kept on the History list. To view the list, click the History button. You can call a person on the history list by double-clicking the name.

It's possible to be too popular. If you don't want calls to come through, choose Call⇨Do Not Disturb. This command stops the dialog box from popping up on your screen. People who try to call you are still listed on the history screen. When you're ready to remove the Do Not Disturb sign, choose Call⇨Do Not Disturb to remove the check mark.

Let's Chat

One-to-one communication seems pretty easy, but how do you get a group of people together? Suppose that you need to meet with four business associates on Monday morning. All five of you are in different cities. You contact the people before the meeting by phone, e-mail, or postal mail and schedule the meeting for 11 a.m. on Monday. At 11 a.m., each person starts NetMeeting. Because you're the person organizing the meeting, you volunteer to call the others. You call them by locating their names on a directory list or by typing their e-mail addresses in the New Call box. As each person accepts your call, the meeting is formed. When everyone is assembled, you start the discussion in the Chat window.

That's really all there is to it. Although you can do additional things — like send a file, have a private side meeting with one person, or draw on a whiteboard — holding a meeting online takes just a little organization and the hardware and software to make the connection.

We hate to give you warnings because communicating on the Internet is such a convenient and easy way to get people together, but you should know that you probably shouldn't discuss company secrets over the Internet. With the vast amount of information flowing across the Internet these days, it's unlikely that someone would pick up on your conversation; if you need to discuss supersensitive topics, however, it's probably better to round up everybody in one geographical location, behind closed doors.

Whenever your meeting includes more than two people, you communicate with each other by typing messages in the Chat window. (During the meeting, you can have a one-to-one audio- or videoconference with one participant, if you want.)

To conduct a meeting by using the Chat window, follow these steps:

1. **Call each meeting participant.**

2. **Verify that all the participants are listed on the Current Call list. Click the Chat button on the toolbar.**

   (Or choose Tools⇨Chat or press Ctrl+T.) When one person opens the Chat window, the Chat window opens on everybody's screen and all participants can start typing messages. Everyone can see the messages instantly, as the messages are entered.

3. **Type the message you want to send and press Enter.**

   Your message is displayed in the Chat window for everyone to see. The default setting places your name before your message.

4. **If you want to add the date or time to your message, choose Options⇨ Chat Format and select the items you want to display in the Information Display area.**

5. **Messages can be saved to a file for future reference. To save the messages in the Chat window, choose File⇨Save and type a filename.**

   If you've already saved the messages once and you want to save them under a new filename, choose File⇨Save As and type the filename.

6. **Messages in the Chat window can be your printed minutes of the meeting. To print a copy, choose File⇨Print.**

7. **When the meeting is over, close the Chat window. Click the Hang Up button on the toolbar.**

One benefit an online meeting has over an in-person meeting is your ability to easily remove someone from the meeting. Unless you have the Do Not Disturb option selected, you can still receive incoming calls. If someone in your meeting accidentally accepts a call from a person who should not be in the meeting, you (as the person who originated the meeting calls) can remove the errant party by right-clicking the party's name on the Current Call list and clicking Remove.

Sending a file

While you're in your meeting, you can do things other than type and read messages. At some point, you'll probably need to send a file to one or all of the participants. Sending a file is a good way to distribute an agenda or topic list to participants.

To send a file to everyone listed on the Current Call screen, choose
Tools⇨File Transfer⇨Send File (or press Ctrl+F). Select the file or type the
filename.

To send a file to one person listed on the Current Call list, right-click the
person's name, and then choose Send File from the menu that appears.
Select the file or type the filename.

On the receiving end, the person you sent the file to sees a Transfer dialog
box. She can choose to open the file or save it to disk.

Although sending a file is most common when you're meeting with a group
of people, you can also send a file to the other person during a one-to-one
audio- or videoconference.

Talking privately

Another thing you may want to do during a meeting is talk privately with
one meeting participant. You can either send a private, typed message or
initiate an audio and video connection so that you and the other person can
talk to and see each other.

To send a private, typed message to another person in the meeting:

1. **In the Chat window, click the down-arrow button at the right end of
   the Send to box. From the list that appears, select the person to
   whom you want to send the message.**

2. **Type your message in the Message box and press Enter.**

   Make sure that you don't type the message first and press Enter while
   the Everyone in Chat destination is listed in the Send To box. If you do,
   everyone sees your message that was intended for one person. That
   could be embarrassing.

To start a private audio or video conversation with another person in the
meeting, click the Switch button on the toolbar and select from the list that
appears the person you want to talk to. A check mark appears next to the
name of the person you selected. When you're finished with the private
conversation, click the Switch button again and click the person's name
again to remove the check mark. (You can also right-click the person's name
on the Current Call list to start and stop the connection.)

You Gotta Have Art

Some people just can't say it all in words. They have to be able to create pictures and illustrations to present their ideas. If you're one of these people (or if you know someone like this), the whiteboard in NetMeeting is for you. With the whiteboard, you can draw as much as you want just as though you were in your company's meeting room. (Well, give or take your skill with paint programs, which is what the whiteboard resembles.) Doing a presentation? Because multiple pages are available on the whiteboard, you can use it to simulate a flip chart.

Whether you're meeting with one person or with many people, everyone can see the whiteboard as soon as you open it. In fact, if you let them, other people can even contribute to your drawing.

Here's how you open the whiteboard and start drawing:

1. **Click the Current Call button, and click the Whiteboard button on the toolbar.**

   (Or choose Tools⇨Whiteboard or press Ctrl+W.) The whiteboard window opens on your screen and on all other meeting participants' screens.

2. **Using the drawing tools on the left side of the whiteboard, create your drawing.**

   Figure 14-6 shows an organizational chart drawn on the whiteboard.

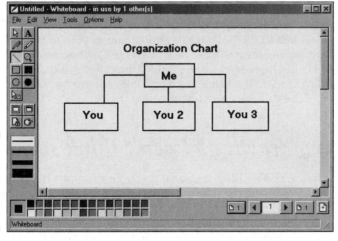

Figure 14-6:
A basic
drawing
on the
whiteboard.

3. **To start a new, blank page, click the Insert New Page button in the bottom-right corner of the whiteboard (the white sheet of paper with a plus sign on it).**

   A new, blank whiteboard appears. Your first page is still on the board. To move backward and forward through the pages, click the Next Page and Previous Page buttons at the bottom of the whiteboard. If the other people who are viewing the whiteboard feel like it, they can add items to the drawing or edit the drawing. You see their changes instantly, as they are entered.

4. **If you create something too precious to throw away, choose File⇨Save and give it a filename.**

   Whiteboard files are saved with the extension .wht.

5. **Need a printout? Choose File⇨Print, and select the print options you want.**

6. **When you're finished using the whiteboard, close the whiteboard window.**

   Participants have to close their own whiteboard window on their computers.

Tempted to change the drawing? Go ahead

Watching someone else create a drawing on the whiteboard is fun. You see each stroke and item as it is entered. If you have a number of people participating in your meeting, the whiteboard can be a place for brainstorming ideas and mapping out thoughts.

As you watch, you may want to jump in and add your own two cents to the drawing. Feel free to do that! (If this action causes pain to the originator of the drawing, he can always lock the whiteboard.) Whenever you see something that should be moved or one little thing that's not quite right, go ahead and change it. The same drawing tools that are available to the originator of the drawing are available to you.

Edit my drawing? I don't think so

Free expression is one thing, but what if you've created a masterpiece and other people are trying to change it? Fear not, for you can lock the whiteboard and keep all other participants from altering your drawing.

To lock the whiteboard, click the Lock Contents button in the drawing tools area. When you are ready to grant dispensation and reopen the drawing to the masses, click the Lock Contents button again. The drawing is once again available to all other meeting participants.

Sharing with Your Friends and Associates

As we all learned in kindergarten, sharing is good. Whether it's your toys or your computer programs, sharing something with others is a nice thing to do. In NetMeeting, you can open a file in its original application and let other people in your meeting see it. Although they can't change it (we discuss that topic in the following section, "Collaborating with Your Partners," they can see it in its original format. It's a good way to relay information without having to retype data in the Chat window or read information to another person. Here's how to share an application with the other people in your meeting:

1. **Open the application you want to share.**

   For example, you can share a Web page you're creating in FrontPage Express. To open FrontPage Express, click the Start button on the taskbar and choose <u>P</u>rograms⇨Internet Explorer⇨FrontPage Express.

2. **In the application window, open the file you want everyone to see (for example, the web page file in the FrontPage window).**

3. **On the taskbar, click Microsoft NetMeeting to return to the NetMeeting window.**

   Make sure that you see the Current Call list. (To get back to it, click the Current Call button on the left side of the NetMeeting widow.)

4. **Click the Share button on the toolbar and select FrontPage Express from the drop-down menu to make the FrontPage Express document visible to everyone in the meeting.**

To stop sharing, click the Share button on the toolbar. Click the application you want to stop sharing to remove the check mark.

 If you're going to collaborate on a document with other people, you must first share the application in which the document is written. If you're collaborating on a Word document, for example, you have to share Word before others can collaborate on the document.

Collaborating with Your Partners

If you've ever tried to co-author a document by exchanging e-mail messages, letters, or faxes, you know how time consuming that process can be. What if you and your co-author could view the document and see editing changes as they are made? Life would be grand.

Get out of the past and fast-forward to the present — now, you and your co-author can access the same document at the same time online. By sharing the document in its original application and electing to collaborate on the document, you can exchange control of it.

While you're sharing a document, the program you're sharing runs on only one person's computer. For example, if you and a coworker are sharing a Word document and you started Word and shared it with your coworker, then Word is running on your computer and the document is stored on your computer. Although your coworker sees an image of Microsoft Word and the document on her screen and can type commands to edit the document, the document is still stored on your computer.

Before you can collaborate on a document, you must share the application in which the document is written. After you complete the steps to share the application, follow these steps to collaborate on a document:

1. **Click the Current Call button, and then click the Collaborate button on the toolbar.**

   The person you want to collaborate with also has to click the Collaborate button on his toolbar.

2. **To gain control of the document, click the mouse button anywhere in the document.**

   Only one person at a time can be in control of the document. You can tell who is in control of the document because the user's initials are displayed on your screen. When you are not in control of the document, you cannot move your cursor, and you see a message telling you to click the mouse button to regain control.

3. **When you're finished collaborating, click the mouse button to regain control of the document. Click the Collaborate button on the toolbar to turn off the collaboration feature. You also have to stop sharing the application, by clicking the Share button on the toolbar and clicking the application to remove the check mark.**

   Your collaborator also has to click the Collaborate button to turn off the collaboration feature.

   If clicking the mouse button doesn't return control of the document to you, try pressing the Esc key.

4. **Go back to the document you were collaborating on, and save the document. (You have to do this step to save the changes that were made during the collaborating session.)**

Be aware that when you collaborate on a document, the other collaborators can open your files from the shared application by using the File➪Open command or save files by using the File➪Save or File➪Save As command. Because you're collaborating, you can see the actions your collaborator is taking, although it's probably a good policy to collaborate only with people you trust.

Chapter 15

Making Your Own Web Pages with FrontPage Express and Netscape Composer

In This Chapter

▶ Web page basics

▶ Graphics and linking

▶ Push your page

*P*erhaps you have noticed all those Web pages for individuals or small organizations and have thought about building a home of your own on the World Wide Web. Strictly speaking, a *home page* is the first page you come to when you visit a Web site, although the term is often used more loosely to cover a collection of pages. People have home pages, companies have home pages, and groups of highly talented authors and speakers have home pages. (You can check out the authors' home pages by following links from Internet Gurus Central, at `http://net.gurus.com`.) If you're ready to build your own home page, read on.

Although creating a home page is not difficult, it may seem complicated for a new computer user. Luckily for you, programs called *Web page editors* or *HTML editors* can help you make your first home page without your even having to know the first thing about programming or HTML. Windows 98 comes with a fine Web page authoring tool called FrontPage Express.

Just so that you know what *HTML* is, in case someone asks, it stands for *HyperText Markup Language*. Web pages are made up of text and pictures that are stuck together and formatted by using HTML codes. In a demonstration of your infinitely good timing, you have waited until now, when you can create your pages without having to understand HTML codes. You can concern yourself with more important things, such as baking chocolate chip cookies. If you decide that you want to be in the Web page creation business, entire books have been written about how to do it. We recommend, however, that you stick to recent titles because older titles may make things more difficult than they have to be. Just to prove how easy all this stuff is, we step you through the process of making your first home page and putting it up on the Web.

Your First Web Page

To create a Web page, we strongly advise that you use one of the WYSIWYG (pronounced "whizzy-whig," it stands for "what you see is what you get") Web page editors. FrontPage Express, which we talk about most, comes with Windows 98. Netscape Communicator includes a nice Web page editor called Netscape Composer. You can get it for free at http://home.netscape.com.

A note about WYSIWYG: In the case of Web page editors, it means that as you create your page, rather than see seriously unattractive HTML codes, you see what it will actually look like. Trust us — you'll like it much better this way. HTML purists point out that WYSIWYG editors churn out less-than-elegant HTML code, although the pages they make generally look fine. If you're planning to create a large, complex Web site, you may want to use more powerful tools, such as Microsoft FrontPage. (The absence of the word *Express* means that FrontPage has lots more features *and* that you have to pay for it.) For one page or a couple of dozen, however, FrontPage Express and Netscape Composer do just fine. Nobody (except John and Margy) writes in HTML anymore.

In a pinch, you can also use your own word processor. Both Microsoft Word 97 and WordPerfect 8 have capable web-editing features built right in!

What is a Web page, anyway?

The first thing you need to know is that a *Web page* is a file — just like a word-processing document or a spreadsheet. You begin by creating your Web page directly on your hard disk. You can see how it looks by telling your browser to view it from your hard disk. Edit and view the page until you have something you like.

After you have your page to the point where you're ready for other people to look at it, you can move it to the Web page server area your Internet service provider allots. If your Web page grows and grows, you may end up having to pay extra for the space it occupies. If your Web page gets extremely popular, you may end up paying an extra fee for the traffic you generate. (You should be so lucky.)

All home pages are Web pages, although not all Web pages are home pages. We tell you how to make a Web page — whether it's a home page is up to you.

The Express route to your front page

Here's our approach to using the Windows 98 FrontPage Express:

1. **Start FrontPage Express by clicking Start and choosing Programs⇨ Internet Explorer⇨FrontPage Express.**

   FrontPage Express displays a window with a big, blank box, as shown in Figure 15-1.

File Save   Insert Image   ┌Create Hyperlink

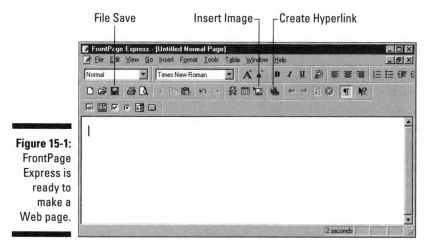

Figure 15-1: FrontPage Express is ready to make a Web page.

Below the menu bar are one or more toolbars. When you point to each icon with your mouse, FrontPage Express tells you what it's for. If you go into mental gridlock at the sight of a blank screen, FrontPage Express is here to help you.

2. **Choose the File⇨New command to display the New Page dialog box. You can choose to start with some predefined pages you can edit, or you can call on the Web Page Wizard, which talks you through the whole process of making a Web page.**

   Whether you battled your own demons or got help from FrontPage Express, you're ready to type on your very own Web page. Typing in FrontPage Express is much like using a word processor.

3. Save your work by choosing File⇨Save As.

When you've done enough work that you wouldn't want to have to start over from scratch if your computer suddenly crashes, save it. Saving in FrontPage Express is a little more involved than saving in your average word processor. For starters, FrontPage Express wants to know the title of your page. If you've typed a title at the top of your page, as we did, FrontPage Express probably makes a reasonable guess. It also wants to know where your page will be stored. In the Page Location box, it suggests a location on your own computer, starting with `http://` and your computer's name. Ignore this stuff for now; we explain it later in this chapter, in the section "Weaving Your Page into the Web." To save your page on your hard disk as a file you can publish later, click the As File button. You see a dialog box that should look much more familiar, in which you can specify a location and filename for the Web page file. The *extension* (the last part after the dot) of the filename should be `htm` or `html` to show that this is a Web page written with hidden HTML codes. Figure 15-2 gives you an idea of what this process looks like.

In principle, when you're done with your page, you save it. In our experience, waiting until you're done to save your work is asking for trouble. Save early, save often — just choose File⇨Save or press Ctrl+S or click the Save button on the toolbar (the disk icon, third from the left).

Figure 15-2:
Saving your FrontPage Express Web page on your local hard disk for now.

Composing your home page

Microsoft and Netscape have been trying to match each other feature for feature in the browser market for some time. Fortunately for us, because their competition has spilled over into the Web page editing market, Netscape Communicator includes Netscape Composer, its own Web page editor. Follow these steps to create your own home page:

1. **Start Netscape Composer by clicking Start and choosing Programs⇨ Netscape Communicator⇨Netscape Composer.**

   Composer displays its own blank screen in which you can express your creative urges. WYSIWYG programs love to make you start with a blank screen. Check out Figure 15-3 for the details.

File Save   Create Hyperlink ⌐ Insert Image

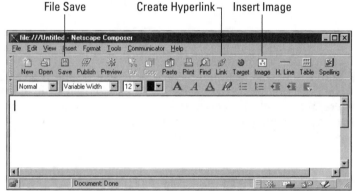

Figure 15-3:
Netscape
Composer
encourages
you to get
creative.

2. **Like FrontPage Express, Composer can help you with your writer's block. Choose File⇨New⇨Page from Template if you want to start with some boilerplate text or File⇨New⇨Page from Wizard if you want Composer to lead you through the process of writing your page.**

   In either case, you have to be online because Composer goes back to its home planet (`Netscape.com`) to get its sample text. You can skip the whole File⇨New business and confront your blank screen with resolve.

3. **Save your work by choosing File⇨Save As.**

   Saving in Composer looks a little more normal than saving in FrontPage Express: You get a regular File Save As dialog box that asks you what you want to call your document. It turns out that after you've told Composer where to save your document, it too wants to know the document's title — so it asks. Take a look at Figure 15-4.

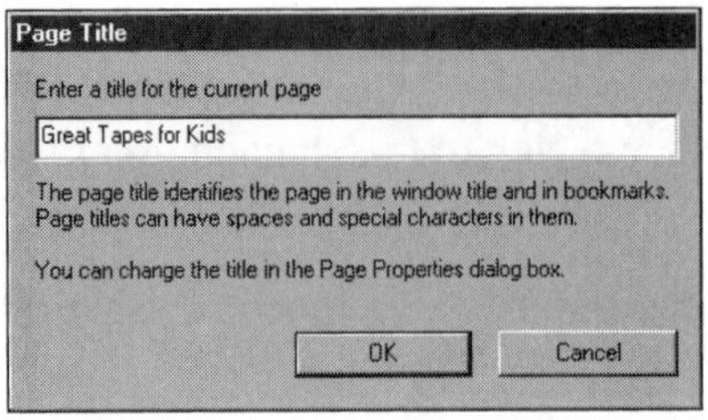

Figure 15-4:
Saving your
web page
on your
local hard
disk.

Page Title

Enter a title for the current page

Great Tapes for Kids

The page title identifies the page in the window title and in bookmarks.
Page titles can have spaces and special characters in them.

You can change the title in the Page Properties dialog box.

OK   Cancel

To say or not to say

Creating your first Web page is easy. Choosing what you put on your page, however, takes a bit of thought. Ask yourself what the purpose of the page is and whom you want to see it. Is it for you and your family and friends and potential friends across the world, or are you advertising your business online?

If your page is a personal page, we recommend that you not include your home address or phone number. If it's a business page, by all means, include your address and phone number. We don't think that the content of your first page is all that important — we just want you to get the feel of putting it out there. You can always add to it and pretty it up. You don't have to tell anybody about your site until you're happy with it.

A Picture Is Worth a Thousand Bytes

Most Web pages contain graphics of some sort. Each picture that appears on a Web page is stored in a separate file. FrontPage Express lets you add images easily and even provides a fair number of images you can pick from. If you want to get fancier, this section tells you a little more that you should know.

Pick a picture format

Pictures come in dozens of formats. Fortunately, only two picture formats are in common use on the Web. These formats are known as GIF and JPEG. Many heated discussions have occurred on the Net concerning the relative merits of these two formats. Because John is an Official Graphics Format Expert, by virtue of having persuaded two otherwise reputable publishers to publish his books on the topic, Table 15-1 lists his opinions about the subject.

Table 15-1	JPEG and GIF Duke It Out
JPEG	**GIF**
Best format for scanned photographs	Best format for computer-drawn cartoons and icons
Handles "true color" better	Can have transparent backgrounds (which we discuss at the end of this chapter)
Files are smaller	Files are larger
Doesn't handle large areas of solid color or sharp edges well	Handles solid color areas well
Some older browsers don't handle JPEG	All graphical browsers handle GIF
Slower to decode	Faster to decode

If you have a picture in any other format, such as BMP or PCX, you must convert it to either GIF or JPEG before you can use it on a Web page. Many graphics-wrangling programs are available; check out the Consummate Winsock Applications page, at `http://www.stroud.com`, for some suggestions. One good choice is Paint Shop Pro, a shareware graphics program that can convert many formats to GIF or JPEG.

Finding the right picture

You can always draw a picture by using a paint program or scan in photographs; unless you're a rather good artist or photographer, however, your graphics may not look as nice as you want.

Fortunately, you can locate lots of sources of graphical material, as described in this list:

✔ Plenty of freeware, shareware, and commercial clip art is available on the Net. Yahoo has a long list of clip art sites; start at `http://www.yahoo.com` and choose Computers and Internet, then Graphics, and then Clip Art. Also try searching for `clip art` in any other Web directory or index.

✔ If you see on a Web page an image you want to use, you can write to the page's owner and ask for permission. More likely than not, the owner will let you use the image.

✔ Lots of regular old software programs totally unrelated to the Internet, such as paint and draw programs, presentation programs, and even word processors, come with clip art collections.

✔ You can buy CD-ROMs full of clip art, which tends to be of higher quality than the free stuff. A commercial clip art collection can be a good investment, particularly considering how many images fit on one CD-ROM.

Clip art, like any creation, is protected by copyright laws. Whether the art has already been used on a Web page or whether a copyright notice appears on or near the image doesn't matter. It's still copyrighted. Some clip art owners grant you a right to use their art royalty-free — that's what the Dover series of clip art books are famous for. Similar arrangements are available on the Web at reasonable prices. Check out our favorite clip art site, ArtToday, at http://www.arttoday.com.

Unless the copyright owner gives you the right to use her art (as Dover and ArtToday do), if you use someone else's copyrighted art, you must get permission to do so. Whether your use is educational, personal, or noncommercial is irrelevant. If you fail to secure permission, you run the risk of anything from a crabby phone call from the owner's lawyer to winding up on the losing end of a lawsuit. One big exception is material created by the United States government, which is generally in the public domain.

Got the picture?

The steps for inserting a picture are much the same in FrontPage Express and Netscape Composer. To insert a picture in your Web page, follow these steps:

1. **Move your cursor where you want the picture to appear.**

2. **Click the Insert Image button on the toolbar (the one with a tiny landscape), or choose Insert⇨Image from the menu bar.**

   Either way, you see the FrontPage Express or the Netscape Composer Image dialog box, as shown in Figure 15-5.

3. **Click the Browse or Choose File button, select the file that contains the picture, and click the Open button.**

   Netscape Composer makes you click the OK button too and may ask you a few questions about your image. FrontPage Express just puts the image on your page. After the picture appears on your Web page, you probably will want to adjust its size and placement so that it looks just right.

4. **Double-click the picture on your Web page.**

   In FrontPage Express, you see the Image Properties dialog box, as shown in Figure 15-6; in Netscape Composer, all those options are in the Insert Image dialog box.

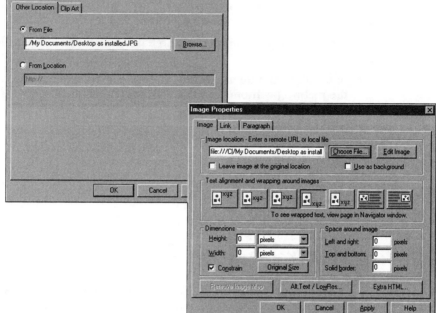

Figure 15-5:
Telling your
Web page
editor
which
picture to
display.

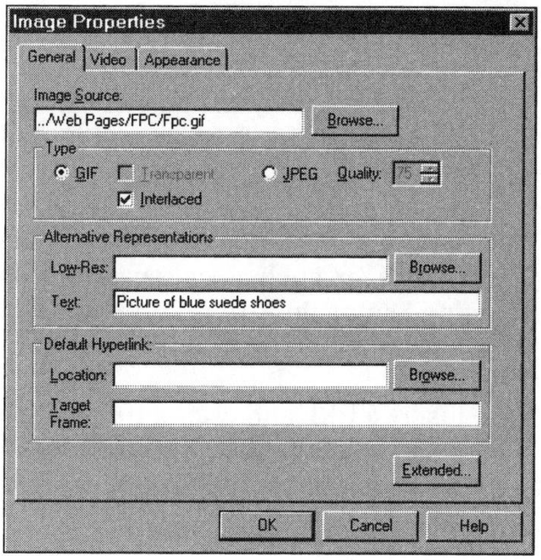

Figure 15-6:
FrontPage
Express
shows you
more
information
about your
picture.

5. **In the Text box in the Alternative Representations part of the dialog box (in Netscape Composer, click Alt Text/Lo<u>w</u> Res), type the text that appears if a browser cannot (or is set not to) display pictures.**

   It's polite to give graphics-impaired people an idea of what they're missing.

6. **In the Text Alignment section of the dialog box, choose how you want the picture positioned on the Web page. (In FrontPage Express, click the Appearance tab.)**

   The most popular options are left, right, or middle.

7. **Click OK.**

You may have to fool around with the properties of your picture until it's in the right place.

Linking Your Page to Other Pages

The *hyper* in hypertext is the thing that makes the Web so cool. A *hyperlink* (or just *link*) is the thing on the page that lets you "surf" the Web — go from page to page by just clicking the link. A Web page is hardly a page if it doesn't link somewhere else.

The immense richness of the Web comes from the links that Web page constructors have placed on their own pages. You want to contribute to this richness by including as many links to places you know of that the people who visit your page may also be interested in. Try to avoid including links to places that everyone already knows about and has in their address books. For example, the common Internet search engines and indexes are already well documented, so leave them off. If your home page mentions your interest in one of your hobbies, however, such as canoeing or volleyball or birding or your alma mater, include some links to related sites you know of that are interesting.

Both Web page editors let you insert a URL and create the link for you:

1. **Highlight the text you want to appear as the link or select the image or graphic you want to act as a link button.**

2. **Choose <u>I</u>nsert⇨Hyperlin<u>k</u> (FrontPage Express) or <u>I</u>nsert⇨<u>L</u>ink (Netscape Composer) from the menu or click the Hyperlink button on the toolbar.**

   You see the Create Hyperlink (FrontPage Express) or Character Properties (Netscape Composer) dialog box, as shown in Figure 15-7.

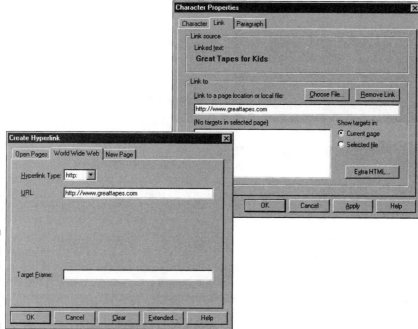

Figure 15-7:
Where do
you want to
link to
today?

3. **In the URL or Link to box, type the address of the page you want the link to go to.**

Be careful to type the address exactly, including all capitalization and the proper prefix, http://, for most links.

4. **Click OK.**

The text you selected in Step 1 is now blue and underlined, to show that it's a link. If you selected an image, it has a blue border.

To change a link later, select the same image or text you selected when you made the link, and then click the Create Or Edit Hyperlink button (or press Ctrl+K) again.

Looking Good

After you have put together a basic Web page, use the tips in this section to avoid some mistakes that novice Websters often make.

Less is more

Don't overformat your text with too many fonts, too much use of font colors, or emphasis with **bold,** *italics,* underlining, or some ***combination.*** Experienced designers sneeringly call it "ransom note" text. Blinking text universally irritates readers. We can't blink text on a printed page, so open and close your eyes a few times to get the effect. Annoying, huh?

Class beats sass

Tiled background images can be cool if they're subtle. Often, however, they make the text on top of them hard to read. Black text on a solid white background (like the pages of this book) has been used for thousands of years with good results.

Avoid the cliché Under Construction sign icons available in many Web art collections. Just leave out the link to your autobiography if you haven't written it yet; or, if you must, include a little note saying "Stop by next month to hear how having Mrs. White in the third grade changed my life." ("Next month" is always safe.)

Missing the big picture

Many Web pages are burdened with images that, although beautiful, take a long time to load — so long that many users may give up before the pages are completely loaded. Remember that not everyone has a computer or Internet connection as fast as yours.

You can take a few steps to make your Web pages load more quickly. The main step, of course, is to limit the size of the images you use. A 20K image (20 thousand bytes big) takes twice as long to load as a 10K image, which takes twice as long to load as a 5K image. You can estimate that images load at 1K per second (on a dial-up connection), so a 5K image loads in about five seconds, which is pretty fast; a 120K image takes two minutes to load, so that image had better be worth the wait.

You may consider putting a small image on a page and give visitors an option (via a link) to load the full-size picture. We know that you're proud of your cat and that she deserves a place of honor on your home page, but not everyone visiting your site will wait excitedly for your cute kitty picture to download. No digitized hairballs, please.

If your images are in GIF files, images with fewer colors load faster than images with more colors. In many cases, if you use a graphics editor to reduce a scanned GIF from 256 colors to 32 or even 16 colors, the appearance hardly changes, although the file shrinks dramatically. If you set up your graphics program to store the GIF file in *interlaced* format, browsers can display a blurry approximation of the image as it's downloading, which at least provides a hint of what's coming.

If your images are JPEG files, you can adjust the "quality" level in the JPEG, with a lower quality making the file smaller. In our experience, because of the limited resolution of most computer screens, you can set the quality quite low with little effect on what appears on users' screens.

You can also take advantage of the cache that browsers use. The *cache* keeps copies of previously viewed pages and images. If any image on a page being downloaded is already in the browser's cache, that image doesn't have to be loaded again. When you use the same icon in several places on a page or on several pages visited in succession, the icon's file is downloaded by the browser only once, and the same image is used for all examples on the pages. In creating your Web pages, you should try to use the same icons from one page to the next, to both give your page a consistent style and speed up the process of downloading its images.

Tips from the pros

If you're looking at other people's Web pages and come across one that's particularly neat, you can look at the source HTML for that page to see how the page was constructed. In Internet Explorer, choose View⇨Source; in Netscape 4.0, choose View⇨Page Source.

Weaving Your Page into the Web

After you've made a page you're happy with (or happy enough with), you have to put it somewhere people can find it. How do you release your page to the world? In principle, showing off your page is easy; in practice, however, a wee bit of confusion is possible.

A home for your home page

For other people to see your Web pages, you have to load your handiwork on a machine with a public Web server. Although nearly every Internet service provider has this type of server, many have limits on how much data you can store for free and start charging you a fee when your site generates more than a certain amount of traffic.

Many companies, such as Geocities (at `http://www.geocities.com`), host your personal or nonprofit Web site for free. Because most of these services are supported by the advertising they display while people are visiting your site, they are glad to get all the traffic you can generate. You can see a long list of free Web hosts by starting at Yahoo (`http://www.yahoo.com`) and choosing Business and Economy, then Companies, then Internet Services, then Web Services, and then Free Web Pages.

The big moment with FrontPage Express

The time has come to step through the curtains and onto the great Web stage. FrontPage provides a Wizard that takes you through the steps required, if your provider lets you use it. After you find a provider who will host your page for you, it gives you a URL (an address on its computer) telling you where you're supposed to put your pages. If your provider works with the Web Publishing Wizard, follow these steps:

1. **Choose File⇨Save As from the menu bar.**

2. **Type in the Page Location box the URL your provider suggested.**

3. **Click OK.**

    The Web Publishing Wizard starts up.

4. **Follow the instructions.**

Unfortunately, hardly any two Internet service providers handle the uploading process in quite the same way. You may have to check with your provider to get all the details you need.

The big moment with Netscape Composer, or when the Wizard fails

If you're using Netscape Composer or if the Web Publishing Wizard doesn't work with your provider, you can also upload your pages with any FTP (File Transfer Protocol) program. Here's the FTP strategy for loading your Web page:

1. **Run your FTP program.**

    We use WS_FTP (described in Chapter 14), although any FTP program or even Netscape Navigator will do. Internet Explorer doesn't handle file uploads.

2. **Log in to your provider's Web server, using your own login and password.**

   The server's name is usually something like `www.gorgonzola.net`, though providers differ. At TIAC, one of the providers we use, you log in to `ftp.www.tiac.net` when you're uploading Web pages. In Netscape Navigator, type the location `ftp://`*username*`@gorgonzola.net/` in the Location box (suitably adjusting both your username and the server name), and type your login password when it asks.

3. **Change to the directory (folder) where your Web page belongs.**

   The name is usually something like /pub/elvis, /pub/www/elvis, or /pub/elvis/www (assuming that your username is `elvis`). Your provider tells you what to use. In Netscape, just click your way to the appropriate directory.

4. **Upload your Web page.**

   Upload both the Web page file itself and the files which contain the pictures that appear on the page. If you're using WS_FTP or another FTP program, be sure to use ASCII mode, not binary mode, for the Web page itself because your Web page is a text file. Use binary mode when you're uploading graphics files. If you use Netscape Navigator, drag the files from Windows Explorer or File Manager into the Netscape window or choose File⇨Upload File.

   If your page on the server is called mypage.htm, for example, its URL is something like

   ```
   http://www.gorgonzola.net/~elvis/mypage.htm
   ```

Again, URLs vary by provider. Some providers don't follow the convention of putting a tilde (~) in front of the name. Others name their users' pages something like /user/elvis rather than ~elvis. You have to check with your provider to find out its conventions.

You should generally call your home page, the one you want people to see first, `index.html`. If someone goes to your Web directory without specifying a filename, such as `http://www.gorgonzola.net/~elvis`, almost all servers serve up the page named `index.html`. If you don't have a page by that name, most Web servers construct a page with a directory listing of the pages in your Web directory. Although this listing is functional enough because it lets people go to any of your pages with one click, it's not cool.

Be sure to check out how your page looks after it's On The Web. Inspect it from someone else's computer, to make sure that it doesn't accidentally contain any references to graphics files stored on your own computer. If you want to be compulsive, check how it looks from various browsers — Netscape, Internet Explorer, WebTV, and Lynx, to name a few.

To update your page, edit the copy on your own computer and then upload it to your Internet provider, replacing the preceding version of the page.

Strut Your Stuff!

After your page is online, you may want to get people to come and visit. Here are a few ways to publicize your site:

- Visit your favorite Web directories and indexes, such as Yahoo (http://www.yahoo.com) and AltaVista (http://altavista.digital.com), and submit your URL (the name of your page) to add to their database. They all have an option for adding a new page. Better yet, go through the list of directories and indexes at http://www.gurus.com/search and submit your URL to each one.

- Visit http://www.submit-it.com, a site that helps you submit your URL to a bunch of directories and indexes. You can get your site submitted to 20 popular searching sites for free or pay money if you want them to submit your URL to a much larger list.

- Find and visit other similar or related sites, and offer to exchange links between your site and theirs.

Getting lots of traffic to your site takes time. If your site offers something different that is of real interest to other folks, it can build a following of its own. A few homegrown sites that keep growing in popularity are Arnold Reinhold's Math in the Movies page, at http://www.world.std.com/~reinhold/mathmovies.html; Margy and Jordan's Great Tapes for Kids site, at http://www.greattapes.com; and John's Airline Information On-Line on the Internet site, at http://www.iecc.com/airline. Just imagine what you can come up with!

Chapter 16

Tips for Effective Web Pages

· ·

In This Chapter

▶ Tips for effective Web pages

▶ Advanced techniques

▶ Creating a home page on America Online

▶ A quick intro to HTML

· ·

*O*kay, in Chapter 15, we explain how to make a Web page. In this chapter, you can discover how to make good Web pages . . . or, at least, more aesthetically appealing pages.

Wickedly Wonderful Web Pages

Making a Web page is easy — so easy that millions of pages are on the World Wide Web. If you want your page to be effective, you have to put some effort into it. Just what constitutes an effective page is a matter of opinion and taste. Much depends on who your audience is. Here are some suggestions you may want to consider as you build your site:

✔ **Look for Web sites you like.** Spend hours at it. See what other people with similar goals have done, and take notes as you go. Imitate the sites you admire, and don't do the things you detest on other peoples' pages.

✔ **Develop a theme and stick to it.** Sure, you can wow the Web with your incredible virtual-reality anthill, but will it sell your ceramic night lights?

✔ **Remember that content counts.** Provide solid information, interesting artwork, entertaining stories, well-maintained links, or something else to make people who visit your site tell their friends about it.

✔ **Make your point quickly.** Try to make your point at the beginning of the first page. Most visitors spend less than ten seconds at your site unless you grab their interest. If you make them do two extra clicks to find out what you have to say, you lose three-quarters of your audience.

✔ **Keep it simple.** Don't let backgrounds and font colors interfere with legibility. Black text on a white background is always in good taste. Focus on the essentials.

✔ **Use color and graphics judiciously.** They should enhance your message, not distract visitors from it. Avoid Web clichés, such as Under Construction signs and animated images that distract visitors from your message.

✔ **Design every page for indexing.** Most people find pages through search engines, and you can do some things to make your pages more visible to those search engines. Include all key words in the first paragraph or two of the text on each page, or use the <META> tag (see the section "META tags," later in this chapter). Secondary pages should have an explicit link to your home page. If visitors get to the secondary page via an indexer, their browsers' Back buttons don't get them to your main page.

✔ **Make your site text-friendly.** Some users cannot use graphics — either because of disability or having an older computer.

✔ **Keep in mind that most information on the Web is copyrighted.** It's true even if no copyright notice is posted. Follow the golden rule.

✔ **Make your site slow-friendly.** Because most Web users connect to the Net through a modem, make the loading of large image files optional and give visitors something to read while they wait for any graphics to appear on their screens. Test-drive your site while using a 14.4 Kbps modem — the slowest modem in common use.

✔ **Treat all browsers equally.** More than a half-dozen browsers are in common use, and the same page make look much different in each of them. At least check how your page looks on both the latest and earlier versions of Netscape Navigator and Internet Explorer. The page displays on these programs can differ greatly!

✔ **Get indexed.** If you want people to visit your page, get it indexed at as many appropriate sites as you can. See also the section "Pushing your page harder," later in this chapter.

✔ **Give visitors a compelling reason to come back.** The Web contains many sites to see, and you want yours to be one of them.

Maintain your presence

Creating your Web site is only half the job. Your site gets stale in a hurry if you don't maintain it. Here are some tips:

✔ **Keep your links alive.** Check all your links regularly by clicking them and seeing whether they still go where they should. Update or delete any that go nowhere. Look at the Web shareware sites for programs that do this automatically.

✔ **Link to the main page of sites wherever possible.** Although Webmasters rearrange the content within a site regularly, top-level addresses don't change as often. For example, link to `http://net.gurus.com` (the Internet Gurus home page) rather than `http://net.gurus.com/toc-i4d98.html` (the page about a specific book we wrote).

Some large sites, however, such as the Internet Movie Database (at `http://www.imdb.com`) suggest safe ways for you to link to individual pages.

✔ **Put information that changes regularly on its own page.** A single simple page in an easy-to-update format is much less work to keep current than five elaborately formatted pages, each containing a few facts that change often.

✔ **See your site through others' eyes.** Every now and then, ask someone else to find your home page and tour your site while you watch. If you can, videotape the visit. Believe us — it's a humbling experience. Many things that seemed obvious to you aren't obvious to a new visitor.

✔ **Commit only to what you can do.** Make yourself a maintenance checklist and schedule that you're willing to follow. A low-maintenance page containing a mission description and contact information — with no time-dependent information and few or no links — is better for an organization than is a complex page filled with expired links and announcements for events that have already happened.

✔ **Solicit advice.** Include an e-mail address on your page, and invite comments and suggestions.

✔ **Stay put.** Links to your site are priceless. Don't sever those links by changing the URL of your Web pages unless absolutely necessary, and provide a cross-reference from the old URL if you do change.

Pushing your page harder

People won't visit your page if you don't let them know about it! We suggest a few ways to get the word out in Chapter 15 (see the section there about strutting your stuff). You can save yourself a great deal of surfing by paying a Web site submittal service. Here are a few:

✔ **Submit It:** `http://www.submit-it.com`

✔ **Go Net-Wide:** `http://www.GoNetWide.com/gopublic.html`

✔ **WebPromote:** `http://www.usaworld.com/WebPromote.htm`

Do it in style

If your Web home contains more than one page, it looks a whole lot better if each page has a similar look or style. Designing your Web page is much like decorating a room in your house. Here are some ways to keep your site from looking like a hodgepodge:

✔ Use a single type font and size for body text.

✔ Use only one type of bullet.

✔ All buttons should use the same typeface, capitalization, color, and border.

✔ Pick a single color scheme. All pages should have the same background and use the same color to highlight links.

✔ Design a standard heading for each of your pages. Using the same basic graphics on each page speeds loading and creates a uniform image.

Feel free to break these rules when you have a good reason to do so. One good reason is to draw visitors' attention to something you want them to notice.

You can find many more listed at Yahoo: Start at `http://www.yahoo.com`, and then click Computers and Internet, then Internet, then World Wide Web, and then Announcement Services.

After you fill out the submittal services form and click the Submit button, you have to wait as each site is contacted and gets confirmation. This process takes awhile, so be patient and don't interrupt the process.

Yahoo (at `http://www.yahoo.com`) is one of the better Web directories, in part because humans review all submissions. It is important to follow the Yahoo submittal instructions carefully if you want to be listed there.

If you ever saw the movie *Six Degrees of Separation,* you understand how easily a con artist can use a small amount of personal information about you to abuse your friends' and families' trust. A kidnapper who sees your kid's gymnastic award online could weave a convincing reason to pick her up early from class. Think before you put detailed personal information on your home page.

Exchange links and join rings

You may be able to *exchange links* with other sites that have similar themes. In return for adding a link to another site to your Web page, the other site promises to add a link to your site. For more information, visit `http://www.linkexchange.com`.

Web rings are groups of Web sites that link to each other to form a circle in cyberspace. Visit `http://www.webring.com` for information about more than 15,000 Web rings you can join or to find out how to start your own ring.

Insert META tags

Some sites, particularly Web indexers such as AltaVista, don't ask for key words and descriptions when you register with them. Instead, these sites get all the information they need from your pages, indexing all the words and using the first sentence or two as a page description. In fact, these indexers visit your page regularly to update their listings.

You can control how these sites index your pages by including a META tag in each page you make. Most indexers use the description you provide in the META tag and add any included key words to those it got from your page's text. A page about this book, for example, may contain these lines:

```
<META name="description"
content="A friendly, easy to understand guide to the
          Internet for Windows 98 users.">
<META name="keywords"
content="book, internet, world wide web, www, e-mail,
          email, windows 98, dummies, dummy, dumby, begin-
          ner, novice, newbie">
```

Include keywords that may not be in the main text, variant spellings, and even common misspellings. You want people to find you, even if they spell a keyword wrong.

Advanced Web Making

This section describes some simple ways to make your Web pages more attractive: transparent GIF images and colored Web page backgrounds.

"I can see right through it"

One simple element is transparency. Whenever you have a GIF of an image that isn't really rectangular, making the area outside the image transparent always makes the image look better. Because transparency adds only ten bytes to the size of a GIF, it doesn't affect the time to load or display the file.

You need to use a graphics program that can mark one color in a GIF as transparent. In Windows, using the shareware program LView Pro or Paint Shop Pro is the most popular way to do that. Some Web pages also can "transparentize" a GIF for you. The following pages are among those that can do so:

✔ http://www.mit.edu:8001/tweb/map.html (United States)

✔ http://www.inf.fu-berlin.de/~leitner/trans/english.html (Europe)

Color me purple

Many Web pages have background patterns. We're reluctant to tell you how to use them because we think that background patterns are almost without exception ugly and difficult to read. (Okay, we relent and tell you how in the next section.)

Plain background and foreground colors on your pages look much better. They let you feature, for example, black text on a white background or vice versa — as long as a user's browser supports that effect, of course. (Although it's another addition that originated with Netscape, it's widely supported.)

You may be enlisted in the browser war

We have mentioned the fierce attack Microsoft is mounting against Netscape dominance in Web browser software. We've usually mentioned this situation in the context of marketing or the legal challenges Microsoft has been facing. One of the areas in which Microsoft and Netscape conflict, however, affects you directly: HTML codes. Because both sides have added their own unique features to the Web's language for building pages, if you use one of these vendor-specific features, your page doesn't look as good on the other company's browser. You've just been drafted into the browser war.

For better or worse, the Microsoft FrontPage Express program makes it all too easy to incorporate Microsoft-specific HTML elements, including background sounds, marquees, and WebBot components. Use them if you like, but remember that they don't work for visitors who use the Netscape browser.

The Best Viewed with Any Browser Campaign, at http://www.anybrowser.org/campaign/ has more information about ways to ensure that your Web site makes a good impression on each and every visitor.

Both FrontPage Express and Netscape Composer let you set the colors for your page. In FrontPage Express, you choose File➪Page Properties from the menu and click the Background tab. In Netscape Composer, you choose the Format➪Page Colors and Properties command from the menu and click the Colors and Background tab. Then click the Background drop-down box to see a list of available colors. *Default* is the dull battleship-gray that someone in the dim prehistory of the Internet (the early 1990s) thought would make a nice background for Web pages. If you don't see a color you like, double-click Custom or Other. You see a new window with a color matrix that enables you to click any color imaginable. Right-click the color matrix for additional instructions. Go wild!

We find that you must always fiddle with colors to make them look good. Remember that many PC users can display only a limited number of colors on their screens at one time. If you use other than basic colors, Windows approximates your colors with dithered colors (by using a geometrical pattern of basic colors) that are utterly illegible. Remember too that because some people are more or less color-blind, you should make sure to provide plenty of contrast between your text color and your background. Although white on black and black on white may seem boring, these combinations have certainly stood the test of time.

What's that behind you?

Okay, here's the scoop on background patterns. Background patterns are really images, just like the ones we discuss in Chapter 15, except that they happen to be displayed behind the rest of the page. Unless you have an enormous background as big as the entire page (not recommended), your background is tiled to fill the window. That is, starting at the upper-left corner of the window, your browser fills the window with repeated copies of the background image. Call us boring, but the only type of background images we have found that work well are ones that are very wide and not very tall — usually wide enough to fill the entire width of the browser window so that they repeat down the window. This type of background image can create a nice-looking border down the left side of the window, for example.

You set a background by choosing File➪Page Properties (in FrontPage Express) or Format➪Page Colors and Properties (in Netscape Composer) and clicking the Background tab. Then check the Background Image box and type the name of the image file you want to use.

Why you would want your own home page?

Here are some reasons to have a home page on the Web:

✔ Advertise a business or hobby.

✔ Help people find you more easily.

✔ Publish your ideas and creations to the world.

✔ Tell friends what's happening in your life (more than one prenatal ultrasound image file is proudly displayed on the Internet).

✔ Carve your initials on the Web as an art form or just for the fun of it.

You may also want to build a page to help an organization you belong to, such as a school, church, synagogue, mosque, or other charity.

Electronic commerce is about to explode. A Web site for your business that at least lets the world know who you are, what you sell, and how to contact you is as vital as a listing in the phone book. While you're at it, reserve a domain name for your business (you can ask your Internet provider to register a domain name for a fee).

Table the motion

After you have played with Web pages for a while, you notice that HTML has a mind of its own about how pages will look. For example, don't bother trying to add tabs or additional spaces to get text to line up in columns — it just doesn't work. One technique that gets around some of HTML's limitations is to use tables. A *table* organizes a section of your page as a rectangular grid of boxes, called *cells.* Although you may think of tables as the way to display the kind of numerical information that comes from a spreadsheet program, Web pros use them for a wide variety of special effects, such as placing text where they want it on the page, setting up multiple columns of text, and creating decorative borders.

To create a table, choose Table⇨Insert Table (in FrontPage Express) or Insert⇨Table⇨Table (in Netscape Composer) from the menu. Both editors display a dialog box in which you can specify for your table the number of rows and columns, alignment (left, right, or center), border size, and width, either in pixels or as a percentage of table width.

The key thing to remember about tables is that the cells can contain almost anything: text, graphics, hyperlinks — even another table! If you want to contrast Abraham Lincoln's Gettysburg Address with George Washington's Farewell Address, for example, create a table with one row and two columns. Paste Lincoln's words in one cell and Washington's in the other. If you want to display a block of text in the middle of your page, make a table with three columns and paste the text in the center cell. Then adjust the width of the right and left cells by clicking each cell and choosing Table⇨Cell Properties (in FrontPage Express) or Table⇨Properties and clicking the cell tab (in Netscape Composer) from the menu.

Finding a Home on America Online

AOL members can have a home page at no additional cost. Each username under your account can store as much as two megabytes of Web information, enough for fairly complex pages if you don't use a number of large graphics or multimedia files.

To find the home page (if he has one) of a member named `screenname`, point your browser to

`http://members.aol.com/screenname`

Note: Some older AOL Web pages may be stored under `http://home.aol.com/screenname`.

You can use FrontPage Express or any other HTML editor to create your home page and then upload the HTML file to AOL. AOL also provides a novice-friendly Web page authoring tool called Personal Publisher. Go to the keyword **Personal Publisher**.

A page created by using Personal Publisher can be edited by using any HTML editor; after you have changed the page in this way, however, it can no longer be edited with Personal Publisher.

AOL has a support area for Web page authors called the Web Diner (keyword **Web diner**) that's worth checking out.

What's All This Stuff about HTML?

Web pages are written in a special computer language called *HTML,* which stands for *HyperText Markup Language.* Programs such as Microsoft FrontPage let you create HTML documents almost as easily as you create printed documents in a word processor. You absolutely, positively don't have to understand HTML to use them, although we give you a quick introduction to HTML in case you're curious or run into a situation in which you believe that understanding HTML may help (you want to impress a date, maybe).

HTML files are text files that are usually stored with the extension .html or .htm. In fact, you can even write a text file in the HTML language by using a text editor like Windows Notepad to create a simple page; it's not all that hard to do.

Most users of personal computers are familiar with the *what you see is what you get* (or *WYSIWYG*) concept of document preparation. In using WYSIWYG, authors are in complete control of how their documents look. HTML, on the other hand, is based on a totally different model. An author or an HTML editing program converts a text document into an HTML page by inserting tags that describe the function of various parts of the text, such as

- ✔ Addresses
- ✔ Lists
- ✔ Headings
- ✔ Quotes
- ✔ Words requiring emphasis

HTML tags are code names surrounded by an open angle bracket (<) and a closed angle bracket (>). After tags are activated, they usually must be turned off by another tag with the same code but preceded by a slash character (/). Text that appears between such pairs of tags is called *tagged text.* Here's an example:

```
<BOLD>This sentence will appear in bold on your
          browser.</BOLD>
```

The Web browser that reads the HTML page decides how tagged text appears on-screen. In particular, HTML ignores return characters and any extra spaces, except in preformatted text marked by the tags <PRE> and < /PRE>.

The HTML concept is a throwback to 1970s text-preparation methods, although extensions have been added to HTML to give authors more control over the appearance of their pages. You need an HTML editor program to take full advantage of these extensions.

Most Web browsers enable you to read the HTML text of any page you find interesting so that you can see how they do it. In FrontPage, choose <u>V</u>iew➪ HTML from the menu bar.

Table 16-1 lists some commonly used HTML tags.

Table 16-1	HTML Codes: Web Page Innards
Tag	*What It Does*
<A> ... </A>	Defines a hypertext link (long, long ago known as an *anchor*)
<ADDRESS> ... </ADDRESS>.	Displays enclosed text in address style
<BLOCKQUOTE> ... </BLOCKQUOTE>	Displays enclosed text as indented block of text — typically used for a quotation from another source
 	Starts new line within paragraph
<H1> ... </H1>	Indicates Level 1 heading, the biggest; used mainly for page titles
<H2> ... </H2>	Indicates Level 2 heading, a medium size; used for main subjects
<H3> ... </H3>	Indicates Level 3 heading, which is smaller in size; used for secondary subjects
<H4> ... </H4>	Indicates Level 4 heading, which is smaller still; used for tertiary subjects
<H5> ... </H5>	Indicates Level 5 heading, the next-to-smallest-size heading; not good for much
<H6> ... </H6>	Indicates Level 6 heading — tiny; used for fine print
<HR>	Draws line (a horizontal rule) across page
<LI>	Indicates item in a list
<OL> ... </OL>	Indicates ordered list; items in ordered list are typically numbered
<UL> ... </UL>	Indicates unordered list; items in unordered list are typically bulleted
<P>	Indicates beginning of new paragraph
<PRE> ... </PRE>	Displays enclosed text as is, using its native spacing and line breaks; a monospace font is normally used, making <PRE> ideal for displaying tables or ASCII art (pictures drawn in characters)
<EM> ... </EM>	Emphasizes enclosed text, typically by displaying it with underlining

(continued)

Table 16-1 (continued)

Tag	What It Does
<STRONG> ... </STRONG>	Displays enclosed text in strong emphasis style — typically in boldface type
<I> ... </I>	Displays enclosed text in italicized style
<B> ... </B>	Displays enclosed text in boldface style
<TT> ... </TT>	Displays enclosed text as typewriter text, typically shown in monospace font
<META> ... </META>	Encloses text addressed to any indexer program; text is not displayed on your page
<TABLE> ... </TABLE>	With additional tags in between, defines a table; don't even think of using tables without a good HTML editor

For more information about Web authoring, see *HTML For Dummies,* by Ed Tittel and Stephen N. James (published by IDG Books Worldwide, Inc.).

An excellent compendium of HTML elements by Ron Woodall is at `http://www.htmlcompendium.org`.

Part V
The Part of Tens

The 5th Wave   By Rich Tennant

Meditations, Inc.
BOOKS · SEMINARS · TAPES

"Sales on the Web site are down. I figure the server's chi is blocked, so we're fudgin' around the feng shui in the computer room, and if that doesn't work, Ronnie's got a chant that should do it."

In this part . . .

There's a lot to know about a lot of stuff before you begin to master the Internet. Stuff we couldn't fit anywhere else we put here, in The Part of Tens. We're fond of quoting Tom Lehrer, who said that "Base eight is just like base ten, really — if you're missing two fingers." So you may find that some of our lists have ten items in them in more of a symbolic than a literal way. We help you with common pitfalls, frequently asked questions, places to find things, and things you absolutely, positively, shouldn't even think about doing.

Chapter 17
Ten Problems and Their Solutions

● ●

In This Chapter

▶ Problems most Internauts encounter

▶ What to do about those problems

● ●

*L*ots of people are afraid of the Internet and of the problems they will encounter. Relax — you'll be a pro in no time! In the meantime, here are the solutions to the problems many readers encounter.

"Loading Web Pages Takes Forever on My Computer"

The Internet promises many exciting possibilities, but it provides nothing except tedium when each page takes half a minute or more to appear. Not all Internet slowdowns are under your control, although you can take steps to speed things up.

✔ **Set your browser to load images only when you ask for them, as explained in Chapter 9.**

✔ **Get a faster modem.** If your modem is slower than 28.8 kilobits per second, it's high time to upgrade. If you're using a 28.8 Kbps unit, however getting a 33.6 Kbps or one of the new 56 Kbps or x2 modems probably will show only a modest improvement.

✔ **Switch to a higher-speed service, such as cable, xDSL, or ISDN.** All these are much faster than ordinary phone lines, although price and availability vary from region to region. Getting one of these services makes your surfing a pleasure rather than an exercise in patience (the so-called "died and went to heaven" effect).

"My E-Mail Inbox Is Filled with Junk Mail"

The best thing to do about junk e-mail, or *spam,* is to get good at deleting it immediately. Don't even read it if it is obviously junk. Look for telltale subject lines like "MAKE MONEY FAST!!!" or bizarre return addresses, like "???@???." If you aren't sure, you should open the message — you don't want to throw out something important. You don't have to read the entire message after you realize that it's junk.

Whatever you do, don't encourage the junk e-mail industry by buying what they are selling. You may even consider getting a different account name to use on mailing lists, chat rooms, and Usenet newsgroups — all places where spammers collect addresses for their lists.

See Chapter 6 for more tips and visit `http://spam.abuse.net` and `http://www.cauce.org` for suggestions for fighting the spam problem.

"I Don't Want My Kids Exposed to Online Porn and Weirdos"

Your kid is probably safer on the Internet than he or she would be at the mall, although enough raunchy stuff is online that parents should actively supervise their kids' Internet use. Here are some tips:

✔ Although software is available that keeps kids from visiting unsuitable sites, you are relying on someone else's judgment about what is suitable. Because most sites tend to err on the side of caution, your kids see a Web that is very watered down. You can find pointers to these filtering services and many other resources for parents at `http://www.smartparent.com`.

✔ Be sure that you talk to your kids regularly about what they are doing online and what behavior you consider acceptable. Make sure that they know not to meet any Net friends in person without your permission and never to give out over the Internet any information that could identify them in the real world. This kind of information includes full name, street address, phone number, school they attend, and hours they travel to and from school or other activities.

✔ The best solution, particularly for younger children, is to have a parent or other adult be with them at all times while they are online. If children are not old enough to go out on their own in the real world, they are not old enough to go out on their own online.

"I'm Afraid to Use My Credit Card Online"

If you are doing business with a reputable firm that offers a secure Web page for entering credit card information, you are probably safer than when you use your credit card at a restaurant or gas station. You can tell whether a page is secure by looking for an unbroken lock or key logo in the lower-left corner of your browser window.

For the highest level of security, we recommend that you try to get a version of your browser with the U.S., or 128-bit, security feature. The international, or 40-bit, versions can be broken by hackers, though with some difficulty.

"My Computer Crashes Frequently While I'm Online"

Computers have no good reason to crash as much as they do, and — hopefully — someday they won't. In the meantime, here are a couple of steps you can take to make crashes happen less often:

✔ Make sure that your computer has enough memory (RAM). We recommend at least 32 megabytes.

✔ Make sure that you have the latest version of your browser and helper software, although you should stay away from beta versions. The word *beta* means that the software has been sent out without complete testing. You can probably wait for the fully tested version, which will have enough problems.

"I Can't Find a Friend's E-Mail Address"

The best solution to this problem is to call your friend on the phone and ask for his address. Right now, no perfect way exists to find out someone's e-mail address. Here are some other suggestions:

✔ Keep an e-mail address book. Both Netscape and Outlook Express have this feature. When someone you care about sends you a message, copy the address, which is in the message's From field, and paste the address in your electronic address book.

✔ If you have the person's business card or stationery, see whether it lists an e-mail address.

✔ Try searching for the person's name by using AltaVista (at `http://altavista.digital.com`) and DejaNews (at `http://www.dejanews.com`).

✔ All the value-added service providers, such as America Online, CompuServe, and Prodigy, have ways for you to look up the addresses of other subscribers to that service. You have to be a subscriber on that provider's service, however. The address directory is one of the added values of a commercial service.

Several groups have set up Internet "white pages" directory services. None is close to complete. Still, you can try any of these services, such as `http://www.four11.com` or `http://www.whowhere.com`, to find long-lost friends or enemies.

"I Keep Getting '404 File Not Found' Messages"

If you typed the URL from a printed source, for example, make sure that you typed it exactly as it was printed, including capitalization.

If you're sure that you typed the URL correctly or if you clicked a hypertext link, the data on the site may have been reorganized. Try "walking up" the URL by deleting the portion to the right of the last slash character, and then the next-to-last slash character, and so on. If you get a "File Not Found" message when you try this address, for example:

```
http://world.std.com/~reinhold/pubs/mathmovies/
```

try this one instead:

```
http://world.std.com/~reinhold/pubs/
```

Then try this one:

```
http://world.std.com/~reinhold/
```

or even this one:

```
http://world.std.com/
```

At one of these levels, you may find a hint about where the file you seek can be found.

You can also use a search engine by including in the URL both the filename or topic you seek and the domain name. In the preceding example, you would search for `world.std.com` and `mathmovies`.

"My Eyes Hurt, My Back Aches, and My Arm Is Sore"

Spending a great deal of time at the computer can be hard on your body and can even lead to debilitating injury. Follow these tips:

✔ Make sure that your computer is set up in a way that minimizes stresses while you work. The top of your monitor should be at or slightly below eye level and positioned to minimize reflections and glare. Your chair should give good back support and keep your thighs horizontal and your feet flat on the floor. Your forearms should be horizontal and in a straight line with your wrists and hands while typing.

✔ A good computer desk and chair are excellent investments if you plan to use your computer frequently.

✔ Take frequent short breaks. Look out the window several times an hour.

✔ If you do notice pain or discomfort, see your doctor sooner rather than later. Treatments for injuries related to computer use are usually more successful if the problems are caught early.

Yahoo has a collection of sites dealing with computer health problems. Start at `http://www.yahoo.com` and then click `Health`, then `Diseases_and_Conditions`, and then `Repetitive_Strain_Disorders`.

"I Don't Have Enough Time to Try All Those Interesting Web Sites "

Give up television. The average American watches 2.6 hours of television and videos a day. Although many sites on the Web are a waste of time, compared to sitting on the couch in front of the idiot box, surfing the Internet is positively purposeful. Some Web sites even tell you what you missed on TV last night.

Unlike TV, the Web can save you time. Internet shopping can be very convenient. More and more government agencies have forms available online. For example, you can get passport forms at `http://www.state.gov`. You can look up zip codes at `http://www.usps.gov`. For almost any kind of information, in fact, the Internet is becoming the first place to look.

"I Spend Too Much Time Online"

The Internet can be addictive. The standard advice is "Get a life!" If you are truly enjoying what you're doing and it's bringing you in contact with others, don't be too hard on yourself.

The best test for whether you have gone overboard in your Internet usage is to ask whether the Internet is interfering with your most important relationships and activities, such as family and work. Here are some suggestions if you think that you are hooked and want to cut back:

- ✔ Talk to family and friends and get their honest appraisal of your online activities.

- ✔ Sign up for real-world activities that get you out of the house and away from the Net, such as evening classes, a health club membership, theater subscriptions, and political groups. Of course, you can spend hours on the Internet finding these activities.

- ✔ Put yourself on an Internet diet — budgeting the hours you are online each week — and stick to it.

- ✔ Pick one day a week when you do not log on, not even to check your mail.

- ✔ Let a family member change your password so that you have to ask her to log you in.

- ✔ If the Internet is ruining your life, give away your computer. People got along fine before the Net existed, and you may be better off without it.

- ✔ Get professional help, but don't look for it online!

Chapter 18
Ten Frequently Asked Questions

● ●

In This Chapter

▶ Straight (but not narrow) answers to vexing questions about the Internet

▶ Our opinions about what's useful and what's not

▶ A few myths debunked

● ●

The Internet is a big subject; it seems like it's a subject that's on everybody's mind nowadays. As a result, we get asked lots of questions about the Internet. Many of the answers to those questions are sprinkled throughout this book, although some of them don't fit neatly under any specific subject. You can find those questions, and our answers, here.

Now, whenever someone asks us one of these questions, we can — rather than answer it — tell them to get a copy of this book and read the chapter. Heh-heh.

If you have more than ten remaining questions after you read this book, surf to our Web site, at http://net.gurus.com, where we tell you where to find hundreds of answers.

It used to be that the most frequently asked questions about the Internet were things like "What kind of computer should I buy?" or "What software should I use?" If you're reading this book, you've probably decided on Windows 98 and a computer that can run it, so we don't have to deal with those questions here. That leaves room for more interesting questions.

"How Important Is This Internet Stuff?"

Darned important. In a minute, we talk about all the wonderful things you can do on the Internet and all the wonderful reasons you *should* bother with the Internet. For now, however, let's talk about why you have to understand the Internet, whether you really want to or not.

Back when computers were just beginning to emerge from their big, glass houses, a visionary friend of ours, Ted Nelson, wrote a book subtitled "You can and must understand computers now!" He was absolutely right. If you don't have a clue about how computers work, you'll have a frustrating day dealing with everything from the microwave oven to the automatic-teller machine to the voice information system when you call the auto-parts store.

The future is about information, and the Internet is about getting information to people. It's not that you *can't* get by without information; of course you can. You can get by without electricity too. If you're in a community where information counts, however, whether it's school, business, or the job market, you have much more access to information if you're comfortable with the Internet. Besides, there's plenty of fun stuff to do on the Internet as well.

"Why Bother with the Internet, and What Can I Do with It, Anyway?"

Our favorite real-life version of this question came from one of our cousins who's not particularly technically savvy. The way he put it was, "The Internet — isn't that the new advertising thing companies are trying to get people to use so that they can sell us more stuff?" All he ever saw of the Internet were the Web addresses that started showing up on everybody's advertisements for everything.

We like to think that what motivates advertisers to put their Web addresses in their ads is a symptom of why the Net is so useful, and not a cynical attempt to force more of their product down your throat. (We suspect that companies put their Web addresses on their ads because it's the with-it thing to do and makes them look like they're on the cutting edge.)

The Internet is about information and communication. In Chapter 1, we talk all about the different things you can do on the Internet, and all of them revolve around getting information in different ways or communicating with people in different ways. If you're not interested in either of those things, chances are that the Internet is not for you. On the other hand, chances are that whatever you *are* interested in has an information aspect or a communication aspect to it, whether it's finding out about the latest product from some company, finding out about the latest design ideas in your favorite craft, chatting with people who share the same challenges you do, or finding people who want to buy your products or services. *That's* why advertisers put their Web addresses in their advertisements: The Net is about information.

If you're curious about some product, chances are slim that you would pick up the telephone and call in for some information and even slimmer that you would still be interested when printed material arrived in your mailbox. With the Internet, however, in a few seconds you can be looking at a page full of information about a product, and in a second or two more you can decide that you don't care about it or that you are really interested. No matter that you live in deepest, darkest suburbia, if you want to chat about keeping chickens, you can connect with other chicken fanciers from all over the world and share stories and advice.

All the things we list in Chapter 1 that you can do with the Internet are not ends in themselves — they're means to other ends. To put it succinctly, it's not what you do with the Internet — it's what the Internet lets you do with the rest of your life. Now that so many other people are on the Internet, relevant information and people are on the Internet no matter *what* you do with the rest of your life.

"Are the Internet and the World Wide Web the Same Thing?"

No. Next question, please.

If you've read Chapters 1 and 8 in this book and the distinction between the Internet and the World Wide Web still isn't clear, we forgive you. People use the terms almost interchangeably, and, in casual conversation, sometimes we do too. We shouldn't, of course, although as it becomes increasingly true that anything you can do on the Internet you can do through the World Wide Web, it's hard to keep the distinction uppermost in one's mind without sounding like a nitpicky academic.

Analogies abound for the Internet, and most of them make some kind of useful point and leave out some kind of important distinction: The Internet is the highway, and the World Wide Web is one kind of traffic that travels on the highway, just as cars, trucks, and buses share the physical highways; the Internet is the engine that powers the information revolution, and the World Wide Web is the dashboard we all use to control the engine; the Internet is like a cable TV system, and the World Wide Web is like the programs that go over the cable system.

Specifically, the Internet started out in 1969 as a way to connect computers. The World Wide Web, born in 1989, is a system of interconnected information (in the form of Web pages) that you can access via the Internet. In the past couple of years, the Web has become the most common way of using the Internet. By now, you can use a World Wide Web browser program to send and receive e-mail (at `http://www.hotmail.com` and `http://mail.yahoo.com`), find Usenet newsgroups (at `http://www.dejanews.com`), and chat with other computer users (at `http://chat.yahoo.com`), all traditionally functions that happened *through* the Internet, by using technologies other than the World Wide Web. So, though they are *not* the same thing, they're beginning to look like the same thing.

"How Much Does It Cost to Be on the Internet?"

At the moment we're writing this chapter, the short answer is "Twenty dollars a month." Obviously, there's more to it than that. Do you need another telephone line just for your computer, or can you share a telephone line between your computer, yourself, and the other people in your house? You have to figure out what telephone lines cost in your area.

Will your telephone calls to your Internet service provider be free (included in your basic service), or will you have to pay by the minute? Or will you pay by the minute and hit some kind of a billing cap? Margy's rural telephone service charges two cents a minute to call the next-door neighbor, so her telephone bill for Internet access works out to about $300 per month, except for the fact that those nice folks at the Vermont Department of Public Utilities put a $30 cap on local telephone fees. Good for her, but not so good for the telephone company. If you're going to be on the Internet frequently, it may pay to really understand your telephone bill.

After you have your telephone straightened out, you'll find that most Internet service providers have an all-you-can-eat plan for about $20, and a pay-as-you-go plan for between $5 and $10 for three to five hours, and about $2 for each additional hour. Early in 1998, some large providers started limiting your trips to the all-you-can-eat salad bar at about 100 hours, charging two dollars for each additional hour, so what you pay depends on what you use (a radical capitalist notion).

If you're willing to hunt around, you may even find access to the Internet for free (at least, free after you make the telephone call). If you're affiliated with an educational institution (university, college, community college, high school, and even some elementary schools) you may be able to get dial-up access to the Internet. If you're not, check out the Organization for Community Networks, at `http://www.ofcn.org`. It's a promotional organization and coordinator for free and community-based Internet access. A free dial-up service may be available in your community. We don't have any experience with them, so we can't vouch for the quality of the service, but it's an intriguing idea.

Finally, check out your local public library. Most of them have computers connected to the Internet, where you can get a taste of what's going on out there. You are, however, stuck using whatever software the library decides to install on its computers.

We can't give you an exact amount, or even an approximate amount. If you can figure out how much you'll be paying for each piece of the puzzle, however, you can do the math.

"Who Should I Sign Up with to Be on the Internet?"

Much of Chapter 2 is dedicated to answering this question, although it would be downright dishonest to claim to have a list of frequently asked questions that doesn't include this question, which we get asked most frequently of all.

The answer, obviously, is that it depends. You trade off four things: price, technical support, local telephone access, and speed. How much of which you get from each Internet service provider may be difficult to determine. The details are in Chapter 2.

"What's an Internet Address?"

Although nobody ever asks this question in just this way, from the amount of confusion we see over slashes, at-signs, and .htmls, we think that it's a question people ought to ask. If they could just figure out that they *are* confused, it's a question people would ask. Two kinds of addresses are on the Internet: Web addresses and e-mail addresses. They're pretty easy to tell apart after you know what they are but can be really confusing if you don't even know that they're different:

> ✔ **E-mail addresses** have at-signs (@) in them. Always. (Okay, some really old-fashioned addresses have exclamation points instead, but you won't run into them.) E-mail addresses almost never have slashes in them, and they don't include www in them or .htm or .html either. They always have the form someone@somewhere.com. Sometimes it's more complicated, like someone@somecomputer.somewhere.com or even Your_Name_at_PO.Jade@smtplink.somecompany.com. The form is always the same, however: something that identifies a person, an at-sign, and something that identifies a computer.

✔ **Web addresses** have slashes (/) in them. They never have at-signs in them, and they usually start with `http://` and end with `.htm` or `.html`. We talk a great deal about Web addresses (also called *URLs*) in Chapter 8, including the fine points about ones that start with things like `ftp://`.

What creates confusion is that almost all Web addresses start with `http://www`, and most of them end with `index.html`. Because we're lazy, most of us forget about those parts. Rather than say "Look for our Web page at `http://www.gurus.com/index.html`," people say "Find us on the Net at `gurus.com`" and assume that you'll figure out the rest. Then, when you hear something like "E-mail me, I'm Joe Smith at `gurus.com`", you're tempted to start putting `https` on the beginning and slashes on the end of poor Joe Smith's e-mail address, when all the mail system is looking for is `JoeSmith@gurus.com`.

Remember: E-mail is `someone@somewhere.com`, and Web addresses are `http://www.somewhere.com`.

"Are There Any Good Places to Shop on the World Wide Web?"

We've been saying over and over again that the Internet is about information and communication. Information is what the market economy is all about: The more information buyers have about products and prices, the better decisions they can make about what they want and whether it's worth the price. That's why Web commerce (buying and selling stuff on the World Wide Web) is such an interesting subject for so many people.

By all accounts, the runaway success in selling things on the Internet has been the bookseller Amazon.com (at `http://www.amazon.com`). It claims to have access to pretty much every book that's in print in English, and its Web site lets you browse the first chapter of many books. It also provides services that may be hard to get from a regular bookstore, like watching out for new books from a particular author you may be interested in. Best of all, Amazon discounts the list price. As you may imagine, its success has drawn the attention of traditional booksellers, and `BarnesAndNoble.com` and `Borders.com` are hot on its heels. Everyone we know who has ordered from Amazon has positive things to say about it.

Intent on duplicating the success of `Amazon.com`, CDNow (at `http://www.cdnow.com`) lists a host of CDs on the World Wide Web. For many of its CDs, you can hear a 30-second audio clip. You'll find, after all the hype is cleared away, that the sound quality is almost good enough to give you an idea of what the music is like. You certainly wouldn't listen to sound that bad for pleasure. Still, it's better than just reading the promo material on the CD case.

If you can buy CDs and books, why not groceries? NetMarket.com has great plans to make it a reality. A division of Cendent Corp. (the same folks who own Century 21 and Avis), it is seriously into Net commerce in many different ways. As of early 1998, the NetMarket site was up, but wasn't really that friendly or inviting. Expect that situation to change. PeaPod (at `http://www.peapod.com`) was one of the first to try this concept and it has worked hard on its user interface. You have to be in one of the seven markets it serves, however.

The idea of putting small shops together in a mall on the Internet is clearly an appealing one. Yahoo (the Web directory) lists no fewer than 811 malls on the Internet. It's hard for us to figure out what value you get from a mall, however, because on the Internet, everyone is next-door to everyone else already. It doesn't cost a small shop much to put up its own store on the World Wide Web, and none of the malls we've seen promotes itself well enough to become a Web destination. Estimates were made in 1997 that many mall proprietors made more money selling Internet commerce seminars than actually selling goods on the Internet.

For a sampling of what small shops can do on their own, check out our entry, at `http://www.greattapes.com`. We specialize in harder-to-find audio- and videotapes for children; we characterize them as the kind you see at a neighbor's house and ask "Where did you find that, anyway?" It has been an interesting experiment in Web commerce, and we must say that we're enthused about the concept. We started it because we were looking for some videos and just assumed that they would be available on the Internet. They weren't! Well, they are now! This site shows how easy it is to run a small retail business on the Web (because it's hard to know less about retail than we do).

Commerce on the Web isn't just about small-ticket items. Edmund's (`http://www.edmunds.com`) is an excellent online version of the venerable car-buying guides; AutoByTel (`http://www.autobytel.com`) can get you a good deal on a new or used car you select. Especially for new cars, with their dizzying array of options, the amount of information you can gather on the Internet from both the manufacturer's Web sites and sites such as Edmund's means that when you walk into the showroom, you and the sales rep are on a much more equal footing.

This discussion is just the tip of the iceberg. Online commerce is changing every day, and, in the main, it's getting better. So, yes, there are many good places to shop on the Internet. You just have to find them.

"Is It Safe to Use My Credit Card on the Net?"

Yes. Could we make that any clearer? Yes, period.

All right, there are subtleties here. In one sense, it's *never* safe to use a credit card anywhere. Anyone at the establishment where you're using your card can copy down the number and the expiration date and even your signature. What's to stop that person from using your card and your number? And then there's your cordless telephone. Any joker with a scanner from Radio Shack can drive down your street and listen to you order from Lands End or L.L. Bean; then that person has the same credit card information you just gave a reputable merchant. We like that example because it's much like what could happen on the Internet: Just as millions and millions of cordless telephone calls are made every day, only a tiny fraction of which mention credit card numbers, billions and billions of bytes of messages are sent on the Internet every day, only a tiny fraction of which mention credit card numbers. Get the picture? It *could* happen, although if you're really worried about credit card safety, stop using your cordless telephone before you stop using the Internet. Your cordless (or cellular) telephone is much riskier.

Now suppose — just suppose — that someone gets your credit card number as you're making a purchase on the Internet. We ignore the fact that at the time this chapter was written, the number of cases of credit card fraud resulting from credit card numbers being stolen from shoppers on the Internet was exactly zero — none — zip — never happened. Suppose that you make history and you're the unlucky first victim. Your liability is limited by U.S. federal law to $50. Although that amount may hurt, it won't wipe out all your assets (or, if it does, you need to think about why you're using a credit card anyway). If you report the theft as soon as you notice it, your liability may be $0.

So why all the hype about fraud on the Internet? It's new, and people are uneasy about new things, especially when it comes to money. That's not unreasonable. Back when buying things over the telephone was new, people worried about the same thing; and back when credit cards were new, people worried about that too. The flames have been fanned, however, by a bunch of consultants out to make a name for themselves by scaring people and a bunch of companies that wanted to make a bunch of money by selling the Internet's next great payment system. Although fearmongering makes for a great reputation, the dismal business results of the companies trying to sell "digital cash" and other such schemes would seem to indicate that people don't really feel that they need them.

If, after this harangue, you still don't want to send your plastic over the Net or you're one of the fiscally responsible holdouts who doesn't do plastic, most online stores are happy to have you call in your number over the phone or send them a check.

"How Can I Make Money on the Net?"

We can't remember exactly how many trillions of dollars of business opportunity the Internet represents according to the people who claim to know about these things. We do see that businesses rely on communication. As a new medium of communication, the doors of the Internet are being flung open for new ways of doing business.

Rather than try to figure out how to make money in the Internet business, spend time getting to know the Net extensively — by checking out newsgroups and mailing lists in addition to exploring the World Wide Web. The more you see, the more you can think about organic ways in which your business can use the Net. Follow your loves: Find newsgroups and mailing lists that excite you. You will meet all kinds of interesting people and get new ideas. We think that what you can find out from the Net can help you find for yourself where your unique opportunities lie.

We have found that the best way to make money on the Net is to write books about it! Then again, we were writing books when dirt was two days old and playing with the Internet for longer than that. If we weren't in the book business, we probably would look at business-to-business commerce, either online services or Net-related "real world" business services, as the most likely candidates.

"Can People Steal Information from My Computer If I'm on the Internet?"

No. This question hasn't generated as much heat and light as credit cards on the Internet, which is surprising. Because, while the answer in general is "No," you can make a number of different slip-ups that do make it easier for people to "tap in" to your computer after you're on the Internet.

The biggest security hole we know of relates to cable modems. We talk about them in Chapter 2. If they're available in your area, we think that they're a terrific idea for fast Internet access. If your cable modem is set up incorrectly, you may find that you can look at the computer of everyone else on your street who has a cable modem. People tend to spot this situation pretty quickly, however, and the cable companies are usually eager to fix it, so it's not a situation that's likely to last long.

Windows 98 occasionally displays a message about disabling file and printer sharing on your Internet connection, usually if your computers are connected in a local-area network. Although it's theoretically possible for someone to gain access to your computer if you ignore this message, they would have to be looking specifically for you and employ a certain amount of technical sophistication. How smart are your enemies? Tell Windows to disable file and printer sharing anyway.

For the rest of us, however, unless you go out of your way to allow people to look at your computer, it's safe. Again, analogies to items we're more familiar with are useful. Your telephone answering machine is connected to the telephone network (just like your computer). Unless it has a remote message-retrieval feature, however, no one can listen to your telephone messages. The same thing goes for your computer: Unless you've installed a feature to access your computer remotely, you're safe.

Chapter 19

Ten Stupid Internet Moves to Avoid

In This Chapter

▶ Stupid things you can do on the Internet to make people wish that you had never showed up

▶ Tips to make you look like an old Net-hand on your first day

▶ How not to annoy Windows 98

*T*he Internet is an exciting place. If you haven't figured that out by now, perhaps you're reading the wrong book. Like most exciting places, however, it's full of excitable people, and those excitable people sometimes go careening off in all directions. One of the surest ways to set them off is to act like a clueless newbie or, even worse, to act obnoxiously even though it looks like you've been around for a while. Finally, although it's true that the Internet is well integrated into Windows 98, you can still do some things that really mess things up on your computer.

In this chapter, we try to keep you out of trouble with some do's and don'ts, for both Net behavior and good housekeeping on your computer. When we're done, you'll look like the coolest Web surfer on your block.

Fitting In

The moment you get your new Internet account, you may have an overwhelming urge to begin sending out lots of messages to mailing lists, chat groups, and anybody else whose online address you can get. *Don't do it!*

Read mailing lists, Web pages, and other Net resources for a while before you send anything out. You then can figure out where best to send your messages, which makes it both more likely that you will contact people who are interested in what you say and less likely that you will annoy people by bothering them with irrelevancies because you sent something to an inappropriate place.

One of the nicest innovations that is creeping from the Internet back to the rest of communications is the list of *Frequently Asked Questions,* or *FAQs.* We talk a little about them in Chapter 12, where we point out that most Usenet newsgroups have one. As we mention there, you can find Usenet FAQs at the FTP site `ftp://rtfm.mit.edu`. You can also find Usenet FAQs at DejaNews (`http://www.dejanews.com`) and Yahoo (`http://www.yahoo.com`), although you have to search for the word FAQ and the name of the newsgroup you're interested in.

Many Web sites also have FAQs. Practically all mailing lists have FAQs. When you subscribe to a mailing list, you usually get the FAQ automatically. It's a long message you'll be tempted to skip over. Don't! It contains a great deal of information that will help you be a valued member of the list rather than a nuisance. After you've read the message, save it (some of us have a mail folder called Reference that's full of these things — see Chapter 6 for tips on how to do it).

Before you go telling other people on the list how to behave, read the rules again. Some officious newbie, newly subscribed to JAZZ-L, began flaming the list and complaining about the off-topic threads. JAZZ-L encourages this kind of discussion — it says so right in the introduction to the list. As you may imagine, that was not a way to become a valued member of the list.

To reiterate: Before you go asking questions in a newsgroup or discussion group or mailing list, read the FAQ. They're not called frequently asked questions for nothing — more often than not, our questions have been answered there.

Netiquette 101

The primary tool you use to make a fool of yourself on the Internet is your e-mail program. Face it — it's hard to do much damage when you're just reading someone else's Web page. After you join a mailing list or begin to correspond with friends and acquaintances or begin to post to a Usenet newsgroup, however, the possibilities for embarrassment are endless. Keep in mind the advice in this section while your fingers do the talking.

Speling counts

Many Net users feel that because Net messages are short and informal, spelling and grammar don't count. Some even think that strange spelling makes them K00L D00DZ. If you feel that wey, theirs' not much wee can do abowt it. We think that sending out a sloppy, misspelled message is similar to showing up at a party with big grease stains on your shirt — although your friends will know that it's you, people who don't know you will tend to conclude that you don't know how to dress yourself.

Many mail programs have spell checkers. If you have installed the Microsoft Spelling Checker (it comes with Microsoft Office, Word, and Excel), Outlook Express uses it to check the spelling of your e-mail messages. While you're composing your message, choose Tools⇨Spelling. If you didn't purchase one of the other Microsoft products, you're out of luck, though.

Netscape 4.0 always comes with a spell checker. After you've composed your message, choose Tools⇨Check Spelling from the menu, or click the Spelling button on the toolbar.

Eudora Pro (the commercial version of Eudora) checks your spelling when you click the dictionary icon (the *ABC* one) on the toolbar or choose Edit⇨Check Spelling from the menu. Eudora can also automatically check outgoing messages for spelling errors; choose Tools⇨Options and find the Spell Checking screen; make sure that the Check When Messages Queued or Sent box has a check mark in it.

STOP SHOUTING — I CAN HEAR YOU

You can shout in your e-mail, just like in real life: JUST TYPE YOUR ENTIRE MESSAGE IN CAPITAL LETTERS. People don't like it, any more than they like being shouted at in real life. It's likely to get you some snappy comments suggesting that you do something about the stuck Shift key on your keyboard. Except for Apple computers, keyboards have handled lowercase letters since about 1970, so avail yourself of this modern technical marvel and aid to literate writing.

Now and then, we get mail from someone who says, "i dont like to use capital letters or punctuation its too much work" You can get away with this technique if you're e. e. cummings; from anybody else, we find it tedious.

If you don't have anything to say, don't say it

Avoid trying to sound smart. When you do, the result is usually its opposite. One of the stupidest things we have seen was on the mailing list TRAVEL-L. Someone posted a legitimate request for information about some travel destination. Then came the edifying comment "Sorry, Bud, Can't Help You." We would have thought that people who don't know anything could keep their mouths shut, but apparently we were wrong.

Each message you post to a list goes to the entire list. Each list member is there on a voluntary basis. If other members are like us, they often wonder whether a subscription to any particular mailing list is worthwhile: Does the good content of the list outweigh the noise and inanity? The more inanity flourishes, the more sensible subscribers unsubscribe and the list deteriorates. What you do *and don't* post has a direct effect on how worthwhile the list is. If you're going to participate, find a constructive way to do so.

"Can someone tell me how to unsubscribe from this list?"

Signing up for a mailing list is a cool thing. We tell you all about how to do it in Chapter 7. We also tell you how to unsubscribe from a mailing list. Still, one of the most common ways of looking like a klutz is to send a message to the whole list asking to be taken off the list. This mistake is doubly absurd: Everyone on the list has to read the message, although it doesn't even get the sender taken off the list.

In case you missed it in Chapter 7, subscribe and unsubscribe requests go to the *list server program* (not the list itself) in a particular format; in the case of lists that are not automated, address them to the list owner. Read Chapter 7 carefully please, lest you be the next person impressing every list member with your newbieness.

The netiquette police: Police yourself

Sooner or later, you see something that cries out for a cheap shot. Sooner or later, someone sends you something you shouldn't have seen and you want to pass it on. Don't do it. Resist cheap shots and proliferating malice. The Net has plenty of jerks — don't be another one. (See the suggestion later in this chapter about what to do when you're tempted to flame.) Be tolerant of newbies — you were once one yourself.

Still, you may be motivated by the best of intentions. Okay, someone makes a mistake, such as sending to the entire mailing list a message that says "subscribe" or posting a message that says, "Gee, I don't know!" in response to a request for help with a newsgroup. Yes, it's true, someone made a dumb move. Don't compound it, however, by posting additional messages complaining about it. Either delete the message and forget about it or respond privately, by e-mail addressed only to the person, not to the mailing list. The entire mailing list probably doesn't want to hear your advice to the person who blew it.

You message doesn't have to be long and preachy either. For example, you can send a private e-mail message saying, "In the future, send subscription and unsubscription messages to `eggplants-request`, not to `eggplants`, okay?" or "This is a list about domestic laying hens, so could you post your message about cats somewhere else?"

Signing off

All mail programs let you have a *signature,* a file that gets added to the end of each mail or news message you send. The signature is supposed to contain something to identify you. Snappy quotes quickly became common, to add that personal touch. Here's John's signature, for example:

```
Regards,
John Levine, johnl@iecc.com, Primary Perpetrator of "The
            Internet for Dummies,"
Information Superhighwayman wanna-be, http://iecc.com/
            johnl, Sewer Commissioner
```

(Yes, he really is the sewer commissioner.) Some people's signatures get way out of hand, going on for 100 lines of "ASCII art," long quotations, extensive disclaimers, and other allegedly interesting stuff. Although this type of signature may seem cute the first time or two, it quickly gets tedious and marks you as a total newbie.

Keep your signature to four lines or fewer. All the experienced Net users do.

Don't get attached

Attachments are a useful way to send files by e-mail. That also makes it tempting to e-mail them to whatever mailing list you happen to be on. "Look, I found this really cool picture of a Barred Rock Rooster. I knew that you would all want to see it, so I've attached it to this message." This idea is a very, very bad one. Your picture (or sound clip or word-processing file or whatever) is probably half a megabyte of information (or more). Multiply that by the number of people who are on the mailing list, and you soon have a very large number of bytes, enough to clog up the mail server and portions of the Internet for some time.

A friend of ours administers a number of academic lists and has just gone through the exercise of smoothing all the ruffled feathers that resulted from an attachment to a mailing list post. One entire university's medium-size Internet connection was tied up for several hours by this multimegabyte message. What's worse (and what's also common) is that the file that was attached was already on the World Wide Web. In a case like that, you have absolutely no excuse — none — ever — to attach the file to a mail message. Just tell people where to get it. "I found this cool picture of a Barred Rock Rooster on the Web, at `http://www.cyborganic.com/people/feathersite/`." On the off chance that people who want it don't have Web access, they can e-mail you *privately* for a copy of the file, and you can e-mail it to them *privately.*

Even if you're just e-mailing a friend, you should remember some things about attachments. First, we reiterate this: Do you really need to send it as an attachment, or is it already on the Web? You would be surprised at how often we get attachments of things we could just as well get off the Web ourselves if *we* decide that it's worth it. Second, remember that your attached file is useful to the recipient only if she uses an e-mail program that can handle attachments done the way your e-mail program does them *and* she has a program that can read the file or files you are sending. For example, if you send a WordPerfect document to someone who doesn't have a word-processing program, the file is unreadable. Ditto for graphics files, sound files, and other files you may want to send around. Third, it can take a long time to download an attachment. Nothing is more frustrating than waiting for an important e-mail message and watching two megabytes of who-knows-what downloading because someone sent you an attachment you didn't ask for. The moral of the story: Ask *first* before sending an attachment.

Warning: Do not use e-mail in the presence of open flame

For some reason, it's easy to get VERY, VERY UPSET ABOUT SOMETHING SOMEONE SAYS ON THE NET. (See, it happens even to us.) Sometimes it's something you find on the Web, and sometimes it's personal e-mail. You may be tempted to shoot a message right back telling that person what a doofus he is. Guess what? He will almost certainly shoot back. This type of overstated outrage is so common that it has its own name: flaming. Now and then, it's fun (if you're certain that the recipient will take it in good humor), but it's always unnecessary.

You have several things to think about here. One, e-mail messages always come across as crabbier than the author intended. Two, crabbing back hardly ever makes the person more reasonable. Three, flaming someone seldom makes him go away and certainly doesn't end the discussion. Instead, he'll get back to you with 150 reasons why he's right and you're wrong. And, if you're talking on a mailing list or in a discussion group, someone else will pick one point of what you said and dispute it. Before you know it, you're spending all your time talking about something you probably didn't even want to talk about in the first place.

A technique we often find helpful when we're tempted to flame (or respond to a flame) is to write the strongest, crabbiest response possible, full of biting wit and skewering each point in turn. Then we throw it away rather than send it. It makes us feel better and saves everybody a great deal of time.

Junk Mail — Retail and Wholesale

Junk mail seems to be one of those facts of modern life — it's hard to arrange your life so that more or less often you end up with something in your physical mailbox that you know should go directly to recycling. The same has become true of the electronic world. Although bits of computerized information are easier to recycle than pieces of paper, you still have to figure out what it is that you're ignoring, and that can take time. You're likely to run into two kinds of junk mail in your electronic in-box: chain letters from "friends" and acquaintances, and industrial-strength junk mail. *You* may even be tempted to indulge in the odd chain letter or unsolicited advertisement from time to time. Don't do it.

The chain gang

Sending a chain letter on the Net is easy: Just click the Forward button, type a few names, and send your letter off. It's a lousy idea. We have never, ever gotten a chain letter that was worth passing along. A bunch of classic chain letters have been circulating around the Net for a decade (see Chapter 6 for details about the boy who doesn't want cards, the phantom good-times virus, the nonexistent modem tax, the overpriced recipe that isn't, and a way that you won't make money fast). Regardless of where they come from, please just throw them away.

Wholesale junk mail, also known as spam

One of the least pleasant online innovations in recent years is *spamming,* or sending the same message — usually selling something that was rather dubious in the first place — to as many e-mail addresses or Usenet groups as possible. This practice is annoying, and we talk all about it in Chapter 6. You should remember, however, that the spammer is liable in many cases for her provider's expenses in cleaning it up. Spamming newsgroups is also ineffective because automatic systems identify and cancel most Usenet spams within minutes after they occur. Even spamming individual mailboxes isn't what it used to be because an increasing number of providers offer e-mail filtering, and most recipients, including us, presume that anything advertised by spam must be fraudulent.

If you do any kind of business on the Net (for profit, nonprofit, or even volunteer), you may find that you accumulate a list of addresses of people who have contacted you for one reason or another. You may be tempted to write to them about some new venture you have, more or less related to the reason they got in touch with you in the first place. Our experience is that this situation is a classic slippery slope, and it's hard to decide where the legitimate "If you were interested in that, you may be interested to know about this" ends and the "If I just send this message to everyone I can find and 1 percent of them respond" reasoning begins. Our advice is to avoid the whole thing. (We're thinking about sending notifications of new editions of this book, for example, to people who write to us at internet98@gurus.com. Let us know if you would like to get news from us or if you would consider it spam.)

Don't Cause a Run on the Bank

The Internet, the telephone system, and the banking system all share at least one characteristic: If everyone tries to use them at one time, there's not enough to go around. Most of us are familiar with this concept when we think of a run on a bank: The bank doesn't have enough money in the vault for every depositor to get all his money on the same day. The telephone system is similar: If everyone picks up her telephone at the same time, there aren't enough dial-tones to go around. The Internet is the same: If everyone tries to download information as fast as her modem can go, the whole Net slows down like molasses on a cold day.

Unlike the bank and telephone examples, you don't have to be there to bog down the Internet. Unbelievable amounts of material are on the Net: programs, documents, pictures, megabyte after megabyte of swell stuff — all free for the taking. All you have to do is set your computer, like the sorcerer's apprentice, to download it all for you. Don't. Go ahead and take whatever you're likely to use, but don't download entire directories full of stuff "just in case."

Your Internet provider sets its charges based on the resources a typical user uses. A single user can use a substantial fraction of the provider's Net connection by sucking down files continuously for hours at a time. Just like a bank, which typically a keeps a small percentage of its depositors' money on hand, Internet providers typically "overcommit" their Net connection by a factor of three or so. In this case, if every user tried to transfer data at full speed at the same time, it would require three times as fast a connection as the provider has. Because real users transfer for a while and then read what's on-screen for a while, sharing the connection among all the users works out okay. If users begin using several more connections than the provider budgeted for, prices go up.

Hang up, already!

This advice applies particularly to providers who offer unlimited connect-time per month. Don't leave your computer connected if you're not using it. Most Net software packages have a time-out feature that hangs up if no data is transferred to or from the Net for a specified period. We leave ours set to 15 minutes on our dial-up connections. Most Internet providers do the same thing from their end: If your connection has no activity for a set period, it hangs up on you.

You can get little programs that fool Windows 98 and your Internet provider into thinking that you're doing something and thus keep your telephone connection open. Call us old-fashioned, but we think that this technique is an irresponsible, dog-in-the-manger approach to the Internet. If you're using your Net connection, great. If you're not using it, however, let someone else use it. That's much nicer than "I'm not using that telephone connection to my Internet provider, but you can't use it either, and I don't care whether you get a busy signal when you try to connect."

Stunts like that have caused many large Internet service providers to put a cap on their "unlimited" connect-time plans, usually at around 100 hours.

Audio and video pigs

Internet Phone and the like present a particular problem on the Net because they put a much, much heavier load on both the local provider and the Net in general than do other Internet services. When you're transferring voice information over the Net, you're pumping data through as fast as your connection will let you. Video connections are even worse: When sites with fast Net connections begin sending video programs around to each other, the entire Net slows down.

Some Web Wisdom

Windows 98 is convenient because it gives you everything you need to create your own pages on the Web and even to put your PC on the Internet as a Web server. (See Chapter 16 if you missed how to do it.) Because what you put on your Web page is all that most people will know about you, this section provides a few suggestions.

Small is beautiful, Part 1

When you're creating your Web pages, you see them right on your own computer. Quickly. After all, they don't have to come in over the telephone line — they're right on your hard drive. Remember that most people who look at your Web page are connected by using a dial-up line and a modem. Those pictures that appeared so quickly when you were creating your Web pages take a long time to load over the phone. If your home page contains a full-page picture that takes $12^1/_2$ minutes to load, you may as well have hung out a Keep Out sign. Keep the pictures small enough that the page loads in a reasonable amount of time. If you have a huge picture that you think is wonderful, put a small "thumbnail" version of it on your home page and make it a link to the full picture for people with the time and interest to look at the big version.

Small is beautiful, Part II

Small pages that fit on a screen or two work better than large pages. Small pages are easier to read, and they load faster. If you have 12 screens full of stuff to put on your Web page, break up your page into five or six separate pages, two screens full each, with links among them. A well-designed set of small pages makes finding stuff easier than does one big page because the links can direct readers to what they want to find.

If we want the White House, we know where to find it

No Web page (or set of Web pages, as we just suggested) is complete without some links to the author's other favorite pages. For some reason, every new user's Web page used to have a link to `http://www.whitehouse.gov` and maybe to Yahoo, Netscape, and a few other sites that every Net user already knows about. Cool Web sites give you links to interesting pages you *don't* already know about.

Let a hundred viewers blossom

Whenever you create a new Web page, look at it with as many Web browsers as possible. Yes, most people use of Netscape or Internet Explorer, but Prodigy and AOL users (close to 10 million possible visitors to your site) use the browsers that come with those services, and users with dial-up shell connections use the text-only browser Lynx. Look at your pages to make sure that they're legible regardless of which browser people are using.

Don't be dumb

Don't put information on your Web page that you don't want everyone in the world to know. In particular, you may not want to include your home address and phone number. We know at least one person who received an unexpected phone call from someone she met on the Net and wasn't too pleased about it. Why would Net users need this information, anyway? They can send you e-mail!

Index

Discover Dummies Online!

The Dummies Web Site is your fun and friendly online resource for the latest information about ...*For Dummies*® books and your favorite topics. The Web site is the place to communicate with us, exchange ideas with other ...*For Dummies* readers, chat with authors, and have fun!

Ten Fun and Useful Things You Can Do at www.dummies.com

1. Win free ...*For Dummies* books and more!
2. Register your book and be entered in a prize drawing.
3. Meet your favorite authors through the IDG Books Author Chat Series.
4. Exchange helpful information with other ...*For Dummies* readers.
5. Discover other great ...*For Dummies* books you must have!
6. Purchase Dummieswear™ exclusively from our Web site.
7. Buy ...*For Dummies* books online.
8. Talk to us. Make comments, ask questions, get answers!
9. Download free software.
10. Find additional useful resources from authors.

Link directly to these ten
fun and useful things at
http://www.dummies.com/10useful

For other technology titles from IDG Books Worldwide, go to
www.idgbooks.com

Not on the Web yet? It's easy to get started with *Dummies 101*®: *The Internet For Windows*®*95* or *The Internet For Dummies*®, 5th Edition, at local retailers everywhere.

Find other ...*For Dummies* books on these topics:

Business • Career • Databases • Food & Beverage • Games • Gardening • Graphics • Hardware
Health & Fitness • Internet and the World Wide Web • Networking • Office Suites
Operating Systems • Personal Finance • Pets • Programming • Recreation • Sports
Spreadsheets • Teacher Resources • Test Prep • Word Processing

IDG BOOKS WORLDWIDE BOOK REGISTRATION

Register This Book and Win!

We want to hear from you!

Visit **http://my2cents.dummies.com** to register this book and tell us how you liked it!

- ✔ Get entered in our monthly prize giveaway.
- ✔ Give us feedback about this book — tell us what you like best, what you like least, or maybe what you'd like to ask the author and us to change!
- ✔ Let us know any other ...*For Dummies*® topics that interest you.

Your feedback helps us determine what books to publish, tells us what coverage to add as we revise our books, and lets us know whether we're meeting your needs as a ...*For Dummies* reader. You're our most valuable resource, and what you have to say is important to us!

Not on the Web yet? It's easy to get started with *Dummies 101*®: *The Internet For Windows*® *95* or *The Internet For Dummies*,® 5th Edition, at local retailers everywhere.

Or let us know what you think by sending us a letter at the following address:

...*For Dummies* Book Registration
Dummies Press
7260 Shadeland Station, Suite 100
Indianapolis, IN 46256-3945
Fax 317-596-5498

BUSINESS AND
**GENERAL
REFERENCE**
BOOK SERIES
FROM IDG

COMPUTER
BOOK SERIES
FROM IDG